LESLEY RIDDOCH is a writer, journalist and b
brought up in Belfast, she spent family summe
Caithness mother. In 1997 Lesley was involved in
by the local community, becoming a trustee of th

Mostly known for broadcasting, after presenting Radio 4's *You and Yours* and BBC2's *Midnight Hour* in the mid-90s, she came 'home' after devolution to present her own daily radio show on BBC Radio Scotland until 2005, for which she won two Sony speech broadcaster awards.

She now runs her own independent radio, podcast and TV production company, Feisty Productions, which produces *Riddoch Questions*, a weekly topical phone-in programme hosted by Lesley on Radio Scotland.

She is a weekly columnist for *The Scotsman* and a regular commentator in other papers. In 2006 she was shortlisted for the Orwell Prize for political writing. During the 1990s, she was founder of the feminist magazine *Harpies and Quines*, assistant editor of *The Scotsman* (where she edited a special edition known as *The Scotswoman* written by its female staff in 1995), and contributing editor of the *Sunday Herald*. She was also founder and editor of *Africawoman*, an online newspaper written by one hundred African women journalists and, with her husband Chris Smith, hosts www.lesleyriddoch.com, where there are audio clips of people interviewed in this book.

RIDDOCH
on the Outer Hebrides

LESLEY RIDDOCH

Luath Press Limited

EDINBURGH

www.luath.co.uk

'The Gaelic Long Tunes' by Les Murray (*New Collected Poems*, 2003) is reproduced with the kind permission of Carcanet Press.

The excerpt from 'The Life of Lord Leverhulme' by Louis MacNeice (Faber) is reproduced by permission of David Higham Associates.

First published 2007

ISBN (10) 1-905222-99-8
ISBN (13) 978-1-905222-99-5

Printed and bound by Thomson Litho, East Kilbride
Typeset in Minion and Gill Sans
Design by Tom Bee
Maps by Jim Lewis
Gaelic proverb illustrations © Laurie Cuffe

Acknowledgements

This book focuses on people. Not facts and figures, perfect histories, or even totally accurate cycling routes. I'd like to thank the various authors who have given me permission to quote from their work. My husband Chris, for maintaining my equilibrium and website during a long, hot summer of cycling, editing, broadcasting and writing newspaper articles. He has also patiently endured a slightly preoccupied wife ever since. Maxwell MacLeod gamely modified his rigorously haphazard approach to life to be my support driver. Against all his best instincts, he called ahead to confirm interview and accommodation details, took a multitude of photographs, learned how to make girl-friendly sandwiches, drove with passion and some sciatic discomfort, laughed when things went ridiculously wrong, charmed anxious interviewees like an islander and never complained. Thanks to BBC Radio Scotland for commissioning the series that got me 'on the bike' in the first place, and to the ever-resourceful Feisty production crew, John Collins and Claire McVinnie. Thanks to *The Herald* for permission to use the columns that accompanied the radio series. And to *The Scotsman* for permission to use extracts of subsequent columns written for them. Thanks to artist Laurie Cuffe for permission to use his cartoons of Gaelic proverbs. Their meanings, I'm told, are often opaque even in Gaelic. So I hope any wildly improbable meaning imposed upon them will be excused. Thanks to photographers Eoin MacNeil and Cailean MacLean, and to the Morven Gallery and artist Moira MacLean; to Maureen MacLeod at the Castlebay Hotel, CalMac, John Randall from the Islands Book Trust, Arthur Cormack of the *Fèisean* organisation and Donald J MacLeod for his painstaking research. Thanks to the Luath team, to my editor Jennie Renton and to Sria Chatterjee. Thanks to all the interviewees who put up with late arrivals, changed arrangements and then broke every unwritten rule of island behaviour by speaking (in English) like no one was listening. Thanks to Hector and Jeannie MacLean who offered a vital communication-free week up beautiful Glen Prosen when I was writing this book and to Malcolm MacLean (no relation) who didn't close his mind to critical thoughts about his beloved Gaelic. And many thanks to my mum and late father, whose epic holiday journeys to the Far North sowed the seeds of my curiosity about their beloved Highlands.

I have read but never written the following words and feel the force of them for the first time: none of the above is responsible for any offence this book creates or any mistakes I've made in spelling, grammar or content – in Gaelic or English.

For the Caithness lass, Helen Miller More

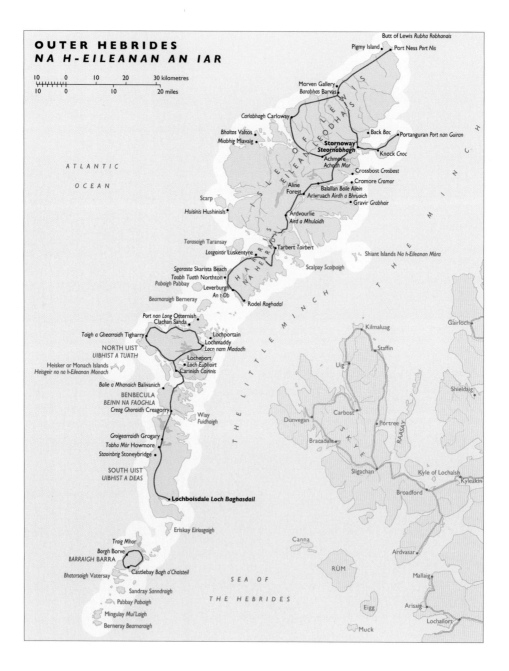

OUTER HEBRIDES
NA H-EILEANAN AN IAR

10 0 10 20 30 kilometres
10 0 10 20 miles

ATLANTIC

OCEAN

Butt of Lewis *Rubha Robhanais*
Pigmy Island• •Port Ness *Port Nis*

Morven Gallery•
Barabhas Barvas•

Carlabhagh Carloway•

Bhaltos Valtos•   •Back *Bac*
Miabhig Miavaig•   **Stornoway** •Portanguran *Port nan Guiran*
                              Steornabhagh
                              Achmore•   •Knock *Cnoc*
                              Achadh Mòr
                                •Crossbost *Crosbost*
                           •Balallan *Baile Ailein* •Cromore *Cromor*
Aline   Arivruach *Airdh a Bhruaich*•
Forest   •Gravir *Grabhair*
Scarp•
Huisinis Hushinish•   Ardvourlie•
                         Aird a Mhulaidh

Tarasaigh Taransay•   Shiant Islands *Na h-Eileanan Mòra*
Losgaintir Luskentyre• •Tarbert *Tairbert*
Sgarasta Skarista Beach•   Scalpay *Scalpaigh*
Taobh Tuath Northton•
Pabaigh Pabbay•   Leverburgh•
                    An t-Ob
Bearnaraigh Berneray•
                •Rodel *Roghadal*

Port nan Long Otternish•
Clachan Sanda•
Taigh a Ghearraidh Tigharry•   •Lochportain
                              •Lochmaddy
NORTH UIST   •Loch nam Madadh
UIBHIST A TUATH
Heisker or Monach Islands   •Locheport
Heisgeir no na h-Eileanan Monach •Loch Euphoirt
                            Carinish *Cairinis*•

Baile a Mhanaich Balivanich•
BENBECULA
BEINN NA FAOGHLA
Creag Ghoraidh Creagorry•   •Wiay
                                Fuidhaigh

Groigearraidh Grogary•
Tobha Mòr Howmore•
Staoinbrig Stoneybridge•

SOUTH UIST
UIBHIST A DEAS

Lochboisdale *Loch Baghasdail*

                      •Eriskay *Eiriosgaigh*

Traig Mhor
Borgh Borve•
BARRAIGH BARRA
Bhatarsaigh Vatersay•   •Castlebay *Bagh a'Chaisteil*

                Sandray *Sanndraigh*
                Pabbay *Pabaigh*
                Mingulay *Miu'Laigh*
                Berneray *Bearnaraigh*

THE LITTLE MINCH

THE MINCH

Kilmaluag•
        •Staffin
Uig•
                Shieldaig•
        •Carbost
Dunvegan•   SKYE   •Portree   RAASAY
Bracadale•   •Kyle of Lochalsh
                Sligachan•   •Kyleakin
                        Broadford•

Gairloch•

Canna
                Ardvasar•
RÙM
                Mallaig•

SEA OF   Eigg   Arisaig•
THE HEBRIDES
            •Muck   •Lochailort

Contents

Foreword

Lesley Riddoch, as her company name proudly boasts, is a feisty woman. This is underlined by her cycle through the Outer Hebrides in summer 2006. By way of contrast I have yet to cycle round one of the smaller Hebrides, my native Barra.

I have known Lesley for many years since we both met on the Island of Eigg sometime last century. Lesley shares with me the feeling that islands are probably the best place a person can live – but in Gaelic, there is a proverb, *Is math an sgàthan sùil caraid*. In English, 'A friend's eye makes a great mirror.'

I know that Lesley Riddoch is just such a friend to the Hebrides. However, she is not an uncritical friend. She will, as she's demonstrated on radio many times, hold up a mirror that will show warts as well as beauty. Her observations, comments and analysis have rearranged my mental furniture. Her book is ultimately an act of social consultancy – I don't agree with everything and she'd be shocked if I did.

She speaks not a word of Gaelic but has an awareness of the language's importance. Which is an important asset amongst English-speaking social commentators. Because we are at a crossroads in the islands linguistically. We have to face up to the fact that we are living in the last area of the Gaelic language on Earth (the language that arguably made Scotland what it is). *Scotti* was the word the Romans gave the Gaels in the same way the Algonquin called the Inuit *Eskimos*. Only a minority of children go to school able to speak Gaelic. And despite the known advantages of bilingualism only about a third of children then go into Gaelic medium education. I am constantly amazed at how many people speak to my youngest daughter Annie Sine in English but will speak to me and my two other daughters in Gaelic. Why is a speechless child perceived as an English monoglot? It is so often not the case and yet it becomes a self-fulfilling prophecy quite unconsciously. It's helping to knock the stuffing from Gaelic.

On the other hand we must be positive and nurture all that is good about our islands so we do not become 'dead end' Gaelic speakers, where the vernacular and perspective of at least fifty island generations stall on our tongues.

Crofting is changing from my own young days. The croft earns less but connects more. I am as well wired to the world on my croft in Barra as I am in my Westminster office thanks to BT Broadband.

I am grateful that someone I admired long before I met her has asked me to write the foreword to her book. One thing I can be certain of – Lesley Riddoch will always be arguing or supporting a position with the best of intentions and with the best interests of the islands at heart. That won't stop respectful disagreement. But at least the debate will be feisty.

Angus Brendan MacNeil, MP *Na h-Eileanan an Iar*

Tuppence Worth by Maxwell MacLeod

A few weeks before my late father's death at ninety-six I was sitting talking nonsense to him, as you do. The nonsense was largely an exchange of family stories, short ones, that we both knew and loved. He was a darling man and it wasn't an easy time for either of us. Eventually I tossed him a juicy worm, knowing he would gobble it up and respond with an absolute corker.

'So, Father, you have walked this road of life before me. What's your advice on life's great journey?'

It was a question he had asked his own father in exactly the same situation half a century earlier. The old boy grinned gratefully for the opportunity to perform and set off on his riff.

'Funny you should ask me that. I remember asking my own father the same question, and he replied that after a long life he had come to only three conclusions. That it is never wise to cross a fence with a loaded gun, stand up in a small boat, or do business west of Crianlarich – and I agree, I agree!'

Lord how he laughed. I tell you this because of that last line.

'Never do business west of Crianlarich.'

Now Crianlarich lies in the middle of Scotland – so my father was suggesting that everything that takes place on the Hebridean Islands is a ridiculous waste of time. The particular perversity of that remark needs a bit of explanation.

My family have lived on the Hebrides for at least four hundred years, quite possibly twice that. My cousins still live in the house in Skye that we came from in 1777. I still have the house in Morvern that we lived in next.

My father, Lord George MacLeod of Fuinary, gave much of his life and money to leading the restoration of the Hebridean Cathedral on Iona, mostly using volunteer labour. He had, in fact, thrown away the family fortune by investing west of Crianlarich. Though I don't begrudge him a penny.

Part of his motivation for that endeavour was wanting young people to become immersed in the experience of working alongside Gaelic stonemasons on high scaffolds as they sang work songs, told tales in the evening of their love of nature and their lack of materialistic ambition, and then crooned exquisite songs, some of them written when Napoleon was but a child.

So that was the great side of the Gaelic culture.

But there was another side too.

All his life George had had to fight against miserable, thrawn folk in the islands who were also Gaels and for whom cynicism or drunkenness were ways of life. Indeed, when I once asked him where he wanted to be buried he had replied: 'Anywhere but Iona.'

Any honest book about the islands must explore the same dangerous territory without painting Gaels as heroes or villains – they are people... with stories.

Storytelling, and this book is largely a collection of stories, is a vital part of our culture. It's how we remind each other of who we are, and of the great truths and mysteries. The truths of Hebridean culture are becoming harder to swallow with each passing generation. The next will not know the culture that has cradled the islands for over a thousand years.

If such cultural genocide had happened to the Inuit or the Aborigines, every child in Britain would know about it. As it is, there is hardly a child in the land who could point to Uist on the map, or say a word in Gaelic, though most can parrot a dozen words in French or German.

But does it matter a damn?

Well, apart from warning me not to invest west of Crianlarich, my father would also observe with a sigh, 'The Gaelic culture is dying and I sometimes want to mourn it, and sometimes am greatly relieved.'

So when my friend of fifteen years Lesley Riddoch phoned to ask if would accompany her on a journey up the Western Isles, I said yes without checking my diary. Anything that was in that diary would have to be cancelled. I would just tell folk the truth and they would understand.

I agreed for two reasons.

Firstly, because I love the woman, and by that I mean that I have an abiding passion for her. She has such conviction and fire for what she does that I admire her very deeply, and yet she is sometimes simultaneously so vulnerable and idiotic that it inspires a deep compassion in me and I also want to protect her.

We irritate each other almost constantly.

We also enjoy each other's company. God knows why, but we do.

Several times during our intensely busy two weeks together on our island venture I seriously considered abandoning her and I know that the number of times she considered sacking me was even greater. Given that we were only working together for two weeks, that probably means there was scarcely a period of forty-eight hours when one of us didn't playfully consider the pleasure that might be experienced murdering the other. In retrospect, I don't think I have ever enjoyed a fortnight more in my life.

Secondly, I knew that this is a vital time in the history of the islands. The Gaelic culture is just about dead and the 'Resties' (we sold the house in the south and bought a cheaper one here, the rest is invested) are arriving in their droves.

Again this poses the question, does it matter a damn?

I think it does, otherwise I wouldn't have gone.

Why does it matter? If mankind doesn't turn away from a global culture based on competitive consumption, our time on Earth is limited. Here on the islands we have people who live different, non-materialistic lives that may teach us something.

Some of this collective lifestyle is based on Gaelic tradition, on religious tradition, and on valuing family above all else. A small part is just based on smoking copious amounts of dope.

But all aspects of island tradition are interesting, all worth examining.

And in this book Lesley examines them by using the very technique that is at the core of Hebridean culture: storytelling.

Through her stories she defines the state of, and to an extent the potential of, some of these glorious islands and the cultures that they have created.

Lesley is not only a great storyteller, she is also a great story gatherer.

During her career as a radio journalist in Scotland she has gained the trust of thousands of people – who listened to her broadcasts, sometimes shouting at her, sometimes whooping with delight as she dismantled some prevaricating politician.

It was my job as her assistant to go ahead and find people prepared to talk to her and it was never hard – often they had been having one-sided conversations with her for years and were anxious to meet their pal.

I may have wanted to kill her, but I still love her.

Though you mustn't believe everything she says about me.

The bitch.

Introduction

A BBC weather presenter has apologised after calling the Western Isles 'nowheresville'. The Western Isles MP Angus MacNeil offered weather presenters a visit to his constituency. The Met Office forecaster said he 'deeply regretted' his choice of words.

BBC News, February 2007

Land Rover is promoting a new colour called Stornoway Grey. A Western Isles councillor claimed the name was 'offensive, inaccurate and inherently degrading'. Land Rover said Stornoway Grey was one of its strongest colours and helped to 'keep' the Western Isles on the map.

BBC News, March 2007

The Outer Hebrides hardly belong to this country or this century. The name says it all. Outer means distant, remote, marginal, unfamiliar.

Hebrides means the place protected by the pre-Christian fire goddess Bride. And the Gaels' decision to revert to this ancient name after thirty-five years as the breezy-sounding Western Isles should tell lovers of shopping malls and bouncy castles everything they need to know.

The Outer Hebrides are different. Nearer than Orkney and Shetland – but stranger. In fact their Gaelic name, *Innse Gall*, literally means 'Islands of the Strangers' – a name given by wary Gaelic-speaking *Scotti* to the Vikings who colonised the islands around 800 AD. Vikings whose descendants are still happy to be called strangers by other Gaels, twelve hundred years on.

The Outer Hebrides are a place apart.

Composed of Lewisian Gneiss – the most ancient and unyielding rock. Populated by unyielding Gaels, who therefore still have Scotland's most ancient language on their tongue. Blessed with natural beauty that is both outstanding, and unpackaged. There are no quaint Tobermory-like towns, no famous Islay-like distilleries and no formidable Cuillin-like peaks to tick off Munro-bagging lists.

A heaven for lovers of wild places. A no-wheresville for lovers of foreign holidays, epicurean delights and managed attractions. Exotic for the few. Grey for the many – a giant, blank canvas, regularly daubed with whatever drab colour of paint a car manufacturer cannot sell.

How has this misrepresentation of Europe's most beautiful island chain been allowed to happen?

In reality the Outer Isles contain stunning landscapes, empty roads, mercifully flat cycling terrain, humour, Gaelic, shellfish, tweed,

tradition, loss, music, boats, fear of depopulation, ferries, kindness, churches and passing places aplenty. If that seems 'grey' to the marketing folk at Land Rover, they should get out more.

But the Outer Isles are easily and often dismissed. For centuries, mainland opinion has tended to be sentimental at best and hostile at worst. The road along the east coast of Harris was dubbed 'the Golden Road' by Scots, horrified so much money had been 'lavished' on peasants. It is a beautiful road, but single track, winding and slow. Hardly twenty-four carat.

Nowadays urban Scots struggle to keep pace with one another and with London – and the slow, low-key, family-based nature of Hebridean life has allowed the island chain to sink beneath mainland radar. Which is generally fine. But the Outer Isles have sunk beneath the living standards of every other Scottish island group too. Which is not fine.

Shetland has been transformed by large-scale trawling and oil. Incomes are amongst the highest in Europe and ferries run day and night to keep outlying islands viable and connected. Wind energy has been embraced swiftly through deals that will give Shetland Islands Council a fifty per cent share of wind wealth. And islanders have integrated incomers attracted by oil money. Witness the spontaneous, defiant and successful campaign to resist the deportation of a Thai sports instructor in 2006. Shetlanders act to defend one another – no matter what rules a distant state tries to impose.

Orkney too has been transformed by the canny combination of heritage and enterprise. Carefully developed branding and intelligently nurtured talent have given Orkney the biggest jewellery industry outside Birmingham. Runic-inspired bracelets, pendants and rings compete for space on ferries and planes with Orkney Cheddar, Orkney Ice Cream, Orkney Herring and Orkney Oatcakes – and the favourite tipple of successive Chancellors, Highland Park. All value-added. All manufactured. All produced locally and therefore all helping to create jobs, profits and skills.

The Northern Isles have got drive, focus and entrepreneurial flair.

The Western Isles have got left behind.

According to the Scottish Annual Business Statistics of 2004, the GVA (a measure of the individual worker's productivity) was lower for manufacturing in the Outer Hebrides than the other five remote regions that compose the Highlands and Islands Enterprise area – Orkney, Shetland, Argyll and Bute, Highland and Moray.

And yet the educational attainment of Hebridean pupils outstrips every other part of the HIE zone. Wherever they are taking their skills, it isn't the manufacturing that would add value to local craft industries.

There is not a local distillery – though a proposal has just been made for a site near Uig on Lewis – and I've struggled to find a local creamery the length of the Outer Isles. Fish are imported and no large-scale trawling takes place. The Hebrides are net importers of energy and have a higher unemployment rate than their northern cousins, a higher incidence of alcoholism and a shorter life expectancy.

Why is life apparently tougher on the Western Isles than elsewhere in the Highlands and Islands?

The Gaels didn't have easy access to oil deposits like Shetland or fertile soils like Orkney. But the Northern Isles grabbed control over production of their natural resources. The Western Isles didn't. The Outer Hebrides continued to export 'raw' fish, tweed and seaweed to middlemen and to mainland manufacturers. And those mainlanders got the jobs, made the profit and learned the skills.

In 1773 Samuel Johnson visited Skye. What he observed there could easily describe the situation on the Outer Hebrides today:

> The clans retain little now of their original character, their ferocity of temper is softened, their military ardour is extinguished, their dignity of independence is depressed, their contempt of government subdued and their reverence for their chiefs abated. Of what they had before the late conquest of their country there remain only their language and their poverty. Their language is attacked on every side.

In their sad songs of departure and loss, in their reverence for 'tradition bearing', in their aversion to expansion and the modern cash-based society, in their dogged independence, in their Gaelic, in their churches and above all in their powerful families demanding obedience or virtual exile – the Western Isles still bear the fruits and scars of battle. Battle against the secular, pluralist, materialist society Scotland has become. Can they survive? Will they adapt? Were they right?

Cycling up the Hebrides in the summer of 2006 for a thirteen-part BBC Radio Scotland series, *On the Bike*, I had modest aims – to stretch my legs and spend some time away from mobile phones, emails, and deadlines.

I experienced much more.

Hermetically sealed in a car, the visitor moves too fast from A to B, and is usually underwhelmed at both ends. No serendipity, no downhill descents into dodgy sheep-grids, no conversations at bus shelters, no skirling bagpipes.

Instead, I spent weeks in touch with two great natural phenomena. The sea, never more than a few miles distant. And the people, unwitting repositories of Scotland's collective psyche.

The plan was that my transit driving companion, Maxwell MacLeod, would carry heavy editing equipment and extra bikes, while I would leapfrog from Barra to the Butt of Lewis, interviewing folk with stories, skills and insights into Hebridean life. The sort of people you never forget meeting but can never coax into a studio. So the great and good are not featured in this book – neither are the large number who spoke but wouldn't be recorded through shyness, diffidence, wariness or basic mistrust.

It would be easy to leave the *Gàidhealtachd* to the Gaels and thereby lose a large chunk of Scottish culture and history. Gaelic was the Scots common language only a few centuries ago. Scots then, like Gaels now, lived rural, clan-based, family-centred, land-focused lives. 'Quaint' Hebridean customs that survive today were mainstream Scottish customs then – from knowing everyone else's business to thatching, communal hay making and ceilidhs.

A trip to the Hebrides today is a trip to Scotland's otherwise inaccessible past. And given the desire for sustainability and stronger community life, it could be a trip to Scotland's future too.

Admittedly, though, I am biased.

I was a Trustee in the first-ever island community buyout on the Inner Hebridean island of Eigg. I bought land intending to build a house and become a hermit in the north of Skye. A plan which was abandoned after I got married on the innermost Summer Isle, Isle Martin, to a Canadian born on the Isle of Wight. My mother maintains our Caithness-rooted family hail originally from Orkney, where the splendidly self-reliant Westray has become our favourite island destination.

I admire the doggedness and distinctiveness of islanders. And the folk of the Western Isles are amongst the most dogged of the lot, hanging on to their population against all the odds. Large chunks of that population still live like large extended families – with all the comfort and connectedness that brings. But the power of island clans can be a formidable obstacle for those stuck on the 'wrong' side of rigidly held views on religion, race, or wind power.

Those views have served to define islanders and exclude strangers. Now many young islanders are feeling excluded too. And yet for traditionalists, the fear of alienating a generation of children is not as great as the fear of change. For some, preservation of island life is a God-given task – a legacy handed down by wronged forebears with whom no easy deal can be made.

But battling the will of God just to surf the net on Sunday isn't an appealing prospect for young islanders. A shift in emphasis is needed. From the over-examined moral side of Hebridean life to its under-examined practical side. Samuel Johnson spotted the islanders' Achilles heel: 'The Scots have attained the liberal without the manual arts. They have excelled in ornamen-

tal knowledge [without] the conveniences of common life. They are more accustomed to endure little wants than to remove them.'

Johnson is still right. In two weeks, I found 'ornamental knowledge' aplenty – erudite arguments about the origins of step dancing, competent pipers in every other household, and people jigsaw-puzzling ancestral DNA across centuries and oceans. All this often without a decent ferry service, a shop or a functioning public toilet for miles around – ornamental or otherwise. The non-materialist, unworldly sense of worth in in the Western Isles is both part of its charm and part of the reason for its population decline, especially amongst its very worldly young-sters.

The current generation of web-connected, well-educated children are leaving the land of Gaelic, crofts, church adherence and seasonal, manual work. Some may return, disillusioned with a materialistic society long on promise and short on delivery. Some may become mortgage slaves and stay close to the promise of steady work. Meantime, incomers are shoring up school rolls and population numbers. But they cannot shore up the cornerstones of Gaelic, crofting, church attendance and weaving. At least not with the 'untaught' flair and unquestioning adherence which characterise the natives.

So what does the future hold?

Can the Hebrideans adapt to survive? Should they?

No society is likely to disappear in a decade or five – not even one as quiet and stoic as the Outer Hebrides. Not even the Iron Lady could manage that. But the Isles won't have quite the same kind of culture if they are not populated by the same kind of people.

Welcoming, colourful, talented, self-doubting and funny. God-fearing, superstitious, polite and fearful, too. Each passing day, cycling, eating, driving and arguing brought me into a marvellously rich human and physical landscape. Each day there were stories, songs and music, told hilariously and fluently by people who would then make panicky searches for someone 'better educated' to speak 'on the wireless'. Each day an exotic 'pick 'n' mix' of language was spoken: English, Scots Gaelic and Macaronic – speech that uses a mixture of languages. Each day there was spontaneous friendliness and knee-jerk wariness. Waves from cars on single track roads evaporating into stony indifference on double track. There was kindness, offers of lifts and cups of tea, if you made a connection – and not so much as a shop selling last week's bread if you made none. But above all for a radio broadcaster, there were glorious turns of phrase. Little sentences summing up life in mini haikus. A year later I still savour them, like aural aromatherapy. Motivation in the morning is delivered by DJ MacKay the Harris Tweed weaver saying, 'Yes it *is*,' in response to my formulaic 'Nice day.'

Calmness returns with Uist crofter Neil MacMillan patiently calculating the last time he spoke English: 'It was not yesterday, nor the day before that. It was not last week nor last weekend. It must have been two weeks ago. Yes – it was then.'

Life-affirming exuberance is delivered by Dr Finlay MacLeod on a day of clear skies and lashing seas at the Butt of Lewis. 'Isn't it marvellous,' he said, all distance swept aside in a shared moment of childlike awe atop the high cliffs.

These Gaels are emotional conductors, with direct connection to the energy found in family, community and nature. Modern mainland life makes that energy harder to source and those connections harder to maintain. It takes time and an absence of distraction to be aware of nature's dynamic.

Sadly, time is one thing mainland minds don't have. We know a few Burns songs, can recite the first verse of a few poems and used to go first-footing – but how do we listen to people, how do we value them, how do we behave towards strangers? How do we perform these least theatrical and most basic acts that underpin human culture?

The Hebridean Gaels are neither perfect nor doomed, but the mix of personality and memory they contribute to the composite character called Scotland is well worth having. It's different. And in a world tending towards conformity, we need all the difference we can get. Particularly when that difference arises from communitarian traditions that used to be the norm across Scotland three short centuries ago.

If human culture is a crop, then the Hebrides have some of the few remaining GM-free fields. Elsewhere, life is full of hybrids. Commerce and culture, materialism and happiness, mobility and dislocation – how well will they coexist in the long term? We need places that offer an alternative – in case our mainland experiment fails or falters. And it might.

Since my original mission was to record enough material for thirteen radio programmes in fourteen days, I had to speed through villages and past whole communities whose stories have therefore not been recorded here. This book is, in every respect, a random set of encounters on the Outer Isles – not a detailed account. Some readers will not understand the term 'croft' – others doubtless drafted the latest crofting legislation. I have the ambition of keeping all on board, though I'm sure each sentence will be subject to instant challenge – especially the following basic definitions.

As my mother says, it's a great life if you don't weaken.

Croft – A croft does *not* necessarily have a house. It's a small parcel of land in the crofting counties north and west of the Great Glen, with protected tenure under the Crofting Act of 1886. The crofter shares rights of access to common grazing and, since 1976, the right to acquire title to the land and become an owner-occupier. The croft is handed down within the family or re-assigned locally.

Free Kirk – The present Free Church (FCs or 'wee frees') dates from an early schism in the 1900s when a minority opposed a proposed merger of churches. When the merger to create the United Free Church went ahead, the Free Presbyterians broke away too (FPs or 'wee, wee frees'). In 2000 another group broke away to form the Free Church Continuing (FCC). The early Free Church backed land reform and opposed landowners choosing local ministers. All branches still use an evangelical style of delivery using only Psalms in their metrical form, sung unaccompanied.

Cráic – Fun or lively conversation, associated with the Irish and Celts. Use it with Gaelic purists (Irish or Scottish) at your peril though – they insist the word was never used in Gaelic society until English speakers implanted it in the 1970s and then Gaelicised the spelling. In Irish *cráic* means arsehole!

Fèis (plural *Fèisean*) – the Gaelic word for a festival or feast. Since 1981 the Fèisean movement has set up around forty week-long Gaelic arts tuition festivals for young local people, which take place mainly across the Highlands and Islands during the summer.

Machair – the Gaelic word for a fertile plain behind a beach covered with a profusion of wild summer flowers. It's formed when calcium carbonate-rich sand is blown inland from beaches and managed by light grazing and haymaking by crofters. The Outer Hebrides has the biggest single collection of this unique European habitat. The beach *tràigh* (pronounced 'try' in Gaelic) is usually fringed with marram – a grass whose extensive root system lets it survive on harsh windswept North Atlantic coasts.

Western Isles Council – has been called *Comhairle nan Eilean Siar* since 1999 and the Western Isles are officially *Na h-Eileanan Siar*. But several other names are used too. And choosing the right one can be as sensitive as getting the great Northern Ireland/ Ulster/ Six Counties naming dilemma right. On the islands, though, no one will ever let you know you've got it wrong. The name Western Isles was used only for Westminster elections until it was applied to the new unitary island council created in 1975. Previously the islands were called the Outer Hebrides which derives from the 'Isles of St Bridgit', the Celtic goddess of fire, whose powerful grip on island communities may have inspired the Christian creation of St Bride the midwife of Christ. In Gaelic though, *Innis Bhrìghde* disappeared from use, giving way to *Innse Gall* (The Isles of Strangers), a strangely derogatory term applied by outsiders during the time of the Norse settlement. Many folk still refer to the islands as *An t-Eilean Fada*, or 'The Long Island'; *Na h-Eileanan a-Muigh* (the Outer Isles) is also heard occasionally. Fabulously few islanders (see Appendix) agree on the best name for their home or the reason for it.

Barra to Vatersay the Southern Isles

Depopulation, missing women and beach landings

Beach-fringed Barra is a mainlander's idea of island heaven. But with a population of just over a thousand at the last census, it's teetering on the brink of viability. Dear knows why. An almost Irish mix of pubs and hotels with busy seafood restaurants greets the visitor at Castlebay. And yet female inhabitants have been quietly leaving Barra for years. Perhaps, as the proverb suggests, island women have found it easier to live with lobsters than island men – fabulous sailors who spend more time at sea than the average crustacean.

Perhaps the problem is far simpler. The neighbouring island of Vatersay was nicknamed 'Bachelor Island' until the 1990s, when a new causeway let island women leave without having to lift a heavy outboard motor or wheedle a two-hour boat journey from an under-occupied passing man.

Whatever the reason behind Vatersay's women trouble – and despite the belated arrival of this 'mod con' – the birth-rate on the Southern Isles is still low and the population's declining. Consequently, there's been mainland pressure to scrap the subsidised air service to the famous Cockle Strand, and no plans to improve the six-hour ferry service that arrives from Oban every other day – not daily even at the height of summer.

Things are tough for Barra. But I suspect tough is what finally gets Barra going.

The hot June day I arrived, the tar on the road was melting. A stream of cars and lorries rolled through the jaws of the ferry onto the pier at Castlebay – probably the best natural harbour in the whole island chain. Caught between the arriving and departing queues of ferry traffic, I leaned on a wall with my bike and overladen panniers, making patterns in the sticky tar with the chequered tread of my trainers. Maybe mainland roads are made of more substantial stuff these days, but I could almost hear my mother telling me to stop making a mess.

Banks of waving yellow flags (irises) flanked the foreshore and white sand glistened beneath every slowly draining, breaking wave. Gulls swooped and a large, animated red-haired family passed – lively with the business of reunion and arrival.

One child, momentarily missed in the swirl, glanced up with those unusual, dark eyes ascribed by Canadian writer Alastair MacLeod to the *Clann Chaluim Ruaidh* – a family group physically dispersed across the world but still genetically united in appearance.

Two old men were squinting into the sun by the harbour wall, watching the Captain hang his jacket over the ship's railing and a deck-hand deftly coil the ferry's thick ropes; all watched, in turn, by visitors stretched out on the lawns of harbour hotels, their eyes fixed on the towering ferry, like Lilliputians regarding an ocean-going Gulliver.

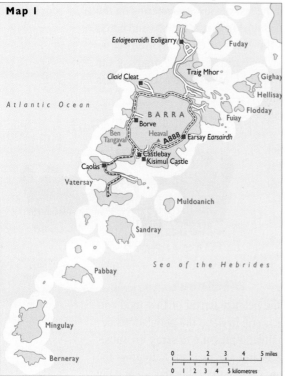

How on earth could such a beautiful and casually eventful place be struggling to keep its people? Of course, summer is deceptive. Islanders trying to attract 'new blood' habitually make incomers stay a winter before making a decision to settle permanently. Even so, it's astonishing how one long, lazy summer day can put the grim reality of rain, isolation, claustrophobia and cancelled winter ferries completely out of mind. I heaved up the hill to check in at the Castlebay Hotel. Minus the weight of panniers and recording equipment, I zipped back down fast, and freewheeled to the only bicycle shop on the island.

Calum was a great find.

'If you went out of here and turned left you'd hit a terrible hill. Then you'd lose heart, come back here and return the bike. So we send people the other way. On the west side it's flat, beautiful beaches, Vatersay if you are energetic: sheep, buttercups, that kind of thing. And of course you have to cycle past three hotels with pubs and food. Everyone comes back at 5pm tired but happy.'

'But you still have to tackle the hill if you cycle round the island.'

'You do still have to tackle that hill, but at the end of the day it's not nearly as big.'

'You find that?'

'I've never been on a bike in my life. Neither has that good for nothing old man who runs this shop, John MacDougall.'

'That's him sitting next door?"

'The very same.'

'Within earshot.'

'Ach he's deaf too. Bit of a dead loss really.'

'So what do you make of my bike for the run?'

'The Claude Butler? You'd be better off with one of ours. The handlebar is too low for you. In fact so is the saddle. Who gave you this bike?'

'Calum, this is a Claude Butler.'

'I can guarantee you'll wish it was a mountain bike when you hit the rough terrain on the west side. And then it'll be too late.'

'Why, what's round there?'

'Well, the site of our new distillery. Up a rather rough single track road. Nothing much to see yet, but it'll be a famous first for the Hebrides. A famous first for Barra yet again. There's also the place you get mobile reception. How long have you been here?'

'An hour.'

'Then a busy, mainland woman like you will have a lot of messages to write down. The signal starts where the road is crumbling. We're waiting for another hurricane to get it fixed. Take a notepad, take in the scenery and take the mountain bike. That's my advice.'

'So if Barra is first with everything, how come it's last to get a mobile phone mast?'

'Don't start. Old folk weren't keen. Part of the rat race. No need for them. But then all the young ones, all our children, started complaining. If they can't text and send pictures of their spots to one another, life's not worth living. And we have to keep them happy because we have to keep them here. To look after people like MacDougall in his old age. So we've changed our minds. Now I've got two mobiles.'

'Do they work?'

'Not yet. I'm keeping them in a drawer for when we get the mast. It won't be long now. We may be a Catholic island, but we've no problem with the colour Orange.'

Calum could sell coals to Newcastle, or the need for a mobile phone

CalMac ferry dominates Castlebay pier

mast to Orange. As it was, he'd just sold a mountain bike. Well, at least a full day's hire.

'By the way, have you seen Donald Manford?'

'Councillor Manford. What a man he is. Have you been looking for him for long?'

'Since I got here.'

'That's not long enough. I can give you his phone number but he's never in.'

'I know, I've been phoning. I need to talk to him about the beach landing…'

'Ach if we'd been meant to fly we'd have been given wings.'

'It's been like trying to find the White Rabbit. Mind you, I've…'

'…no mobile reception. I told you. Get cycling. And take a notepad.'

Castlebay is a circular bay rimmed with islands, promontories and white sandy beaches. Its cycle shop provides the services of one stand-up comedian and one long-suffering (and perfectly fit) boss, John, who finally adjusted my hired bike so well I tried to swap it for my posh-at-one-time-touring Claude Butler. The island is small enough for a three-hour circuit by bike, which is indeed leisurely – till you hit that final hill. The east is rocky, with boats nestling beneath a hill topped by a statue of Our Lady of the Isles – a delicate reminder that these are Catholic communities, where the Sabbath does not bring physical life grinding to any more of a halt than it's been all low-key week long. Legend has it that proselytising Free Kirk ministers from Lewis were on their way to convert the people of the Southern Isles, but couldn't get further south than Benbecula, thanks to islet-, sandbank- and current-ridden straits. It strikes me that Presbyterians were poor negotiators, even then.

The bike shop boys John (Iain Rod) MacDougall and Calum Clelland

I take Calum's advice and opt for the flatter road on the island's west coast, where daisies and buttercups form a carpet of machair behind miles of white sand. I remember suddenly that I once watched an Island Games here, at Borve Point. The highlight was 'Barra wrestling': two men shuffling inside a roughly-drawn circle on the daisy-carpeted grass,

Cycling at Borve, Barra

aiming to catch their opponent off-balance and flip him out of the ring. Some amiable competition had taken place, but the final bout was serious. The two young men were locked together, and after some nimble footwork and consequent loss of balance one had the other locked between his legs in a rather ungainly scissors position. At which point, the bout was interrupted by a small dog repeatedly hurling himself at the centre of the locked arms and swelling chests, tugging unhelpfully at the belt of his wrestling owner.

Amidst much laughter, the dog was hauled off and held with some difficulty while the bout re-started. Within minutes the men were locked in their own intimate tug-of-war once more, lifting and pushing one another round the ring like slightly drunken dancers.

Finally, the two were on their knees, faces taut with exertion and just inches apart. Suddenly the dog owner smiled, and kissed his opponent full square on the mouth. Over-keen to prove his heterosexual credentials, the rival lost his balance and was effortlessly flipped out of the ring.

The two ended up in tears of laughter on the grass, trying vainly to fend off a hopelessly over-excited dog and acknowledge the applause of the crowd. The rules had been stretched, the contest animated by wiles and barefaced cheek, and there was no loser, because there was also no formal winner.

On the Southern Isles, trophies, cups and medals are rare and competition is not the name of the game.

Past Borve Point, there's a road into the rocky interior where building work on the Outer Isles, first distillery will apparently *not* start soon. Another hitch.

Plans for whisky making have rumbled on for years, along with plans for a hard aircraft landing strip near Eoligarry in the north of the island, which would end use of the world-famous Cockle Strand.

The on-off threat to Europe's only beach landing has, for more than a decade, united islanders in joyous, sociable and near total opposition.

Meetings are called, neighbours share cars so some can have a dram afterwards, halls fill and the island's single track roads are a living stream of orderly, one-way traffic. And until now, the islanders have always won. When it comes to fiddling with the Cockle Strand, mainland politicians have been strangely unwilling to force the issue. It could be because of the persuasive powers of the man I'm trying to 'bump into' on the road – local councillor Donald Manford. I'd like to think it's also because interference feels like very bad *cráic*.

Barra has perfected the art of the laid-back (the sign for *Dà Ablach* grocers reads, 'open except when closed') and the island is nearing perfection of the musical riot (it was their 'lively' inaugural *Fèis* to revive traditional music learning amongst local children that kicked off the *Fèisean* movement in 1981). As a result there are just too many happy people – even happy politicians and happy council administrators – with too many happy memories of chaotic island nights to mess lightly with the winning formula.

Historically, very few people have messed successfully with the *Barraich* (Barra folk), especially with Clan MacNeil at the helm. These brilliant sailors spent as much time travelling to Ireland as to the Scottish mainland, reinforcing the Catholic tradition of the Southern Isles, and were not above a spot of piracy should 'alien' boats stray into their waters.

One larger than life Chief was *Ruairi an Tartair* (Noisy Rory), who survived a charge of piracy against Good Queen Bess herself, as John MacPherson recounts in *Tales of Barra*:

> A famous old warrior who flourished at the end of the sixteenth century, Ruairi was said to have committed an act of piracy on a ship of Queen Elizabeth of England and Roderick MacKenzie, a well known highland diplomat of those times, was commissioned to apprehend him. MacKenzie arrived so unexpectedly

**Machair at
Tangasdale, Barra**

MacNeil was sitting in Kismul Castle built on rocks in the sea a hundred metres from Castlebay – without food. He decided to kill two dogs and paint the inside of sheepskin rugs with the blood in the hope MacKenzie would say to himself, 'I may as well clear out – if MacNeil can kill all these sheep I will never starve him out.'

DA A BLACH
Licensed Grocers
Open except when closed.

The trick worked. When MacKenzie found out several years later, he was furious, and planned revenge. He sailed down the coasts of Portugal and Spain and came home with every kind of wine available. He called on MacNeil, tempted him on board with the wine, got him drunk and sailed him off to court in Edinburgh. Happily for MacNeil, the Sheriff was a blood relation – although he did not let on: 'Ruairi was brought before King James VI and I, who asked why he had raided Queen Elizabeth's ship. To which Ruairi replied he was only avenging King James' mother, Mary Queen of Scots, whom Elizabeth had executed. Taken aback by this reply King James allowed him to go free.'

I rather like this tale. Hebridean islanders like Noisy Rory are portrayed as confident, crafty and calm in the face of danger. And like many other pre-Culloden snapshots, island life sounds eventful and unpredictable, with moments of violence and great civility intertwined. Enemies made one day may be entertained the next – people are changeable and passionate, though blood feuds over trifling offences can fester for decades. It conjures up an island chain more *Whisky Galore* than Pastor Jack Glass, with vibrant, colourful characters – not the grey, forbidding personalities mainlanders have come to associate with the Outer Isles. My belief is that somewhere beneath their guarded exterior, modern Hebrideans are still nurturing a healthy disrespect for mainland rules.

My elusive quarry for the day has certainly acquired some of Noisy Rory's wiles.

An Irish correspondent on Radio Scotland once described Charles Haughey as 'a foxy auld whore' (pronouncing that last word to rhyme with stour). He was bestowing the ultimate Celtic accolade upon a man able to duck and weave his way out of trouble and past bureaucrat obstacles, sometimes for the sheer hell of it, sometimes for the common good. I can think of few more genuinely useful civic skills.

Donald Manford, now Transport Convener of Western Isles Council, exhibited his own 'foxy' flair in 1996, when the first closure threat hit Barra's beach landing. He prompted Neil MacPherson, son of a famous local character, the Coddie, to summon me to cover the islanders' plight for Radio Four, not Radio Scotland. Craftily, Donald figured associations with *Whisky Galore* would make the campaign more appealing to sentimental, smog-drenched English commuters than Gael-averse, deep-fried-Mars-Bar-loving Scots.

He was right.

The day I tottered off my first Twin Otter flight I had to beat my way through a throng of Manford-prompted islanders, who had assembled such an array of facts, figures and winning anecdotes they could convince any Doubting Thomas that tampering with the Cockle Strand would cause World War Three and possibly Global Meltdown. It was impressive. In the old days the strength of a clan chief was measured not by the land he owned

– he didn't – but by the loyalty of his fighting men. Donald was taking a leaf from a very old book. There was the writer Sally Beauman, married to actor Alan Howard, whose uncle was Compton MacKenzie and who still has vivid memories of summer visits to the MacKenzie house that overlooks the *Tràigh Mhòr* (the 'big beach' in Gaelic but Cockle Strand in English).

Twin Otter, Cockle Strand and proud Loganair Captain

Sally reliably informed me that Compton MacKenzie would turn in his grave if the diggers attacked even a part of the precious vista to build a 'hard landing strip'. A local cockler explained – with graphs – that the lucrative shellfish trade would be destroyed, because every self-respecting winkle, cockle and crustacean would leg it elsewhere with the changing tidal patterns caused by construction. Next in the airport queue was George Macleod, the redoutable proprietor of the Castlebay Hotel. George was unstoppable. Tourism would be destroyed by a boring piece of concrete replacing the world's most romantic, shell-based beach landing. And the new planes would only be able to land when the wind direction matched the single direction of the strip, so the new service would be less reliable. Sticking with the beach/ Twin Otter combination would guarantee landings in any weather, into any wind direction, with happy pilots landing on a miracle of nature.

The outcry worked – plans for that hard landing strip were shelved, though not abandoned. And even though the damned Twin Otter was so unreliable it broke down for my own return journey, I could only marvel at the speed with which Donald instantly offered the services of one of his brothers with a speedy boat to connect me to the bus over on South Uist and a trip home via Benbecula airport instead. Bouncing across the choppy waves of the Sound with another entertaining Manford at the helm, it occurred to me the brothers had almost planned this too. What the hell, I thought. Job done.

Well, not quite.

Although the proposal was shelved, the problem of the Cockle Strand is back on the agenda today, which is why I'm cycling round Barra looking for Donald Manford once again.

The snag is the plane – De Havilland of Canada stopped making the Twin Otter thirty years ago, which means every time there's a fault, the plane and the service is grounded. Sometimes the replacement part can only be found in Canada and must waltz its way across the Atlantic (in a 'proper' plane) while frustrated islanders and tourists embark on a six-hour ferry journey to Oban (and thereafter a two-hour drive, or three-hour bus journey to Glasgow by road); the alternative is a three-hour journey across the Sound of Eriskay and up South Uist to the indestructible RAF landing strip on Benbecula. Balavanich airport is served by a fleet of very sensible and slightly soulless Shorts 360s, which cannot land on Barra's beach because their undercarriage retracts during flight, allowing the ingress of salt water, rusting and corrosion.

Why isn't there a modern Twin Otter? It seems Britain insists that small planes have two engines, whilst Canada and the rest of the world need only one. So De Havilland abandoned much twin-engine production thirty years ago, concentrating on single-engine models like the Cessna. And that has left 'wet' British landing environments, like Barra, high and dry. Strange. If one engine is good enough to get Canadians across dodgy mountain-, bear- and forest-strewn habitats, why isn't it good enough for us? I don't know, but cycling round Barra that sunny day I knew I did need to quiz Donald Manford about the latest terminal-looking challenge to the Twin Otter. I was now employing my Pleiades technique. The star cluster tends to disappear when directly viewed – a bit like Donald. So I stopped trying to find him and headed south for Vatersay.

Vatersay

Vatersay is an island just south of Barra. In 1991 a causeway was built linking its flat, fertile land to its hilly, more populous neighbour. This meant no more prize bulls like Bernie drowning whilst swimming across the Sound of Vatersay to the 'mainland'– the incident in the late eighties which guaranteed the causeway's construction.

But Vatersay's problems aren't over – the island could soon become two, if sea levels continue to rise. Those hurricane force storms that bashed Barra's main road also forced waves right up the stunning, white beaches on either side of the narrow isthmus of land, and in January 2005, the island temporarily became Inner and Outer Vatersay.

It was a moment Michael Campbell was dreading. Almost as much, it transpired, as our interview.

When I met the young islander and his sister Mairi outside Vatersay Hall, I realised I had exchanged a slightly breathless hello with Mairi as she stood talking with a friend half an hour earlier. And Michael had driven past with no more than a non-committal Hebridean wave.

'Ach, we weren't sure it was you.'

'Right enough, there must be hundreds of lone forty-something female cyclists over here.'

'You'd be surprised.'

Michael Campbell is a member of the Vatersay Boys – a former Vatersay bachelor and now proud father of two girls. 'It was all just a bit of a laugh to get into the papers really – now there are women everywhere.' The Boys appear to be the nearest thing in the Southern Isles to the early Rolling Stones. Not exactly trashing rooms on tour or guitars on set, but gaining a reputation for playing into the wee small hours, reaching venues by improbable means and conducting gigs in a 'robust' manner. You can almost imagine Hebridean bedrooms with youngsters practising air-accordion in the mirror – that's how croft-credible the Vatersay Boys have become. A status which doubtless relies upon not giving interviews to random 'lady journalists'. I quite understood Michael's reluctance to speak. As a wild man of Hebridean rock, he had a reputation to maintain.

So it was all the more impressive when we finally gathered chairs and tape recorder in the suntrap beside the newly extended village hall and Michael let rip without further prompting about the coastal erosion now threatening the island.

'In the old days, the *Bhatarsaich* (Vatersay folk) hauled wrecked boats or old machinery onto the sand to stop the dunes retreating further inland. In a few months they were covered, but in the meantime they didn't look too good. Some tourists didn't like it – the beaches looked industrial, they said. So they complained and now the authorities say only biodegradable material can be used. That pile of wooden pallets is all we can use to stabilise the sand now. It's ironic really, because the same visitors are wandering all over the dunes, breaking off tiny bits of marram. It's not their fault – but how can we stop them?'

I was suddenly flooded with guilt. I had just put Calum's mountain bike through its paces with a helter skelter slide down a whole crumbling slope of sand dune before standing by my machine for some pictures taken by Crofters Commission cum part-time photographer Eoin McNeil.

With predictions of sea levels rising twenty-three centimetres by 2050, the *Bhatarsaich* are in a valiant but losing battle, which Michael believes they are facing largely on their own. His mum maintains the dunes have moved thirty metres inland since her young days, but there are no photographs to prove it and so locals can only get help to combat the most recent damage. Meantime, Mairi's main summer task is to organise a ceilidh to celebrate a famous victory, not against the sea, but against overpopulation and the accompanying threat of migration and depopulation.

In 1906 men from overpopulated Barra and Mingulay, including Michael and Mairi's forebears, seized land on Vatersay which had been cleared by the owner, Lady Gordon Cathcart, to make way for a sheep farm. The 'Vatersay Raiders' were arrested and jailed in Edinburgh, but released after a public outcry. The island was bought by the state and fifty-eight crofts created for its new inhabitants, carefully excluding the original raiders, it's said, who died landless and unaided in the poorhouse. A cautionary tale about the dangers of being first to stick your head over the parapet, but a great triumph for Southern Islanders whose ancestors had been hunted down for removal by Lieutenant Colonel John Gordon of Cluny sixty years earlier. Francis Thompson in *The Western Isles* quotes government sources who reported conditions on Cluny's Barra:

> The scene of wretchedness which we witnessed as we entered the estate of Colonel Gordon was deplorable, nay, heart rending. On the beach the whole population of the country seemed to be met, gathering the precious cockles. I never witnessed such countenances – starvation on many faces – the children with their melancholy looks, big looking knees, shrivelled legs, hollow eyes, swollen like bellies – God help them, I never did witness such wretchedness.

Between 1849 and 1851 about 2,000 people were forcibly shipped from South Uist and Barra to Quebec – Colonel Gordon's answer to the problem. Some embarked voluntarily, with a promise that they would be conveyed free of expense to Canada where on arrival government agents would give them work and grant them land. These conditions were not fulfilled. They were turned adrift at Quebec and compelled to beg their way to Upper Canada. The Canadian newspapers teemed with accounts of the miseries endured by those unfortunate immigrants, who could speak only Gaelic. Those unwilling to accept the Colonel's promises found themselves hunted – men were attacked and thrown, often unconscious, arms bound, onto the waiting ships. Members of families were torn apart and put on to ships with different destinations in the Americas. In February, 1851 a group of [the remaining] sixty-one destitutes made their way from Barra to Inverness and sat down helpless in front of the townhouse.

Freewheel in prospect to the Barra–Vatersay causeway

This desperate plea for help stoked the land reform movement, but somehow Colonel Gordon's ruthless behaviour on Barra hasn't embedded him in Highland folklore in the same way as the Duke of Sutherland or his notorious factor, Patrick Sellar.

That might be because the absolute numbers evicted on the islands was small. It might

**Wondering whether
to go on to Vatersay**

be because remoteness kept the tales local. Or it might have been because of the wholesale nature of the evictions.

As Harris-based historian Bill Lawson points out, many parts of Lewis are very bitter about the Clearances, despite having fewer evictions than neighbouring Harris – but more Lewis folk were left to bear witness to what happened. In areas where people were removed lock, stock and barrel, there is less anger because no one was left to fuel it with memory and tales.

Survivors are largely elsewhere, in Cape Breton and Nova Scotia, not exactly 'nursing their wrath to keep it warm', but keeping Gaelic and the culture of clanship alive. It is a supreme irony.

Many of the 'losing' evicted families built large houses and small ranches in the New World. Many of the 'winning' families who stayed have lived in the same substandard housing stock for generations. It's a problem that's been largely ignored until very recently. As if the prize of being allowed to remain on the islands two hundred years ago should be enough for their 'lucky' descendants today. As if hopes for a warm, watertight, dry house is a greedy step too far.

The outlook of the lairds has somehow become enshrined in the planning philosophy of today's local authorities. The enduring aesthetic of emptiness means 'cleared' glens are considered too beautiful to be marred by the council houses, low-cost homes and static caravans locals can afford. The historic absence of services like mains water and electricity means the price of house building is prohibitively expensive anyway. And local would-be house builders are still forced to fight on the margins, with both hands tied behind their backs, for tiny parcels of overpriced land – just like their forefathers and mothers.

Unable to compete with crofters for their land or common grazing, unable to fight topography for what remains, unable to challenge habitat designations that have turned many areas into Sites of Special Scientific Interest, and unable to compete with wealthier incomers for the occasional house plots that become available. It's as if Scotland's Victorian landowners are having the last laugh.

Even Scotland's land reform legislation, which is transforming ownership patterns across the islands, fails to bite in the most extensively cleared areas – because there are no communities left to exercise a right to buy.

But back to Barra.

Thirty-five years after the *Barraich* walked to Inverness, the Napier Commission produced 3,000 pages of evidence, which resulted in the Crofters Act of 1886. Many celebrate that date as the year fairness finally entered island land dealings. In fact, there was no relief for the most overcrowded areas. The Act gave security to those already on croft land but created no new crofts and therefore did nothing to help families sharing land with landless relatives (cottars). In the eyes of the factors, they could simply have evicted their own kith and kin. Culturally, that was unthinkable. That's why, twenty years after the Crofting Act 'settlement', men from overcrowded Barra and Mingulay embarked on dangerous land raids – to avoid disease, malnourishment, and family break-up. That's probably also why, within days of war being declared in 1914, those same men signed up to fight for the state that had finally helped them gain land on Vatersay.

Perhaps because of those brutal Clearance Days, the *Bhatarsaich* are more conscious than most of the need to commemorate lost souls. There's a memorial marking the burial site of 350 people, including children, who drowned when the *Annie Jane* sunk en route from Liverpool to Quebec in 1853. And just along from the village hall lies the wreckage of an RAF plane, which crashed in 1944 killing three of the men on board. According to Mairi, one of the survivors returned recently and was grateful the crash site had been left undisturbed. These small, respectful gestures are also the self-defining acts of a confident island culture. But little Vatersay is a self-contained island no more. The causeway means Vatersay folk must share schools, community centres and even their church with Big Brother Barra. Mairi concedes connection has its downside. For one thing, it's a lot less fun.

'It was like the Wild West over here before the causeway. No police, no MOT – I was driving when I was seven, sitting on a cushion to reach the wheel.'

'Aye I was driving when I was five. [See younger brothers – see competitive?] We used to sail across to dances at Castlebay in appalling weather…'

'And the amazing thing is, our parents let us go. Mind you, we had an engine on board – they used to sail across. They were so hardy. It's only now I have kids of my own I realise how much they trusted us. That was the only way to learn. I remember one night it was howling a gale. I was dressed up to the nines – mini skirt, platform soles, leather jacket – the works.'

'Aye, and we were determined to go to this dance. So Dad came out with us to the slipway and pointed out the route we should take. Stay close to the shore, he said, watch for the rocks. And off we went.'

'It was absolutely hair-raising. We were soaked by the time we got to Castlebay and had to go and dry off at my auntie's, but what an entrance we made!'

'Aye they all knew when the Vatersay crew had arrived.'

'Aye.'

And there was clearly a moment of regret there for wild times past.

'Och, we all calm down in our forties,' I try to offer helpfully.

'Speak for yourself. I'm thirty.'

'Right. Do your kids sail?'

'No.'

There's no finessing the hard truth. Times change. And islands are not exempt.

Vatersay ways may be less adventurous but they are also more female friendly. I'm sure the seven-year-old drivers inside Mairi and Michael would hate to admit it, but the thrill of a two-hour boat voyage wears off pretty fast when you need to get a sick kid to the doctor. Mairi herself works as a nurse in the Castlebay practice.

'The causeway has certainly let women take decent, non-crofting jobs in Barra.'

And, despite the undoubted charm of young guns like her brother, the causeway is probably more responsible than any other factor for getting local women to stay. And all joking aside, that matters. Because there is no doubt, it's young women who are about to sink the Western Isles.

Broken pallets near a Vatersay beach

Road-sharing, island
style

Women

The 2007 Outer Hebrides Migration Study states baldly that twice as many young women as young men are peeling away from the traditional crofting areas on the Western Isles; and 71 per cent of the incomers are men. If the current trends continue, there will be more males than females by 2009.

Now this demographic role reversal may sound like heaven for women wanting a bit of prospective partner choice. The Western Isles have been 'woman heavy' since the 1930s, when the combined force of First World War casualties and emigration removed proportionally more young men from the islands than from any other part of the UK. Traditionally on the Hebrides, men have left and women have stayed. That bedrock is now shifting and the whole infrastructure of island life is being shaken. Fewer children are being born, the population is ageing and these old people need care – traditionally supplied by women, who have left.

Why are they leaving?

If anyone could answer that question, rural societies across the world wouldn't be sharing the Western Isles' problem. Ten years ago, Norway's first female Minister of Agriculture, Gunhild Øyangen, had a try. She surveyed areas losing population and discovered that contrary to local mythology it was women who were leaving first:

> The young girl dreams of another life than her mother's. A professional career may be easier to obtain in the cities. The small villages are felt to be narrow-minded and with no space for untraditional or unconventional behaviour. The girls lack relevant female role models, and few local jobs fit with their future plans. Many social and cultural activities are those that men favour, like hunting and fishing, and this does not necessarily attract younger women.

Spot on.

The Norwegian solution was truly radical. They introduced quotas to get women into local planning and politics: 'Women can be a vitamin injection in the democratic process'. They paid remote mums or dads who wanted to bring up their children full-time. They gave special funding to women setting up businesses in remote areas: 'Women's ventures tend to add value to the raw materials produced by male labour.' They backed places for socialising, other than the sheep fank. They put public money into creating challenging indoor jobs, not just producing more jobs at fish farms. And they paid for good public transport to stop women feeling trapped without access to boats or cars.

At least the causeway to Vatersay means women can work elsewhere.

But in a society which still calls girls Hughina and Williamina (because they might have been boys) few seem to understand that the new generation of young women might take offence at being offered second-class status. This may partly be because women have accepted it for decades, opting to leave quietly rather than risk family wrath by questioning the Island Terms of Trade.

I have to say gals, it's time to risk that wrath and have that argument. If island ways don't change to suit the women who're leaving, they'll change to suit the incomers who are arriving. And that will be a profoundly bigger shift. But I see very few women openly arguing.

From Barra to the Butt, many women with whom I had hugely enjoyable private conversations bolted the minute I even mentioned the microphone… and made me promise I would divulge nothing of their inner thoughts. Happily – and I began to fear, symbiotically – most men had no such misgivings. One husband even told me to delete the perfectly innocent interview I'd just completed at the breakfast table with his wife about the trials and tribulations of running a B&B. I pointed out the series of radio programmes would give the impression no women lived on the Isles.

'So be it,' he said. And the fabulously effusive lady of the house stood there, eyes downcast, embarrassed to the core. Women don't argue back in public here. I don't know what happens in private. But that absence of public dissent may be mistaken for widespread female satisfaction with the 'old ways'.

Wrong. Women don't argue – they either accept the deal or leave without warning when the impenetrable brick wall is finally revealed in its full archaic glory. Excuses will be given, punches will be pulled, but no one close to the decision will be in any doubt. Intelligent women are leaving the Isles just as intelligent women are leaving Africa as nurses or Belfast as students. Rigid, macho societies that offer no challenge to capable women will lose them.

In a survey of Scottish Councils in 2003, for COSLA (the Convention of

Scottish Local Authorities) the Western Isles and Orkney Islands Council tied for the lowest percentage of women councillors – at 10 per cent, less than half the Scottish average. More women in island government would not in itself turn the depopulation problem around – the fact it is currently unthinkable speaks silent volumes. Doubtless some Gaels will think they're better off without demanding, 'modern' women. But if independent-minded young women do feel forced to leave, the language will leave with them. So too the chance of creating another generation of native Gaelic-speaking children. One of the biggest and least discussed problems for the language is the loss of Gaelic-speaking mums and their replacement by English-speaking women. Some have learned Gaelic, many have tried, but most know only a few words. And that can be enough to stop Gaelic being used informally by their children – even though the dads may be native. Ironically again, the more 'traditional' the household, the more it falls to the women to inculcate language skills and prompt basic, intimate communication with children. So Gaelic is losing sassy, young, native would-be mums, at its peril.

What can be done?

Apart from some radical Norwegian moves to haul women to the centre of civic life, there needs to be a power shift between the generations. Youth has always bowed to experience on the Isles and with the spectre of depopulation the natural tendency for the older generation is to exert authority and ground kids to stop them breaking the rules that have hitherto made life on the margins possible. It's a natural tendency and a completely counter-productive one. Happily, the canny *Barraich* are already doing the opposite.

Barra's elders are fighting for their children's right to party. That means a mobile phone mast campaign, a broadband campaign and an endless campaign to improve transport. The *Barraich* know that easy leaving promotes easy returning. It's only when people feel forced to choose that they quit the islands forever. I'm told by a young woman at the Castlebay Hotel, for example, that a wonderful café serving curry on the pier is doomed because it has removed the main legitimate excuse for going to Glasgow.

The white, white sands of Vatersay

Young islanders like coming and going. The only reason many of them stay is because they can leave. It may sound paradoxical but good transport stops depopulation. The Aran Islanders off Galway, who have taken over their ferries, make sure the first trip every morning is outgoing, to get locals to mainland jobs – not incoming, to facilitate tourists. Seems to me this is the right way round.

Many politicians seem to think a happy islander is a remote islander. Give them an expensively constructed linkspan or a regular ferry, and they'll simply use it to leave. Where they do, the islanders have been made to wait without hope for too long. Like the people of Mingulay – the next day's destination, and a journey which will fulfil my own grandmother's hopeless dream.

Pabbay not getting to Mingulay

Caithness and ghostly piping

Like any good Caithness woman, my mum regarded Wick as 'home' and (confusingly for Belfast-based children adjusting to the news we were actually born in Wolverhampton) talked endlessly about what we'd be able to do, how much fun we'd have and what a world of enormous value we'd reconnect with when we went 'home' for the summer. I really liked Belfast (despite the constraints of living in a city undergoing a civil war) but understood that Mum was basically marking time. She went to events at the Presbyterian (and therefore largely ex-pat Highland) church. She attended the Women's Guild and faithfully came to our school concerts. But adventures, connection, laughter, being bundled into cars, sitting on people's knees, Sunday School picnics, sunburn, races on the beach, prizes for having the biggest collection on Gala Day – these all happened in Wick not Belfast. In Wick, with family, we belonged. In Belfast, with neighbours, we simply lived.

IS FUAR AN GOILE NACH TEODH DEOCH

IT'S A COLD STOMACH THAT DRINK WON'T WARM

SEAN-FHACAL
GAELIC PROVERB

The penny dropped slowly but it settled hard. 'Home' was generally somewhere else, almost always out of reach. Those were the days before any motorway north of Glasgow or any bridge above Inverness. Our trips started with a drive to Larne, a three-hour sea crossing to Stranraer and a slow progress towards the monster that was Glasgow – a crazed asphalt octopus that sucked cars in and spat them out again at random, almost anywhere. Sometimes the post-Glasgow journey north found us on the Loch Lomond road, sometimes the A9. Sometimes we wound up in the Sma Glen, sometimes at the Devil's Elbow (where I once tried to collect cloud in a jam jar and gave all my pocket money to the lone piper in the

car park). We were always heading north, detouring occasionally to visit Dad's parents in Banffshire – hardy and hardened souls who lived in a dark council bungalow – one of ten built at a crossroads in the middle of nowhere after the war. There was lino beneath the hair mattress beds, hard loo paper, green carbolic soap, and a shelf behind a curtain in the kitchen where things like milk always stayed lukewarm. Everything in the main room was dark brown, including the plastic tablecloth, which was carefully laid when we ate lunch – always broth followed by sliced ham and

Posing in Banffshire, aged 7

31

Granda Riddoch and me in front of his 'Chinchilla' shed

tomatoes – and tea – always boiled hare/ rabbit/chicken or mince. Churchill looked down from one wall, the Queen from the other. People appeared at meal times to insure everything – my granda was a farmer who became the first insurance broker in rural Banffshire, when he was warned more heavy work would damage a weak heart. So he bought a motorbike and sidecar and drove round Banffshire persuading farmers to buy policies. He bought a monkey while he was at it and the monkey and my young dad were often squeezed in the sidecar as well. Between them they saved half the county's farmers by insuring their stock against Foot and Mouth disease just before an epidemic. After that people wanted to insure everything. Houses, cars, tractors, even false teeth (though that could've been another of Dad's embellishments).

The house at Ordiquil wasn't our favourite place. Tatties and tea bags sat inexplicably in tin buckets of rain water outside the back door. Together with my brother Graeme (a year younger) we had to make our own entertainment because the staring neighbours' kids simply wouldn't speak to us on principle. Luckily, though, my granda was an eccentric. Deprived of regular contact with farm animals he bought exotic pets instead.

After the monkey died he bred Chihuahua dogs (unsuccessfully) and Chinchilla rabbits to make fur coats. He couldn't bring himself to kill them and ended up with hundreds in cages lining the walls of an old barn at the back of the house. For no reason (other than to alert them to our presence) the door was kept locked and the mere sound of the huge key turning was enough to send their grey backsides diving for the safety of their wooden boxes. All we ever saw of them in sixteen years was a hundred fat, furry bums disappearing with a soft twang and the sound of a hundred mesh cage wires being stretched and released like guitar strings by two hundred nervous back paws.

Once they'd leapt into the boxes, hours of watching would yield nothing. They could hear our very existence. Although I'll grant you, at the age of six or seven our existences weren't exactly quiet. We only banged on the boxes in frustration once. They didn't come out for days.

Once Chinchilla-baiting was over, we could look for fish in the burn – devoid of fish, I later discovered, because it was part of the local sewerage system – or niggle dad to go to Aberchirder, a neighbouring village where a sweet shop sold packets of chewing gum with highly collectable and swappable pictures of (inevitably) English football players, extensive acquaintance with whose pictures has left me with a Tourette's-like need to bark out their names when certain towns are mentioned. Burnley means forever Ralph Coates. East Fife is Eddie McCreadie. Huddersfield is Frank Worthington.

Occasionally we got to the swimming baths at Huntly – where we knew no one – the shop in Banff where we each bought a summer hat (and wore it once), and Tarlair, the outdoor swimming pool that we resolutely refused to enter because of rats – and that was it.

Joy without ending began two weeks of crushing boredom later, when we left Banffshire and headed first west and then *north* again, past intriguing roads leading to other parts of the enormous mystery that was the Highlands – a mystery we never had time to uncover.

As we drove, Dad invoked his annual rituals – feigning brake failure as we whizzed down the ski-jump-descent to Berriedale in Caithness, past sandpit escape routes that ended abruptly in battered-looking kick boards. And then he'd pretend we'd run out of petrol chugging and chuttering up the steep hairpin bends on the other side. Past the signpost to Badbea, where Mum would tell us the Duke of Sutherland forced people to live on clifftops. Past the Whaligoe Steps where Mum told us evicted families had to carve steps out of the cliff to reach the sea to fish and women walked barefoot into Wick with the fish baskets on their heads, to sell the fish for next to nothing. On we went, past the blowhole at Thrumster, where, according to Granda More, we got our family name and Mediterranean ancestry. It seems rescuers of a Spanish Armada ship in a terrible storm during the seventeenth century were asked by exhausted local res-

The Caithness mafia – grandparents, aunts, sporrans and mum (far right)

cuers if there were still people to save onboard. The answer came, 'More, More' – and so all the Moors saved were called Mores instead. Perhaps. Past Hempriggs Loch where some giant water beast lived. Past the Old Man of Wick, a castle on a clifftop promontory about which Mum would recite, 'The Old Man of Wick was a very old man when the Old Man of Hoy was a Boy.' Quite what it meant was a mystery. But a mystery along with so many others, it didn't really matter.

Arrival at my grandmother's council house in Wick was a very different affair to arrival at Cornhill. Nana More was out in the street waiting for us and wept when we arrived. She wept when we left. Thrust money into our hands when we went anywhere.

And though she was tough as nails, having brought up five children on a baker's wage, her council house was covered in roses. Roses in clumps of three on the wallpaper of the back bedroom, where Graeme and I tried to sleep in a double bed with a bolster pillow down the middle to stop him provoking fights (okay, it was probably the other way around). Faded lavender roses on the comfortable chairs and settees in her front room and, during the summer, curtains of the same flowery material, which were changed back to sombre winter curtains after we left.

Granda More was a big smile of a man. Even though a straightforward operation had gone badly wrong in the seventies and he had lost a leg and gained a colostomy bag, I never recall a complaint or a frown. He sang constantly, stashed quarter-pound bags of Callard and Bowser toffees behind ornaments in glass cases and offered them round when Nana wasn't watching. I remember him trying to get on the trampoline at the Wick Playing Fields on the basis that he weighed the same as a child minus his wooden leg, which he was quite prepared to un-strap. He went every other day to the Fishermen's Rest overlooking Wick Harbour and sat with his cronies, judging the size and cut of the new trawlers, commenting on landings and chewing toffees non-stop.

A six-foot thirteen-year-old, mum and brother

My Caithness grandmother – on the long haul between Granda's death and her own – kept cuttings from the *Scots Magazine* in her bible. About one place, mostly. The island of Mingulay. She held the cuttings before me one day, as if the dramatic, over-colourised snapshots were the Crown Jewels. It was more than a place to her – it was an idea of perfection. She had once had the chance to go to the Western Isles and visit the home of the Gaelic herring gutting women she knew in her youth. She didn't take that chance then – now oesteoporosis and age made the journey impossible. Although, in an attempt to cheer her up, I suggested once that we just get in my car and go.

'You go.'

She died a few months later.

Now, finally, I'm going.

Or maybe not.

It's 9am, I've left another set of messages on the various phone numbers of the White Rabbit, and I'm down at the pier on another cloudless, warm summer's day, hearing that the north-easterly wind direction is guaranteed to make landing impossible at Mingulay's only landing spot. I simply refuse to believe it. The sea looks flat calm.

Once we leave the shelter of Castlebay I have to accept it's not.

Pabbay

Skipper Donald MacLeod suggests we land on Pabbay, five miles from Mingulay, to see if the wind calms while he goes back for the second boatload – more members of the Islands Book Trust, whose redoubtable organiser John Ran-

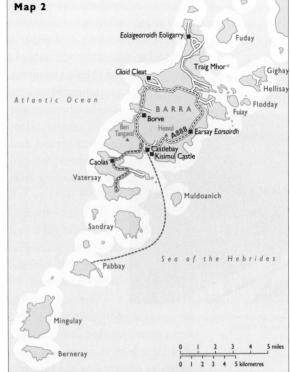

dall (former Registrar General of Scotland) has organised the trip. Calum MacNeil, the folk historian of Barra, who talked movingly the previous night about his forebears on Mingulay, has opted to stay behind for the second boat. Realising I need an expert local voice to interview, I ask him on the pier if the guide on the first boat, Mairi Ceit, can speak.

'She can fairly speak,' says Calum. 'You'll be fine.'

It's only when the small party has landed on Pabbay and assembled round a strange burial mound overlooking the empty, white beach that I realise I have asked the wrong question. Mairi Ceit can certainly speak, but she will not be recorded.

In deep, dramatic tones the Barra native explains the long history behind the grassy knoll and neighbouring ruined house. She tells us the inhabitants of the house in the nineteenth century believed it to be cursed. Some had premonitions of a disaster at sea. Others believed bodies interred in the burial mound had been disturbed. A carved stone at the base suggests the vertical cemetery – created that way because soil was so precious and the earth so hard to dig – has been in use for over 800 years. Whatever the truth, no one would live in the house, and this at a time when men were risking imprisonment to raid land on neighbouring islands, so chronic were problems of homelessness and overcrowding. Miles away on Barra, no one would re-use the lintels of the house. It was fascinating stuff, her voice and accent were beautiful, but when I pleaded with Mairi Ceit to repeat the tale with the tape running, she looked me squarely in the face.

'I've been asked before and I don't think it does any good. The answer is no.' As another woman of iron resolve once observed, this lady was not for turning. Since there was no sign of the returned boat, Mairi Ceit went on to tell us about the island we had missed.

Changing boats to land on Pabbay

Mingulay was first named 'the nearer St Kilda' in an article written in 1883. Like its more famous and distant island relative, Mingulay's inhabitants depended on eating seabirds and their eggs (guillemots, razorbills, puffins and cormorants) gathered by men crawling along ledges on the towering cliffs, dwarfed in Britain only by the sea walls of Hirta on St Kilda. Until the eighteenth century, it was a good – though isolated – place to live, with peat for fuel, fertile soil for crops, fish in the sea, eggs on the cliffs and fertile grazing for cattle and sheep. It was not a cash economy. The inhabitants paid their rent in shearwater meat and feathers.

One year when the rent collector arrived from Barra, he was puzzled by the complete absence of people awaiting the ship. He sent ashore MacPhee (from Colonsay), the clan chief's right-hand man, who came back shouting that everyone was dead. Too late. Fearing the worst, his companions had already set sail without him. MacPhee buried those who had had no one left to bury them and spent the winter on the hill, sleeping in a crevice which was subsequently named after him. In the spring the boat returned and left stores, the men reportedly shouting to MacPhee, 'You've managed the winter. Another six months won't do any harm.'

MacPhee survived what writer Ben Buxton considers might have been Britain's first recorded case of bird flu and MacNeil gave him a dispensation from rent for his own lifetime and let him re-colonise Mingulay with people of his own choice from Barra. The settlers built a new village near the shore, and these are the ruins we would have seen – slowly being overwhelmed by the sand. Back in the days of the MacPhee though, these ruins would have been very busy. Overcrowded in fact. There were fifty-two people in 1764, 114 (living in just eighteen households) in 1841, and 160 in the 1880s. As Ben Buxton writes in *The Decline and Fall of Mingulay*:

> The rising population led to overcrowding in the village and there were outbreaks of disease such as typhoid, measles and influenza. It was often impossible to get to Barra to summon the doctor or just as importantly the priest. Fishing was by line, for cod and ling – the fish were cured on the rocks and the fishermen sold them as far away as Glasgow and Northern Ireland. Their efforts were hampered by isolation and the lack of a sheltered landing place for boats. People and goods were landed on rocks, and boats had to be hauled up onto the beach. This was quite an operation and necessitated wading out to chest height in the

water. For much of the winter launching boats was impossible. The larger boats needed for catching herring were too big to land on the beach and two owned by Mingulay men had to be left at anchor in Castlebay. A visitor reported, 'it is no unusual occurrence for islanders to have to throw their bags of meal into the sea and drag them ashore by means of a rope. It is easier to reach America than to get there.'

In 1896 every man on the island signed a petition taken by their MP to the Secretary of State for Scotland on behalf of a 'sorely-distressed community'. They appealed for a 'boat slip with a boat hauling convenience'. Five years later they got a small crane instead. It may have been useful, but the big problem of landing boats remained – and there is still no fixed pier or slipway.

With these constraints on fishing, land pressure due to a rising population, and a new demand for rent paid in cash, islanders left to earn money: men to the shipyards and gas works of Glasgow, women to the herring towns along the east coast of Scotland and England. These jobs opened the islanders' eyes to the living standards and ways of the outside world. But the final spark which led to the desertion of Mingulay in 1912 was seeing somewhere like home but better – Vatersay. And the islanders moved as they lived – together.

Nowadays Mingulay has become a magnet for 'radical climbers', citylubbers who climb for fun on cliffs locals once had to climb for seabird eggs and survival. Life's strange.

Pabbay is strange too. Despite the holy connection of its past, the island was famous locally for illegal distilling. According to Calum MacNeil, the last recorded distillers were the Glanceys from Co. Leitrim in Ireland, who used Pabbay's crevices to hide their distilling equipment. And it was big trade. The Glanceys became so respectable they married into Calum MacNeil's own family on Barra. In the 1840s, the priest's account book showed entries for mixed and distilled whiskies. As the proverb says, *It's a cold stomach that drink won't warm.* Evidently locals weren't fond of cold stomachs.

John Randall of the Islands Book Trust

Everyone tried to protect the bold distillers from the excisemen – even though the taxmen included sympathetic figures like Alexander Carmichael, who was assigned to Skye and the Uists and joined the team of pioneering folklorists collecting tales for the four-volume *Popular Tales of the West Highlands* (1860–62) compiled by John Francis Campbell. Later Carmichael published *Carmina Gadelica*, a collection of prayers, hymns, charms, incantations, blessings, runes, and other literary-folkloric poems and songs collected between 1855 and 1910. The men crewing the boats (usually lighthouse boats doubling as excise transporters) were a match for all officialdom. If

On Vatersay, Pabbay's nearest inhabited neighbour

they hoisted a light brown sail, the Pabbay distillers would know there was no danger from the boat as it rounded the coastline of neighbouring Sandray (an island currently earmarked for long term storage of nuclear waste). A white sail meant danger – exciseman aboard. But for some reason this large illegal trade never blossomed into a fully-fledged, legal business. To this day, there is not a single distiller along the entire length of the Long Island. Calum MacNeil believes that's because of the hardline nature of the clergy – Catholic, Kirk and Free Church. He maintains the Catholic Church was no less rigorous with its flock than the notoriously strict Free Church. On Sundays he remembers having to attend Mass at 9am (one old sailor took Mass every morning before heading off to sea) – then Sunday School in the afternoon and Rosary and Benediction in the evening.

Some of our landing party had decided to go and look for the old distillery site on the high cliffs of the west side. As they peeled off, life for me got considerably stranger. Mairi Ceit and I sat on the flower-studded grass beside the cursed ruined house **waiting for the boat** (now four hours late) and starting to feel a little like the abandoned MacPhee (in Gaelic, 'black fairy') of Mingulay. She pointed out a prehistoric site a hundred metres away above the beach. Always one for a prehistoric potter, I got up and, starting to walk across, distinctly heard the sound of pipes floating in from the sea. Not random notes: certain phrases were being repeated.

As I walked on across the hummocky bog, the music stopped abruptly. The prehistoric remains were beyond, and I lay between the narrow walls for a while, as if in a stone coffin. By the time I got up to return to Mairi Ceit, I was humming an old waulking song to myself and had forgotten the piping. Until I reached the same place at the side of the house and the same pipe tune started drifting up from the sea. I stood there long enough to take a rain check – was the sound inside or outside my head? Was I visualising the music or hearing it? I have been hypnotised quite easily in the past – had Mairi Ceit unwittingly planted a suggestion?

The sound continued until I walked on to sit beside our island guide, who for some reason took my hand in her own and held it softly while – for some other reason – I started crying. I told her about the music.

'You have heard it,' was all she said.

And in fact that was all that needed to be said. She had politely refused to be recorded half an hour earlier– after which I had been given a vivid demonstration that machines are not the only means of recording sound.

My emotional encounter and subsequent ascent of the largest hill on Pabbay meant I was exhausted when half an hour later the boat pulled into sight round Sandray. While Mairi and I had been disentangling the past, one of its engines had become entangled in seaweed and a diver from Castlebay had been called out to free the propeller. We had a bumpy return journey (just as well no one had eaten all day), reflecting on the hardiness of the people from Mingulay, who scaled cliffs, sailed in open boats to Ireland, and sometimes to their deaths, but who failed to grab the headlines like the St Kildans, because no mainland cruise ships came by to witness their situation and write them into history.

And as for the haunting 'Mingulay Boat Song' which probably charmed its way into my grandmother's imagination – it was composed in 1938 by Hugh Roberton for the Glasgow Orpheus Choir, and was never sung by the island's inhabitants.

When I got back to the Castlebay Hotel, I told Maureen MacLeod about the failed landing. Her father was one of a syndicate of local men who owned Mingulay, Bernera and Pabbay and eventually sold the islands to the National Trust after decades tending sheep there.

'I've been over many times but never managed to stay overnight.'

The way she said it aroused my curiosity.

'Why not?'

'Because the girls in the family just got the house ready for the men. We never slept there.'

'Did you want to?'

Barra's 'Odd Couple' – Donald Manford and Eoin MacNeil

She gives me a long look and turns away.

There's a phrase in the oft-criticised 'Flower of Scotland' – mourning 'land that is lost now, which those so dearly held'. This kind of attachment to land, this kind of holding is almost personal. It's like holding a child or a lover. And despite my years as a Trustee of Eigg, and despite many close encounters with fabulous places, I'd never felt the strength of that desire to hold and be held by land – until now. I didn't even get to Mingulay and yet feel cheerfully possessed by it and everything and everyone to do with it.

Outside, a car stops. At last it is the smiling Donald Manford with Eoin MacNeil.

'So you had a long stop on Pabbay?' he shakes hands, grinning.

'Word gets round.'

'That's what word is for.'

'So tell me this. Is the Twin Otter going to stay or going to go?'

At this point Donald talks opaquely and uses such uncharacteristic jargon I know he's up to something, which will be revealed in his own good time.

'Okay – but if mainland folk ask why Barra should have its own airport when Benbecula is just a car ferry and a thirty minute drive away, you'd say…'

Clouds gather, Donald frowns, the temperature drops a few degrees and he hollers into the microphone, 'I'd say we can't walk on water.'

I click the off button and Councillor Manford smiles again.

'Now, do you need a lift with that bike?'

'Ach, go on.'

Lochboisdale to Daliburgh South Uist
Ceolas, step dancing, dating and traditions

Lochboisdale pier is empty. The CalMac ferry left twenty minutes ago. The ripples, still swirling, suggest no wind (great) therefore no respite from midges (bad) but also no other boat traffic (puzzling). This must be the quietest harbour I've ever seen. In fact it's not a harbour – and that explains the village's unnatural stillness. Harbours have people peering over edges, boats heaving catches onshore, kids guddling for small fry, signs advertising seal spotting trips, restaurants with fresh seafood, B&Bs with vacancies – even the odd ice cream van. Not here. Lochboisdale. Somehow from the length of the name I had imagined something... bigger. At least a proper port. Perhaps this is the curse of the sixteen summers in Wick – these crude lumps of concrete bear no comparison to the small intricate sandstone ports that line coastal Caithness.

Something here is missing. Like fishing boats anchored against a harbour wall – or indeed fishing boats, or in fact a harbour wall. The single concrete exclamation mark that is Lochboisdale pier was built in 1880, not for local fishermen nor for passing yachters, but for the use of pleasure steamers.

'It doesn't work for anyone apart from CalMac,' says local businessman,

Councillor Angus MacDonald and Angus MacMillan on windy Lochboisdale pier

community buyout leader and salmon magnate Angus MacMillan. And as if to prove the point, he and local councillor Angus MacDonald have to shelter crouched behind a ferry gangway out of the wind to make an audible tape recording.

'The fishing boats have to come into the pier to unload their catches, take on fuel and then moor away from the pier, over there.'

Map 3

Now what I don't know about boats could be written on the pages of *War and Peace*. Like there's a lot of ignorance going on. In contrast, my newly arrived colleague and transit van backup driver, Maxwell MacLeod, gets uncontrollably excited in the presence of wooden planking, smashed up bits of wood, abandoned old boats or smelly, diesel-washed puffers. Despite being a 'Sir', Maxwell worked on the last ocean-going puffer distributing coal all the way up the Western Isles. I have a weary sense that he will mention this Herculean feat on our Hebridean trip as often as I will point out that he is the son of the redoubtable Reverend George MacLeod, who set up the Iona Community after the Second World War. Not that the fiery-eyed, sandy-haired Maxwell is anything but a proud chip off the old block. It's just that famous Hebridean fathers have a way of constantly upstaging their offspring. Nonetheless, as I looked at the tranquil waters where ten fishing boats were moored, I couldn't quite see the problem.

'It's a nightmare, this harbour,' says Max (who likes his full name being shrunk as much as he likes being introduced as his father's son). 'The last time I was in here with a yacht I had to stay awake all night to make sure the anchor didn't drag – and it did, constantly. The rocks in here are jagged and they can tear your boat to shreds. You would give anything to have a decent mooring – and there's no reason for it. There's no reason why this pier has been built like this and left like this – half finished, from the point of view of local people. Why isn't there a fishermen's hut on the pier? Why do they have to coordinate fuel supplies with a local lorry driver? Why is there no fuel storage?' Fair enough. Even I am getting interested.

'It's simple. The pier belongs to CalMac and local people can't leave anything on it,' says Angus.

'Have you tried?'

'There's no point. That's why we want the land buyout, to have some control – there's no point arguing with people who have the upper hand and who always say no.'

Now it would be fair to say this is as far from my own outlook as it's possible to get. People with the upper hand **who always say no just bring out the beast in me**. But maybe that's **because I wasn't** brought up with a constant experience of unfairness and being made to feel marginal. The feelings of angry impotence I was picking up in South Uist, reminded me of wise words written by Paolo Freire and discussed by some of the Assynt Crofters before their pioneering purchase of the North Lochinver Estate in the 1980s – the first Scots to buy their land back from a laird.

In *Pedagogy of the Oppressed*, the Brazilian Freire suggested that living without power or control is an art that has to be learned, not just a series of 'normal' aspirations that have to be repressed. And like any artform, practitioners need to employ and refine their skills. 'Inferiorism', as Freire calls it, stops marginalised people 'feeling free' or 'taking responsibility' or 'thinking big' – even when circumstances change. Because a whole series of 'marginalised' life skills need to be abandoned first. Skills like spending next to nothing, making do with second, third or fifth best, leaving instead of speaking out, and discouraging potential troublemakers or personal qualities like defiance or ambition. Freire's contention is that behaving like a second-class citizen or inferior requires a skillset that needs to be consciously unlearned before things can change.

I once had a memorable discussion about Freire and his uncompromising views about the emotional legacy of poverty with Allan MacRae and Issy MacPhail of the Assynt Crofters. It was a Force 8 gale and the two crofters were trying to herd sheep into a fank. Somehow Allan was managing to read the well-thumbed paperback whilst gathering sheep, rolling a cigarette and staying upright.

The 'road' to Glendale, South Uist

'This man is right,' he muttered.

But how do you unlearn being marginalised? Especially when you must simultaneously demonstrate that you can run the land of your forebears better than generations of private landowners, in the full, unforgiving view of the whole of Scotland?

Whatever feelings of apprehension locals are struggling with, they aren't showing – yet. A £15 million marina at Lochboisdale and development of Askernish Golf Course are the twin peaks of Europe's largest com-

43

Ceolas fiddlers, dancers, pipers and tutors during a refuelling interlude

munity land buyout plan, for the 9,300-acre estate of South Uist. According to Angus MacMillan, the previous landowners weren't bad – they just didn't build infrastructure. Why should they? They only came here on holiday. The syndicate of Borders and Oxfordshire financiers agreed a friendly buyout so that they could fish in peace while the community got on with upgrading nineteenth-century services and facilities. It's a big task. There's a lot of grumbling. And whilst much of it is justifiable, simmering resentment eats up energy fast, especially when the subject is the biggest Southern Isles complaint – the cold shoulder from Stornoway. One businessman was refused cash to set up a local brewery – the same proposal in Stornoway reputedly got backing in weeks. CalMac runs a four times daily service to Stornoway, but there are only sailings on alternate days to Lochboisdale.

Meanwhile, the village of North Glendale has a more basic transport problem – it's the only township in the Outer Isles without a proper road. The dirt track means nine crofts get little or no refuse, postal or emergency services – and oil is painstakingly decanted into barrels to refill central heating tanks.

Without proper infrastructure, the little things in life become time-consuming and bothersome. And that phrase from Samuel Johnson echoes again: 'The Scots… are [more] accustomed to endure little wants than to remove them.'

But change is in the air. On St Andrews Day 2006 the community gained control of South Uist and have till 2008 to raise £0.5 million of the £4.5 million asking price. With luck and hard work they should be laughing. The marina, some windfarms and of course Askernish are all developments that should make money and secure bank loans. But loans take confidence, thinking big, and unity of purpose. Not a set of characteristics *Uibhistich* (Uist folk) currently have in spades – until the subject turns to music.

Ceolas Music Festival

The Ceolas Music Festival is celebrating its tenth year at Daliburgh School. For a decade students and teachers of pipe music, fiddling and step dancing have been sailing, flying and driving from all over Canada to revive the vigorous traditions of music and dance exported to Cape Breton during the Clearances. The ceilidhs are apparently all-nighters and the quietly spoken *Uibhistich* start singing, playing and step dancing like no one's watching. Of course, a gathering of musicians also brings a great opportunity for argument about the 'authentic' nature of tradition.

'The culture we call Scottish has been Balmoralised. Did Scots step dance? Of course we did – but everyone thinks that stepping is Irish. How else could people have danced in low croft houses? If they'd been doing dances like the Highland Fling, they'd have taken one another's eyes out. And as for pipes – the piping tradition was so powerful the government had to use them to recruit beaten Highlanders into the British Army after Culloden.' A point Calum MacLean embellishes in *The Highlands*:

> The Hanoverian regime recognises the fact – which most Highland historians have chosen to overlook – that every Gaelic-speaking Highlander, irrespective of creed or denomination, was a potential nationalist, a Jacobite and rebel. Towards the end of the century there was formulated the brilliant policy of enlisting the 'secret enemy' to destroy him as cannon fodder. Highlanders were again dressed up in kilts and, by the ingenious use of names such as Cameron, Seaforth and Gordon old loyalties were diverted into new channels. The end of the Napoleonic wars necessitated another fresh policy... the horror of the Clearances was now to be let loose on the luckless Gaels.

The *piob mor* (big pipes) were banned along with tartan and Gaelic after the '45 Rebellion. Except in the new regiments formed with clan names to lure Highlanders into His Majesty's Service. And it worked, partly because life was so tough post-Culloden, without land or the freedom to live as before. Ironically, it's that 'war' tradition – the massed pipe bands

Step dancing at Ceolas

– that's packing them in at the Edinburgh Tattoo; almost everyone has forgotten the 'peacetime' Northumbrian pipes.

'They're not just Northumbrian,' one of the pipers corrects me. 'People played them indoors everywhere to accompany dancers. Go to Cape Breton and you'll see Scotland's traditions thriving. You just won't find them easily here – except at Ceolas.'

A young piper called Tibor from Cape Breton is starting to look slightly restive in the corner.

'It may be true all this – but hey. We didn't just have Scots immigrants, y'know. There were French and Germans and Italians too. That's where

my name comes from. And what worries me more is that the language is being lost right now. Our culture has roots in the Gaelic language, but no one back home cares so long as they can dance. It's easier.'

Katy Shaw, a step dancer fresh from her class, draws a deep breath and disagrees.

'Tradition isn't just carried in language. Back home there's almost no competition – people play for enjoyment. And pipers

**Piping starts early
on South Uist**

play to accompany dancing. In fact dancing is tradition – it's at the centre of everything.'

And as if to emphasise her point, the Canadian turned Edinburgh resident slips into a spirited step dance.

'Working men with big boots coming out of the forests – lumberjacks I guess – would all dance to one man playing a fiddle tune. The way we'd learn – on kitchen tables. I once got a tape recording from a teacher, an old lady. You couldn't write down the moves, you could only hear them.'

And what does she make of what we call 'traditional' Highland dance?

'It's a bit… sedate. A bit… boring, really.'

Certainly there is a difference between the informal instrument-based atmosphere of Ceolas and the formal, voice-based atmosphere of the Mod – Scotland's annual competition-based festival of the Gaelic language. That could be explained by religious background – there is mention of Free Church Ministers burning fiddles in centuries past. By contrast, priests in Cape Breton bless instruments in the pulpit, and some local priests have actually played the fiddle at Ceolas. The Free Church has a strong belief in a direct experience of God – unmediated through instruments or hymns. Their preference for unaccompanied singing has created the awesome power of precentor-led psalm singing on Lewis and Harris. And the Mod still manages to put a lot more Gaelic bums on seats than Ceolas. Though there again, the Mod is well timed to offer Gaels the chance of a break after the short, frenzied tourist season.

Maybe this is all fine. Even to my untutored eye I can see the islands have different traditions. Barra has fabulous singers and accordions everywhere. On South Uist, pipes are the thing. Every house I visit can produce a chanter (the pipe used to produce the melody on bagpipes) and Calum MacAulay from the Lochboisdale Hotel shows me the chanter a friend bequeathed to him in his will, even though they hadn't met for years and the friend had lived and died hundreds of miles away in the south of England.

If each island felt more comfortable about neighbouring traditions, the Long Island would be an epicurean feast of different musical types. As it is, each island community looks warily over its shoulder towards its neighbours across the Great Religious Divide on Benbecula, where the Protestant North and Catholic South mingle, meet and assess one another still.

Neil Fraser, a former Head of Radio Scotland, once said that *Radio nan Gàidheal* created the Western Isles – as a unitary council and as a concept. Before the radio station went on air, Gaelic speakers were prone to hearing the differences in pronunciation between different island groups instead of the overwhelming fact they were all speaking the same language. Why do we expect the language of music to be any different?

Writer Angus Peter Campbell at Ceolas

With dancing, fiddling, piping and singing all woven together, the Ceolas gigs were more like one endless session than wholly separate events. But then the source for much of this musical intelligence is Maxwell, who has become hopelessly besotted with the beautiful young step dancer, Katy Shaw. As I sit in the Lochboisdale Hotel into the wee small hours piecing together recordings of the first few programmes on my laptop for transmission within days, Max is out having a 'high old time', as my mother would say. Although I was rather grumpy about this, I was impressed that he needed no second bidding to party. And he did come back laden with detail (mostly unusable), names and phone numbers of new folk to interview (pity it wasn't just a radio series about Ceolas) and dozens of suggested detours for the following day. The more he became the footloose, fun-loving laddie, the more I became the pedantic, grimly cycling and tomorrow-focused old bag. Hey ho.

I did take one detour, to call in at the home of the redoubtable Mairi B – or Mairi McInnes – one of the Ceolas organisers. She, along with Mary Schmoller (a Uist native who married an Austrian) and prize-winning Gaelic singer Paul McCalum, are piecing together a project to bring international experts to a conference in Daliburgh in celebration of

Ceolas participants

Margaret Fay Shaw, the great collector of Uist songs, cures and proverbs. I sit listening to them discuss the hurdles they will have to overcome. There will be a struggle to find any accommodation – every summer, the few B&Bs and the two hotels are full.

Distinguished American academics will therefore be horrified at the 'basic' standards of accommodation they get, even though it will be a Herculean struggle to find anything. Officials from the Western Isles Council will probably find they can't spare the time to come – and that means there will be no official publicity to support the Margaret Fay Shaw event, which will also come straight on the heels of the manic, three-day musical and cultural extravaganza we have just been witnessing. But all agree – the show must go on.

It's almost as if Uist folk feel the need to erect some kind of cultural headstone for this remarkable American, who was buried at the grand old age of 103 at Hallan on South Uist, beside the Macrae sisters whose lives she shared in the 1920s. Her husband, John Lorne Campbell, from whom she was inseparable in life, died ten years before her in Italy and his remains were finally interred on Canna in 2006. Those precious years on South Uist inspired Fay Shaw's life, and locals fully appreciate the statement made by her own choice of burial location.

Somehow all these gentle, delicate understandings and connections must find their way into the cold words and figures of an Excel spreadsheet.

As Mairi prepares dinner, I take a look in her bookcase. Half of the books are in Gaelic, the rest are seminal tomes I would now struggle to find off the island in the massive book emporiums which assure us they stock everything of relevance to modern Scots. There in one corner is Margaret Fay Shaw's masterwork, *Folksongs and Folklore of South Uist*. As

I leaf through, I read a description of the landscape written nearly eighty years ago and unlikely to be bettered today:

> In summer the Atlantic, which on fine days is also an extraordinarily deep blue, breaks on the beach of white sand. The machair is carpeted with wild flowers, the air filled with the songs of skylarks, the call of lapwing and corncrake. In winter it is swept by fierce westerly gales and the tremendous seas threaten to break through the dunes and flood the land, some of it well below sea level. The east side of the island is wild and rises to a line of high hills of strange contour that run the length of the island. Three long sea lochs, Skiport, Eynort and Boisdale open into the Minch and cut through these hills… Innumerable fresh water lochs are studded over the island, often with small islands on which are ruins of prehistoric forts…

The crofting life Fay Shaw describes was physically hard, and depended on a keen awareness of the natural cycles that run in people, land, sea and weather:

> The spring work began in February, when seaweed, used as fertiliser, was cut. It was towed ashore on a full tide so high it could be left on the grass verge. The crofters then carried it on their backs to the field, where it was left in a heap for a fortnight until black and dry.
>
> The fields were too small to use a horse-drawn cart, so the ground was dug with a foot plough. The clods were then broken up with a heavy wooden rake and the field was hoed by hand before the oats were sown.
>
> The crofters planted their potatoes in 'lazy beds' or *feannagan*. A strip of seaweed 3ft wide was spread down the center of each bed. The crofter then turned a foot-wide clod and laid it on the seaweed so the strip was covered by a foot of earth on each side. The ditch between the beds would be deep to drain the ground, which was largely peat and often waterlogged. The potatoes were then planted.

49

Karen and Calum MacAulay, owners of the Lochboisdale Hotel

In June the peat was cut… At the end of the summer, when dry enough for burning, [the peats] were carried home to make the great stack by the house for the year's use. In midsummer the hay and oats were cut with the sickle and made into stacks in the field until they were carried home and built into great stacks [*Cruachan*] – the tops thatched with bracken and secured with ropes against the winter gales. The potatoes were dug in October and stored in the byre.

The women… carried the creels, helped with much of the planting, harvesting and carrying home the peats.

Big, active, co-operative physical lives – where women made up their own minds about who to court, based on a thorough knowledge of their patronymic (the names of their fathers, forefathers and very occasionally foremothers).

Mairi McInnes can still demonstrate.

'I am the daughter of Angus John, and the sister of x. I am grand-daughter of x and y and of a and b.'

As she chants the details in Gaelic – triggering Mary Schmoller to do the same – it seems for a moment the heavy hand of the family has made a sombre entry into this light-hearted company. Not to mention a touch of the Old Testament.

'Not entirely – it was just useful to know who your cousins were before you went… dancing shall we say.' And both women throw their heads back and laugh like Hebridean drains.

'Yes, we had to recite our patronymic as young women before we went out courting – just to make sure we would avoid falling for… the wrong people. Members of the extended family, if you like.'

'Yes – we didn't always succeed though!'

More laughter. And it all makes perfect sense. With as many as a half of all births occurring out of wedlock, the 'official' family lineage would literally provide only half the story. And in an aural and oral culture, the recitation of pedigree would prove far more useful – especially in a tight spot.

Formal courtship rituals were quite equal and elaborate, as Margaret Fay Shaw recounts:

> The young man took another friend with him to call on the parents of the young woman. The friend would extol the young man's character and his qualities for making a good husband. She would make her feelings known by staying in their presence with obvious pleasure or by leaving the room. Whatever the opinion of the parents, the daughter made her own decision. Her father would say, '*ma tha ise deonach, tha mise ro-dheonach, agus mura bi sin mar sin, cha bhi so mar so.*' (If she is willing, I am very willing, and if that weren't so, this wouldn't be so.) The young man would catch the girl's hand and they would divide a dram between them, drinking from the same glass.

I put the book back on the shelf. Beside it there's the Batsford edition of Francis Thompson's *Western Isles*, dated by the fact that only eight of its seventy-nine photographs are in colour (but they are by master photographers Sam Maynard and Murdo MacLeod). Next to that, Finlay J Macdonald's *Crowdie and Cream* tells the story of life as a crofter in Harris. Another book records the memoirs of a schoolteacher on the island at the turn of the last century.

Stories, stories, stories.

I stand flicking through these pages for the best part of two hours. The history of these islands is told not in facts, figures or famous battles, but in stories – an approach that is probably too anecdotal for an English-speaking world with measurement mania.

Mairi McInnes with a teacher colleague

Mainland Scots haven't heard half of it – their own people's history.

I wonder again – why not?

It's as if Hebridean history is shrouded behind a veil of Gaelic that simultaneously shapes island identity and guarantees its isolation from mainstream culture.

He that waits long at the ferry will get over sometime.

Once again, the old Gaelic proverb is absolutely right.

But how many Scots are queuing up to try?

The exclamation mark that is Lochboisdale pier

Daliburgh to Balivanich Benbecula

Gaelic, golf, Transport Ministers and archaeological remains

Transport Minister Tavish Scott, his advisor Andy Myles and I are standing in the chalky sunlight of a corridor in Daliburgh School on South Uist. It's the venue for Ceolas and we are warily preparing to enter Angus Peter Campbell's advanced Gaelic class. Tavish is keen to show that he takes Hebridean culture seriously with a fleeting immersion in the language – and just as keen to rebut suggestions the Executive is anti-cyclist by then chumming me on the bike for twenty miles to Benbecula.

MA'S MATH LEAT DO MHOLADH, FAIGH BAS ;

IF YOU WANT TO BE PRAISED, DIE

SEAN-FHACAL
GAELIC PROVERB

The Minister's surprise decision to prove his cycling credentials has caused a slight change of plans. Tavish and Andy had a 'one-day window', which could only be unlocked at an airport with regular, reliable flights. That said Benbecula or Stornoway. And since I was also keen to keep up with two younger, fitter men, that kinda screamed Benbecula – the flat terrain from Daliburgh to the airport at Balivanich was ideal. Both ends offered great food, Ceolas offered opportunities to throw the gallus Shetlander in at the deep end of Gaelic culture and Benebecula offered a Ministerial-quality room and a plane out the next morning.

Suddenly it was a scramble to reach the airport fast. Maxwell jumped in the trusty transit. I cycled from our gaffe at the Lochboisdale Hotel to Daliburgh, meeting Tommy from Rothan Bikes at the school to get the bikes for 'the boys'. And finally, after an inexplicable detour past Daliburgh to Lochboisdale – 'Whoops, we weren't supposed to tell you' – the Minister and his minder finally arrived.

'So before we go in, what's the festival and who is Angus?'

Tavish orients himself impressively before every meeting or chat.

'Angus Peter – don't shorten it – is probably the spikiest poet in Gaeldom and the festival is a Hebridean/Canadian cultural love-in swapping songs, arguing about piping methods, drinking, and doing most of it in Gaelic…'

'Right. How do I say hello in Gaelic?'

'*Ciamar a tha sibh* [Kimera ha sheeve]. Only don't say *sibh* to Angus Peter. It's like *vous* in French or *Sie* in German – it implies age and respect and he doesn't like it.'

'What?'

'Try *cimara ha thu* [kimera ha oo]. It's more familiar.'

'What?'

We knocked and went in.

From the second that familiar hush descended – ten Gaels silenced by the mere presence of three English speakers – I knew we were dead meat. Angus Peter had been rudely kept waiting too long, the suspension of fluent Gaelic conversation was too irritating and being recorded was too stifling to be tolerated by self-respecting Gaels for long.

Having said all that, I was hoping for a little forbearance to simply stuff some words of Gaelic into a Scottish decision-maker's head.

The enigma that is Gaelic

Gaelic and Scots speakers are not currently happy bedfellows. And making common cause might be useful, because the linguistic jewel of Gaelic is not in good health. According to the 2001 Census, there are just 58,652 Gaelic speakers in Scotland. This is just 1.2 per cent of the Scottish population. In 2001, 7,000 kids aged 3–15 spoke Gaelic in Scotland, while 184,000 kids of the same age spoke Welsh in Wales. Which puts Welsh well above language-group reproduction levels – and Gaelic well below.

Why? In Scotland decision-makers still see Gaelic as a loser language, even though fluency in *any* second language is currently worth its job-seeking weight in gold. In the long run though, if the author of *The Language Instinct*, Steven Pinker, is correct, Gaelic and Welsh, along with 90 per cent of the world's other 6,000 languages will be dead by the end of this century leaving only a Big Ten spoken nearly everywhere.

And strangely, that unites the parents battling for and against Gaelic medium education. Language activists fear extinction and doubting parents fear their kids are engaged in pointless learning.

Minority languages are probably on their way out whatever we do, because beyond the school gates, Gaelic isn't a language in the communities young people frequent – the home, the internet, the secondary school and the TV. But do parents oppose immersion in Gaelic because they know the language is limited to 100,000 speakers worldwide, and falling? Or because immersion in anything other than English just sounds weird? Would the row evaporate if children were to be immersed in Mandarin Chinese?

I suspect not. In fact, Gaelic is the only language where fluency almost guarantees a job. It may be 'only' for reasons of state support, rather than burgeoning natural demand. But for a language and culture staging a long-overdue fightback, it's a good start. Fluent Gaelic-speaking graduates are in great demand in the media and government – so sought after, that few trickle beyond the relatively high pay and bright lights to the education system that is crying out for their specialist expertise, and so few head back to the place of their birth, the Outer Hebrides, that it cannot fulfil its pledge on Gaelic education, because of a lack of teachers. It is the ultimate irony.

A few fluent Gaels have great scarcity value, and are unlikely to opt for teaching. But if they don't, Gaelic will become so marginal that their prestige jobs will dry up. The dearth of Gaelic teachers means only one new Gaelic medium primary unit has opened since the millennium, and the number of primary pupils being 'completely immersed' has increased by fewer than 200, taking the total to just 2,000. Not because of a funding gap or lack of demand, but because there simply aren't enough teachers.

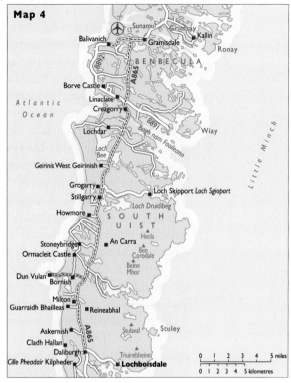

Map 4

The majority of Gaelic speakers live in the Outer Hebrides. But Scotland's only Gaelic medium school – where every subject is taught through the medium of Gaelic – is in Glasgow, not on the islands. It's a vicious little Catch 22. And as long as Gaelic medium remains a minority interest, objecting parents can't be blamed for feeling wary. After all, if immersion in a second language was such a great educational thing, why wouldn't the Scottish Executive make it compulsory? Indeed, if language skills genuinely mattered one iota in the real world, why did our political masters make foreign language study an optional extra, not a core piece of the Scottish curriculum in 2001?

Gaelic is not an easy language to master and non-speakers who've failed to pronounce so much as a confident '*failte*' will doubtless project this difficulty onto child-sized minds and wonder if the effort of learning Gaelic and English will simply exhaust them for all the other tough learning work that lies ahead. These are understandable concerns. But they have no grounding in fact.

Children under six can learn up to three languages easily. And their improved language skills make them better general communicators. Even the boys. The Welsh have proved it. Roughly a quarter of Welsh kids are in Welsh medium schools. In Gwynedd 90 per cent of children are in Welsh medium primaries. Children who move into that area are offered intensive Welsh courses at special centres before attending their local school. In English-speaking Rhondda, 40 per cent of kids are in Welsh primaries – almost all have non-Welsh speaking parents.

The motives of the parents are simple. They know the Welsh schools get better results, view the language as an important asset for children in a competitive job market and buy the educationists' line that learning two languages improves almost every aspect of linguistic ability. The fact Welsh medium schools also tend to possess enthusiastic teachers and a self-selecting group of parents who make sure the little darlings do their homework is icing on the Welsh cake.

Gaelic now is where Welsh was forty years ago.

A decade of rebellious activism by the Welsh Language Society brought the cash and control to establish Welsh medium education. And what they've achieved since then is astonishing.

Scotland's Gaels must fight for their right to party – but be careful lest the sense of injustice that motivates them, alienates everyone else. Even in Wales, fluency peters out fast – at GCSE and 'A' level only six per cent of students are fluent in Welsh. The figure drops to 1.6 per cent at university. In short, Welsh even for Welsh speakers is a language more like French or German – not the native tongue of the hearth, or the heart.

The biggest selling Welsh language book shifts only 5,000 copies. Welsh, like Gaelic, will not make Stephen Pinker's top ten surviving languages; according to Welsh veteran, Geraint H Jenkins, 'a language network is not a community. And a language which is not a community language will die.'

But then, we all die and we all learn things at school which we hardly use on a daily basis. The decline of Gaelic is not a reason to rule out learning the big, beautiful, frustrating thing – just for the *cráic*.

If you can find the immersive learning experience, that is.

Sadly, most Hebridean children can't. There are some Gaelic medium classes within twenty-four primary schools across the Islands. And Gaelic is compulsory for two years at island secondary schools – then optional.

It's not a patch on the language provision offered to Welsh children.

Perhaps that's because there are not one but two language traditions at work in Scotland – and both are under threat. Scots may not be a full-blooded language, but unlike Gaelic its evocative vocabulary *is* used by almost everyone. Remember the notorious case of the man who was found guilty of contempt of court for replying 'Aye' to questions in the witness box? That happened in 1993, not a hundred years ago.

So try suggesting to Scots, struggling for formal acceptance of their own 'mither tongue', that the 'real' language spoken by their forebears was Gaelic, and stand well back. Even though there is strong circumstantial evidence of widespread Gaelic speaking – the place-name Scotstoun, for example, describes a Scots-speaking community in a sea of Gaelic – there is little love lost between the Scots-speaking descendants of Gaels living in Glasgow, and the lost language many now deride. 'Who dura who dura helicopter', they mock – 'Gaelic isn't even a proper language.'

In a calmer mood they might concede that helicopter is a foreign word in English too. Though the occasional Greek borrowing doesn't seem to undermine English.

The real problem for Gaelic is that its sentences, grammar and pronunciation often bear no resemblance to anything the average Scot can understand. And being made to feel stupid doesn't leave the average Gael, Scot or Greek feeling very happy.

Our 'national' greeting, for example, is *Ceud Mìle Fàilte* – a hundred thousand welcomes. But few Scots can say it with any confidence. Complex rules mean words starting with an M like *Mhairi* are pronounced with a 'v' in certain circumstances sounding like Vairi. In fact, the very use of *Mhàiri* as a first name is grammatically incorrect. According to Gaelic scholars, she should be called *Màiri* but addressed as *a Mhàiri*. Fine – without a grounding in Gaelic grammar, the average Scot cannot confidently pronounce even this common girl's name.

What does a majority population do when it tries to use a minority language and is constantly corrected? It doesn't generally like it.

This is not spite, it's just human nature. I wonder how Gaels would react to the notion that everything important about their culture is enshrined in a language they cannot understand, and regard as the outdated relic of an agricultural past?

The more Gaels explain to the Scots-speaking majority that an understanding of Gaelic is essential for national identity, the more their own ignorance of the language annoys the majority of Scots.

It may not be fair, but it's a reaction Gaelic campaigners might do well to consider, before language creates an unintended meltdown in Gaelic/Scottish relations.

Of course, many Scots have learned, or tried to learn, Gaelic at night classes. I was one, until the combined effects of an overheated school, a long day and a long drive from work in Glasgow meant I consistently fell asleep after forty minutes, slumping (and possibly dribbling) on the next guy's shoulder. That and a complete failure to do any of the homework meant that after nine weeks I did a Captain Oates.

During that short learning curve, though, I made some amazing discoveries – for me, anyway. Gaelic has no yes or no. It simply uses the verb employed by the questioner. Thus, 'Did you go to church?' is answered 'I did' or 'I did not' – the words 'yes' and 'no' are simply not heard. Eureka! This finally made sense of my Irish background, because they famously do the same thing in English – 'You will, you will, you will. You did, you did, you did.' I was hugely encouraged by realising I actually had experience of this 'strange language' – albeit second hand, through its impact on Eng-

'**It's gone that way.'
Donald MacInnes
and Tavish Scott**

lish. I could also see how Gaelic words like '*bròg*' for 'shoe' had crept into Scots. And that the Gaelic word for trousers, '*briogais*' (pronounced bree-kis) had either travelled to or from the Scots word 'breeks'.

This cheered me up enormously. Almost enough to propel me through another few weeks of overheated learning. Almost – but not quite. But even in a few months, I could see that Gaelic isn't just a bare translation of words – its vocabulary describes a different way of seeing the world. And that raises a new level of intrigue and difficulty for the learner.

Take colours, for example.

Gaelic names are applied to the spectrum in a subtly different way to English names. *Gorm* (blue) is also the word used to describe the colour of grass, but *Uaine* also means green. *Dearg* (red) covers from scarlet to orange. *Ruadh* is a reddish brown, *Donn* is a dark brown. *Liath* (grey) can also cover light blue. *Glas* is a dark grey which also covers grey-green.

It's no wonder Gaels recommend immersion in learning centres like *Sabhal Mòr Ostaig* on Skye. The language is at times so particular to the landscape of the islands, it's hard to see how it could be learned and applied properly outside them.

The night class experience did at least make me curious and sympathetic towards Gaelic. Usage of a language always does. When Brits go to Greece, the Greeks have the common sense, commercial savvy and confidence to let us play in their language without scything beginners down with correction, explanation, reference and historical lecture. That's why people like going to Greece.

If Angus Peter Campbell could use these island programmes to encourage repetition of a few Gaelic phrases, I reasoned, some closed minds might open towards Gaelic too. So despite the growing tension in Angus Peter's Daliburgh classroom, I tried to coax a few beginner's words from him to repeat, and let me try to ram home, during the course of the bike ride and radio broadcasts. He made a valiant attempt. *Madainn mhath – matin va –* is simple enough – it sounds like the French word for morning, *matin*. *Feasgar math* [fesker ma] – sounds like the day is starting to fester, which by the afternoon it generally is. *Oidhche mhath* [oyche va] – is the one we have all heard Gaels use for goodnight – and the three would at least give Scots a confident trio of greetings. Angus, the dangerously honest soul that he is, simply couldn't pretend that these

Anglophone greetings had any home in his Gaelic head.

'I wouldn't say to my wife 'good morning' in Gaelic. I would say something like, 'There you are. How are you feeling today?' – and that isn't *Madainn mhath*. This isn't real Gaelic. This is English Gaelic. Your ancestors have taken the words from our mouths. Now you are taking the time from our lives.'

I was slightly surprised Angus Peter was so completely unimpressed with our stumbling efforts. But then, as the Gaelic proverb puts it in a fabulously blunt way, *If you want to be praised, die.*

Five minutes later we weren't exactly dead but we were out on our ears; told kindly but firmly that Gaelic speakers had so little time together, we shouldn't waste theirs with half-hearted learning efforts, even if 'we' did include a government minister.

Back in the corridor, Tavish was completely unruffled and happily practising the Gaelic words for ferry, plane and bus. 'John Farquhar Munro (a Gaelic speaking Highland MSP colleague) *will* be impressed.' Though one new phrase, 'I will give South Uist the finest transport links in Scotland', was deemed too hard to repeat.

Golf at Askernish

As we cycled into an unexpected headwind towards Askernish Golf Course, I noted with relief that the forty-year-old Shetlander was not much fitter than me. He's a fair weather cyclist coaxed out by his kids. Tavish on the tee, however, is a different story. Transformed like Superman by slipping on his golf shoes, (the only thing he was carrying in a tiny rucksack), the Minister squared into a 40 mph gusting northerly and whacked a powerful drive against Club Vice Captain Donald MacInnes. Clearly the grinning local had some idea of the extra obstacles Tiger Scott was about

Askernished!

Tavish and I have clearly got bikes – but do we use 'em?

to face. Cyclists weaving through the first hole on a shortcut, a transit van delivering an urgent message to Donald on the second, and cow plops near the third tee left by grazing cattle. And of course the Askernish secret weapon – 'The Rough'.

With a knee-high mixture of clover, orchids, buttercups and poppies, a ball that lands here is cheerfully lost forever. And when Tavish's advisor, ex-RSPB man Andy Myles, was ordered to find the Minister's slightly sliced drive, he fell to his knees making an articulate and emotional tribute to the 'most wonderful rough in the world'.

Never mind Tavish finding his swing on Askernish, Andy had found his emotional home. After his experience with 'The Rough', Andy fired around the greens like a man possessed. Or perhaps like a twenty-a-day smoker finding an outlet for nature and nicotine in the same glorious outdoors (the Scottish indoor smoking ban having come into effect three months earlier).

The sense of freedom delivered by romping around in brisk waves of fresh air was making us all a little giddy. As Andy cycled madly before the van through a track in the foot-high machair, a small bird tottered out and became part of a mad dash to keep ahead of the vehicle wheels.

'It's a baby!' I seem to come over all maternal.

'It's a Dunlin!' says Tavish authoritatively.

'It's a baby Dunlin.' Once the maternal thing has kicked in there is no stopping it. 'It's an inch long – it doesn't know what to do.'

'Look, there's its mother.' Tavish clearly has kids. 'She's saying come over 'ere, Barney.'

'What?' The spell is broken. 'Barney?'

'Well, it could've been a girl I suppose.'

Jings – am I that nippy? 'It's not a gender issue, it's just that Barney's hardly very Hebridean.'

'Well, he could be a twitcher bird not a local. His family could've flown in from down south.'

I look at Tavish. He's serious about Barney. And I realise with great delight, we've all been Askernished. Romping round like big kids for the day had removed every vestige of our usual 'professional' reserve. We plonk ourselves down in a flower-covered bunker for an interview, shielded from the stiff breeze. I have simply never seen anyone I'm interviewing look happier.

I can only hope the place has the same therapeutic effect on golfers. I realise I was on Askernish links years ago for the South Uist Games – at the time I had no idea we were on Holy Ground. Seems I was in good company. Old Tom Morris, regarded as one of the world's finest course creators, laid out eighteen holes here in 1891.

Time, sand and an RAF base then covered up nine holes, until a chance holiday for golf course guru Gordon Irvine confirmed the whole course was the long lost cousin of Muirfield and Carnoustie. Martin Ebert's firm of golf design specialists glowingly reported:

> It is not an exaggeration to say the duneland to the south of the existing course is the perfect terrain over which to route holes and it is hard to imagine there has ever been better raw material for the laying out of a golf course anywhere else in the world. The combination of the dunes, the local undulations, the vegetation, the wet dune slacks, the seaside views, the views of Barra and the inland views to the heather clad hills make it the perfect land for a golf course. It could be the equal of any links in the world. If the potential is realised, it will allow golfers to savour many of the qualities of the great courses of the early part of the twentieth century.

Getting into the swing of things

Putting on the style

Donald insists the course won't be spoilt – they won't have a massive swanky Clubhouse, there won't be a helicopter pad and locals will still be able to play cheaply.

Strange that such a jewel lay half-discovered for so long. Not as long, though, as another neighbouring jewel, which looks destined for another long period of obscurity.

Cladh Hallan and archaeology

Cladh Hallan is where Britain's first barley porridge and only mummified remains were found five years ago in a dig organised by Sheffield University. Thanks to the lengthy business of academic study, there are still no fully analysed artefacts and therefore no academic papers, and therefore too few conclusions to warrant an 'official' exhibition at the local Kildonan Museum, the exhibition space for the Southern Isles on Benbecula, or at the 'central' Museum of the Isles in Stornoway… or even an official sign at the site. So locals are fundraising for exhibition signs themselves.

Our bumpy transit journey behind the small car of crofter Neil McMillan took us through sand and machair to the outline of Bronze Age terraced houses occupied between 1400 and 400 BC. Two mummified adults were found here with three children, ranging in age from newborn to adolescent – one in each dwelling. The north house contained the remains of the two adults, one male and one female. Both of these skeletons had been buried in a crouched posture, with arms wrapped around the knees drawn up against the chest. Describing the find, Neil stood close to us, shielding the frisky wind from the microphone with his wiry frame. The softly spoken crofter didn't seem to feel the chill – but then, Neil was beside a piece of ground that meant a lot to him.

'You know the first porridge was made on this site and we've been eating it ever since… the recipe spread all over the world, right from where we are standing.'

Neil spoke as though he knew it, but still couldn't quite believe it. A single summer's excavation work by Sheffield University unearthed a heritage so rich and productive at Cladh Hallan, locals could scarcely recognise it as their own.

To everyone's surprise, no weapons were found – though the excavation team did find, in the porch of the biggest house, fragments of moulds for swords and spears, as well as dress-pins and razors. Some beautiful Bronze Age swords had been found years earlier in a nearby peat bog. All evidence of skilled craftsmen and traders; the ores needed for bronze production had to be imported from much further south.

According to island-based archaeologist Kate MacDonald, 'The swords would have been status symbols, a bit like having a Porsche today. You can't drive a Porsche at the speed it was designed for, but owning it says a lot about how much wealth or power you've got.'

Neil's probable ancestors were peaceful, resourceful and smart. Not devoid of sophistication, constantly warring and untouched by progress, as many islanders had come to believe.

Neil, who hadn't spoken English for a fortnight before our visit, politely urged Tavish to find the cash to restart the Cladh Hallan dig and went on to demand the Lochboisdale ferry service be upgraded to a daily service landing in Mallaig (a two-hour trip) not every other day from Oban (six hours). Tavish sounded positive – though CalMac later said that would mean £20 million for a new boat. Wait till the golfers want fast access to that Old Tom Morris course; I suspect, everything will then suddenly become possible. Askernish Golf Club could fast become the engine of development on South Uist.

If only Hebridean archaeology could find a similar world-acclaimed 'Golden Goose'. Arguably, of course, it did. The Lewis Chessmen, discovered on Uig Beach in 1831, were hauled off to Edinburgh and London, never to return on a permanent basis. There are still no plans to bid for more than periodic loans of one or two pieces.

Is this realism or lack of ambition?

Western Isles Council has given help in kind but no one can recall council funding for an archaeological dig on the Uists. Orkney Islands Council has rarely failed to support any of their local excavations. Orkney, of course, has oil money. The Western Isles may or may not get wind money. But I've a feeling it'll take more than cash to transform official attitudes towards the artefacts of the Southern Isles.

One barley-encrusted pottery fragment changed Neil's view of himself and his inherited world. It could do the same with island history. Or Scottish history. But not unless it impresses a succession of historians prone to keeping important artefacts in vaults, or in cities where they can be viewed by the maximum number of people. You can see their point. Almost.

With sea levels projected to rise dramatically by 2100, our undiscovered links with the past are quietly submerging. Time and tide wait for no man – and they're no more patient with archaeological sites. Even though the Hebrides is dripping with them.

In North Uist, an Iron Age chamber or *souterrain* was discovered just after we cycled past, when a hole opened beneath the wheel of a tractor. Experts believe there are thirty-seven other stone circles around Callanish awaiting further excavation – Scotland's most famous circle was itself covered by peat until the mid-nineteenth century.

Let's face it. If stones were lighter, we'd be examining the Lewisian Gneiss of Callanish in some London gallery today.

The use of technology around key sites like these could fire the imagination and bring to life past landscapes and peoples – with or without the original artefacts. Archaeology is becoming a general fascination. The latest VisitScotland figures show the top draws are not the Edinburgh Festival or golf at Gleneagles but heritage – castles, museums and battle sites. Surely the time is right for a series of bold projects to offer curious punters an alternative to the fabulous but tourist-trampled sites of Skara Brae or Maes Howe on Orkney? In six months, people on North Uist have raised money to hire archaeological experts to preserve a wheelhouse.

By contrast, the gold plated 'nose-ring' found at Cladh Hallan five years ago is still in storage at Stornoway Museum and cannot be displayed until the lengthy 'disposal process' is complete. No one knows when that might

be. Time. It's the one thing these island sites haven't got any more. Storms and rising seas have dislodged the hiding places of centuries but now threaten to replace discovery with destruction.

At the ruined broch of Dun Vulan, near Bornish, the hurricane of 2005 washed the sea over the massive circular structure and unplucked the final bit of road connecting it with the mainland. Subsequent storms have mixed the ancient stones with recent pebbles. But the waterlogged nature of the site is not a disadvantage for archaeologists – it's a positive gold mine. In dry sites they find bits of pottery and bones. Household and personal items like clothing, leather goods, etc are more likely to be preserved in the watery peat bog.

Sheffield University archaologist Kate MacDonald at Howmore

According to Kate MacDonald, 'These are the most impressive dwellings ever built in the prehistory of Northern Europe: multi-storey houses that would have dominated the landscape in the Iron Age, representing a renaissance of cultural creativity and architectural achievement in northern Scotland not seen since the days of Maes Howe 2,000 years earlier.'

So Kate is preparing to run down the beach picking artefacts from the jaws of the next and maybe final big storm at Dun Vulan. And it may come to that. Scotland's embarrassment of archaeological riches means Historic Scotland hardly knows where to start. Without better national funding more Uist excavations will just mean less for somewhere else, like Shetland.

Dun Vulan shows what is happening out of sight all around Scotland's coastline. Irreplaceable archaeology is daily being washed into the sea in the most remote areas because these are the last to have stone monuments intact. In other words these are not just the remnants of remote island people – these are connections for all Scots with their own collective past.

After Dun Vulan we visited a graveyard beside the Gatliff hostel at Howmore which appears to house no fewer than five different churches or chapels. Perhaps the best tale surrounds the Clanranald stone. Taken from nearby Ormacleit Castle before that building burned down, it was thought that the heavily inscribed stone was cursed. A young visitor in the 1970s saw it lying at Howmore and decided to make off with it to adorn his city flat. He was found dead some time later and one of his friends, who worked in a museum, recognised the stone as historic, looked up the stolen artefacts register and it finally found its way back to South Uist and the Kildonan Museum.

It takes a skilled eye to see the patterns of the past, especially when they have been superimposed with buildings of later civilisations. The first small chapel at Howmore sat unnoticed until the Hebridean dig-meister, Professor Mike Parker Pearson of Sheffield University, brought in Andrew Reynolds, who recognised it as an Irish design for a monk's cell or chapel.

The giveaway features to anyone in the know are the low, spreading doorway (narrower at the top than the base) and the tiny window above. Nearby fallen standing stones carry the simple crosses that tend to denote monasteries. Around the graveyard, the shape of the cross shouts from half a dozen facades – some incorporated into more recent designs, some partly demolished and some evidently missing from church centerpieces.

'Nose-ring' found at Cladh Hallan (image reproduced courtesy Museum nan Eilean)

All along the west coast are remains of monasteries, chapels and places of study and worship. Kate tells me we are standing at the Early Medieval equivalent of St Andrews University.

Today monasteries are for the removed, and marginal. In times gone by they were used by the thinkers who created the modern Europe. Two thousand years ago, the Outer Hebrides were not backward, isolated islands on the margins of Europe. In a world of international, sea-based trade, these excellent boat builders reigned. And where boats, traders and islanders gathered, the intellectual skills of civilisation flourished.

Site of a former lobster pen

A Lewis Chessman (image © the Trustees of the National Museums of Scotland)

At Howmore, without signposts, fanfare or acknowledgement, we are standing at one of the birthplaces of our modern world.

And getting cold. And it doesn't do to deplete the energies of a Minister. Especially one who's gamely squared up to every challenge and conversation of a long day.

It may be, however, that the bikes were not used as fully on the remainder of the journey to Benbecula as had been expected. (Gaelic's slightly elliptical sentence structure has its uses.) And it may be that the moral of the day was hastily rewritten – *If you don't care about being praised, don't die.*

Specifically, don't force yourselves to cycle fifteen miles for nothing when there's a perfectly good van beside you and food stops being served at your destination in roughly forty minutes.

Suffice to say that the lobsters, scallops and prawns who gave their lives for our dinner in Benbecula were delicious, praised, and stone dead.

Balivanich to Lochmaddy North Uist
Second sight and the power of the family

Tavish Scott and Andy Myles are about to climb into the transit with Max for the short drive to the airport and a plane back to Glasgow – clutching a CD of audio to edit for the first programme. They'll hand it over at the airport to my own secret weapon, husband Chris, who will drive to Fife and deliver it to sound editor John Collins.

At least that was the plan. Suddenly at 7am, copying audio files from the laptop onto a CD in my room at the Dark Island Hotel, I realise a vital bit is missing. In all the excitement of getting to Askernish and taking a massive sod out of the hallowed turf with my first ever golf swing, I completely forgot to introduce the famous course. At this point in proceedings there is no 'later'. The first programme is on air in days and Tavish is not only the main interviewee but also my only dependable means of getting the audio material off the island in time.

MA'S MATH LEAT DO CHAINEADH PÒS

IF YOU WANT TO BE ABUSED, MARRY

SEAN-FHACAL
GAELIC PROVERB

Because we were outside at Askernish, the ambience of the room doesn't sound right. I try hanging out the window – but keen not to wake the neighbours, my voice is strangely subdued.

So I get dressed, stand outside the hotel, and attempt to record the missing link. The twenty seconds of speech end up taking almost twenty minutes to record, because, believe it or not, Benbecula has a rush hour. And of course, the greens of Askernish do not. Every time I start to wax lyrical a car pulls out of the hotel car park, or along from the airport, or in the other direction to the school. The only help is the long open vista – at least I can see the atmosphere-ruining motors racing towards me. I finally manage to gabble out my little speech without the sound of car exhausts backfiring anywhere. The CD is complete, handed to the resigned looking Tavish and Andy – 'ah well, back to the office' – and I slump in to breakfast mightily relieved.

Unlike anywhere we've been so far, there is a buzz here. The RAF and Army bases on Benbecula have at least bequeathed businesses, population,

school and busy roads, even if the landscape is otherwise empty and truly flat as a pancake.

It seems the lochan-studded, bird-encrusted islands of North Uist and Benbecula have a madcap two-month tourist season, and islanders aren't universally keen to lengthen it. Folk talk about the rising tide of ferry traffic with equal parts pride (we're popular) and fear (we're full).

The Hebridean welcome

Sandra MacSween is sitting at Reception in the Dark Island and we start chatting about the absence of signs for the glorious, endless beach that's invisible from the road but runs the length of the Uists' west coast. Sandra suggests visitors should forget looking for signs and leaflets and relearn the lost arts of exploring and asking locals. If the *Uibhistich* could muster a slightly more effusive greeting style, that would indeed be the answer.

If I had videoed the line of underwhelmed faces that greeted us on arrival, I think everyone here would be shocked.

And it's not as if people are unable to smile.

When a familiar face appears, the decibel level rises, hands gesticulate, eyes light up and expressions change.

On the positive side, perhaps people here so rarely fake emotions they don't switch smiles on and off the way mainlanders sometimes do.

The Editor of *The People's Parliament* (a Channel Four programme I presented in the 1990s) once asked if I thought I smiled during filming. 'Why yes,' I answered, drawing my face into what I supposed to be a Mona Lisa-esque hint of happiness. Highly appropriate for serious current affairs TV, I thought. Not a grin, but a playfulness around the eyes that suggested inner contentment.

Then I looked at the playback. The grumpy-looking woman sitting in the presenter's chair was a shock. Mouth down-turned, edgy, even wary, I did not appear as I imagined.

'It's just one of those things,' he said. 'TV puts ten pounds on people and takes the bulk of their expressiveness away. You've got a gloomy default setting. Lots of people have. You could smile like a Cheshire Cat and still be looking slightly serious.'

What a discovery. So we practised... I smiled until my fillings showed and the fang-like incisors inherited from my father were on full display. I smiled until I imagined I looked like a maniac. And Peter was right. I looked just about normal. But the revelation for me was hearing how that smile transformed my voice. I've been using it ever since, especially on radio. Because a smiling voice doesn't just suggest confidence, humour and a slightly wicked streak – it actually brings it forth in others. In just the same way a flat, un-modulated voice, which can be how islanders sound speaking to strangers in English, brings forth nothing. And visitors don't generally rave about nothing, come back for nothing or buy nothing. Nothing doesn't endear itself to decision-makers or folk with cash either. But it's easier to produce a low-key, unexpressive hello than attempt a possibility-creating greeting. It gets easier still to elevate that deadpan expression into 'just the local way'.

If you smile, you try. That's what modern culture says – and those who don't smile are deemed not to be trying. Believe me, I have no doubt that is *not* what's going on inside, but how things look from the outside matters too. I'm reminded for the second time in days of Johnson's observation about 'ornamentation of the mind' being valued above all other things on the Hebrides. Sometimes ornamentation of the face is a useful sideline.

If the Hebrideans could just fake it like the Irish for a few summer sea- sons, they could have half the world on their side too. Maybe that's my mistake. The *Uibhistich* don't nec- essarily want Irish-sized success.

Sandra said she was pleased (in a slightly smiling way) that Trans- port Minister Tavish Scott got the message about the need for short- er ferry sailings to Mallaig instead of Oban. But she was worried that the long unsignposted Uist beaches would become overcrowded, 'like Ayr, or Nairn, or Skye'. Never mind that Skye has virtually no sandy beaches. To remove this deeply ir- rational fear, I ran the Glasgow perspective on Uist past her.

Several times.

'Picture it. You're sitting in Pol- lok and yer old man says let's drive four hours to Mallaig (where we've never been) and take the ferry for several hours to an island (where we've never been) and it'll cost as much to reach as Magaluf (where we've been every year for a decade). Let's take the tent and midge repellent 'cos the B&Bs are full. And there's no shop- ping or broadband, so bring yer knitting. C'mon, Sandra – you're never going to get flooded. Relax!'

But she doesn't. I feel for the *Uibhistich*. They live in fear of inundation by heat-seeking Central Belters who hardly know they exist.

Sunamul and second sight

I cycle to the edge of Balivanich runway and the route across the sands to the tidal island of Sunamul – once home to the North Uist ferry (before the causeway), the airport (before Balivanich) and the family of Alasdair MacEachen (before he became the Council's local Environmental Services chief). Alasdair has come loaded with documents, pictures, certificates and cuttings. We're after stories, so I persuade him onto our spare bike. He's off like a bullet, giving a guided tour of islands, disused RAF buildings and even an explanation for the black bin-bag fringed barbed wire (it's dried

Cycling to Sunamul

seaweed that's been there since the high tides of 1005). The cycle over the machair and blinding white sand to Sunamul is fabulous. It's low tide, the sun is warm and until the mudguards of my Claude Butler touring bike start clogging up with grass (and the smiling face of Calum from Barra appears once again, saying 'you'll wish you'd taken our mountain bike') – all is well with the world.

On the tiny island, which Alasdair is vexed to see unnamed now on maps or even in Hamish Haswell-Smith's definitive book *The Scottish Islands,* we stand by the overgrown vegetable patch where Alasdair's grandparents used to barter for tea and coffee with airmen during the Second World War. The family seem to have been the transport kings and queens of the Uists. His grandad and uncle worked the ferry and helped flag down the aircraft, which his grand-aunt used to get to her job as a housemaid in Renfrew near Glasgow.

'She literally walked down from the crofthouse, got into the plane, flew to Glasgow and walked up to her job at the other end. They didn't have running water or a power supply but they had excellent transport links and were practically self-sufficient.'

Alasdair fishes in his pocket and comes up with the *Daily Record* medal for the best garden in Benbecula, 1936.

Now that we've got into family stories, and I've stopped irritating Mr MacEachen by rhyming his surname with 'quiche', he embarks on stories

of second sight possessed by his uncle and father.

'One night when my uncle was staying with his own grandfather on the island of Wiay, east of Benbecula, he heard the sound of something heavy thud to the floor inside the house. Some time later his grandfather found a sailor washed up dead on the shore. He wanted something to cover the man while he went for the police, so he came back

Alasdair MacEachen

to the house, pulled a sail from its storage place,

and it made the same thud as it hit the floor. The thud brought my uncle back to the sound he had heard earlier... On another occasion I was with my father in a car and he insisted we stop driving. It seems he had seen a car come over the hill and go into the ditch. I'm still half-waiting for something to happen. In fact there were several stories in the local papers about a ghost car seen in the vicinity. He never made a big fuss about it or spoke a lot about these things.'

'Do you hear anyone younger with these stories, or has it gone with the last generation?'

'The most recent was a neighbour who said she could see lights in the sky. Afterwards the airport came – right beside the woman's house.'

There's certainly something unusual about the speed of life here and the amount of time previous generations would have spent observing the natural environment. Second sight may be an ability to visualise what could happen based on a super-sensitivity to patterns, natural cycles and other phenomena. After my own Pabbay experience I want to believe all of this so much, I become perversely sceptical.

'Mind you, in sea-going communities like this there are bound to be sailors drowning in storms. And even now most casualties worldwide happen on roads. As for the lights in the sky...'

Alasdair has almost turned away, as if vexed to have given me the benefit of the doubt with these stories of his much loved family. So I tell him about Pabbay – and later find Margaret Fay Shaw's account of second sight:

> Second sight, which is the ability to foresee what is to happen, is well known, and the possessor is never envied. There is no doubt that it exists and that it is inherited. In most instances the seer foresees tragedy, as in the case of the girl who saw seaweed about the necks of two young men at a dance at Garrynamonie and they were drowned together soon after. There are two types of phenomena. One is known as *manadh* or a supernatural warning from inanimate objects. You hear a knock at the door and find no one there. Later, the same knock comes

Sunamul crofthouse and former transport hub

and there is someone there. Or dishes move about, the chest lid flies open and soon after a death comes – and those same dishes and supplies from the chest are needed. The second is the *taibhse,* which is an apparition described as 'seeing yourself standing at the house six years before you came'.

I sense Alasdair is almost back onside again, when a tick bites me. The interview is abruptly over while I hop around urging Alasdair and Max to look for matches to strike and apply to the tick's backside. I'm convinced this will get the little blighter out in one piece with its greedy little jaws intact. I've no idea if this is correct, but quite enjoy the palaver. And since reading about the increasing prevalence of Lyme Disease spread by ticks, I'm not taking any chances.

Half a packet of matches later, we are back on the 'mainland'.

It's fascinating to realise how quickly being on an island off an island changes perspectives.

In just one hour on tiny Sunamul, the road on Benbecula seems to have been transformed from the quaint, single track symbol of a slower, less car-oriented lifestyle to a grubby conduit of materialism.

Grimsay and the Monach Islands

Heading on to Grimsay, I meet the singer, lobster fisherman and last man to leave the Monach Islands, Lachlainn – Lachie – Morrison (eighty-two). The Monachs, four miles off the west coast of Uist, are called Heisgeir locally but were renamed to avoid confusion with a small lighthouse rock of the same name between Oban and Lochboisdale. Local tradition maintains that the islands – abandoned after the First World War – were once connected to North Uist, reachable at low tide by horse and cart. Like all the Uists they have spectacular white beaches made up of crushed seashells along their Atlantic coast.

'The place seemed like a paradise to the Grimsay fishermen; the machair would be a blaze of flowers. We'd go ashore from the boat, the cattle would be standing in the sun, the waters teeming with fish.'

No wonder the young Lachlainn was delighted when his dad and three other men decided to move their families across to the Monach Islands and start again. But the other three families never arrived. Sitting now outside his spectacular Grimsay house on a grassy island knoll surrounded by a glorious tidal lick of swirled sand, Lachie looks away and speaks of his enduring regret about not being able to fulfill his father's dream. This might sound sentimental anywhere else, but on the islands family is the superpower.

The old proverb *If you want to be abused, marry* characteristically overstates the case – a lot. But family obligations have certainly tended to over-rule the wishes of individual family members here. Back in the 1940s, the Morrisons on Heisgeir made a decision. If the mother stayed, the girls would stay and give up their careers to work with her and teach their brothers while the men fished. They decided that would be unfair, so they all left – together. Clearly, individually, Lachie would have chosen differently. But it was a family decision. And yet Lachie's puzzlement all these years later endures. Why didn't the other families come? Life could have been so very different.

Why didn't he ask them?

He shrugs. I hesitate before enquiring further. We are surrounded by people, including his son, Padruig (ten), sitting at the back of his house in the sun, sheltered from the slight breeze. The past seems very close to Lachlan, maybe too close to dip in and out of on a fleeting visit.

Somehow I feel I haven't earned the right to know more. I had hoped to be talking with Lachie on Heisgeir itself, having waded through grey seals (it is the world's second largest colony after Newfoundland) and perhaps brewing a cup of tea in the schoolhouse, which has been refurbished largely through the organising energy of the American 'local' Mary Norton, who's also helped restore the boat-shed and the tradition of boat-building at nearby Kallin pier. But there are no suitable piers on the west side, so Lochmaddy-based Neil Johnston, who runs boats to the Monachs, must sail round for three hours to reach islands maddeningly visible from the west, or divert his speedy rib from a far longer and more profitable run to St Kilda. Finally, the tin lid on the proposed expedition, Lachie has to travel elsewhere the next day. With the 'not Mingulay' experience fresh in my memory, I know that even in summer, sailing weather cannot be 'booked'. And we didn't have time to wait for a weather window. Quite the contrary.

Max and I had started to realise my timings for this journey were hopelessly optimistic, based on interviewing people in twenty minutes, not the three hours each encounter was tending to fill. It's not just a question of things going slower on the islands, although they unquestionably do. It's also a discovery that people are more confident, articulate and

Mary Norton, Padruig and Lachlainn Morrison

funny doing something outside rather than thinking about it inside. And the business of doing takes longer than the business of thinking. Once written, that seems obvious. I think again about that picture of Tavish Scott and Donald McInnes laughing their heads off on the machair at Askernish. Studio-based broadcasting may be quick-witted, amusing and incisive – on a good day. But unless interviewees have the descriptive powers of David Attenborough, the passion that

Neil Johnston after a flying visit to St Kilda

has brought them to the table is usually stored beneath layers of fear, politeness, disorientation, nervousness and slight boredom.

Lachie consoles me about the missed Heisgeir trip.

'You wouldn't have seen the seals anyway. They breed in October and then there are tens of thousands. Strange thing, though – they weren't about when we were still living there. It's as if they waited for us to go before they took over. Like the new folk coming in when you move house.'

I try to steer Lachie back to those last island days. I'm not quite sure what the fascination is with 'the last people to leave' a place. Maybe the drama created around St Kilda's evacuation has something to do with it. Maybe the last person leaving is like a little moment of death. Islands that lose people completely very rarely regain them. And yet Heisgeir has not been completely abandoned. Lobster fishermen still use the schoolhouse each summer and shepherds from North Uist and Benbecula keep sheep on the islands (which became a National Nature Reserve in 1966).

Lachie remembers his years fishing for lobsters with great affection and sings an unusually feisty and upbeat Gaelic song about rowing.

His memories of the Billingsgate middlemen are not so affectionate – traders who took their lobsters down to the London markets and simply refused to pay if the creatures died on route. Sometimes they charged fishermen for the cost of carrying 'dead' lobsters.

If indeed they did die. With no other outlet, these sharp Londoners had Lachie and his colleagues over a barrel. Literally. But were there no other options? Was it not possible for the Hebridean shellfish producers to work together and take control?

Lachie shrugs again.

My questions are starting to feel like a cross-examination. I don't want to put Lachie under pressure about his long life at sea, but since shellfish was big business, even in the 1940s, how could producers have had so little clout? Was the problem lack of cash to expand, or unwillingness to take on debt, or the product of the islanders' centuries' long attachment to tiny patches of almost unworkable land?

That Hebridean bond with the land has been well nigh unbreakable – even Lord Leverhulme couldn't entice crofters away to become waged, full-time fishermen. There's a great story in Roger Hutchinson's *The Soap Man*, which illustrates the failings of the soap magnate who bought Lewis and Harris in 1919 to perform a fish-based transformation of the stuttering island economy:

Leverhulme… shipped a small group of village elders to Port Sunlight to witness there the bricks and mortar of prosperity, to see how one year's vision could become next year's reality. They were suitably impressed and admitted as much to their host. But upon their return agreed with one another that 'there is nothing there but slavery'.

Later Leverhulme lost his castle piper, Donald MacLeod, over the need for time off to plant tatties on the croft:

Leverhulme refused him the holiday. 'You are now in regular employment. You earn as much money in a week as will buy sufficient potatoes for you and your family for a year. If you go without my consent you should understand that by doing so you will lose your job.' A fortnight later Donald left word in the castle kitchen that he'd gone home to plant potatoes and would not be coming back.

In many ways Hebridean land is 'super' known. It's as if centuries of hard graft and constant exposure to nature have helped imbue every rock, boulder, stone, bay, promontory and square inch of bog with special qualities. And maybe that process has been enhanced by Gaels to compensate for the apparent disdain of the rest of the world. A local crofter remarked that 'cleared' Hebrideans often travelled to the other end of the world. Once the connection with their own land, home and family was destroyed, the brokenhearted were free to roam wherever they wanted.

The French Lieutenant's father…

One such story, uncovered by Parisian turned part-time Benbecula resident, Jean Didier Hache, concerns the celebrated son of a Uist exile, Marshal MacDonald, whose father was Neil MacEachen of Howbeg (almost certainly related to Alasdair MacEachen from Sunamul).

It starts about twenty miles south of Laclainn's house, on the inaccessible east coast of Uist:

Glen Corrodale has no road access. By land, it is surrounded by a chain of high hills – Ben More, Heckla, Ben Corrodale – which makes foot travel a hard job. By sea, it has no proper anchorage. There are a few houses, but no major settlement of population. So you would expect Glen Corrodale to be this kind of place where very little has ever happened.

Nevertheless, in July 1815, a ship dropped anchor in the bay, and a rowing boat brought ashore a passenger. He was Jacques Joseph Etienne Alexandre MacDonald, Marshal of France, Duke of Tarentum, Arch Chancellor of the order of the Légion d'Honneur, Chevalier Commandeur du Saint Ésprit, Grand-Croix de Saint Louis, French Minister of State, Member of the Privy Council of the King of France, Second Major General of the King's Bodyguards, etc… and, incidentally, Deputy Grand Master of the Free Masons in France. The purpose of his presence was… to visit Scotland and to discover the land of his ancestors, since his father, Neil MacEachen of Howbeg, was a native of South Uist.

When he travelled to Uist, Marshal MacDonald travelled on a British Navy ship on direct order of Lord Melville, First Lord of the Admiralty. Had the same British Navy got hold of his father, some 80 years before, they may well have hanged him from the highest mast after extracting information on the whereabouts of Prince Charles Edward Stuart – for Neil MacEachen was the very person in charge of arranging the Prince's escape in these islands, after Culloden.

Neil Etienne MacEachen was born in Howbeg, South Uist, in 1719 – a family with strong connections to the Clan Donald, which is probably why Neil changed his name from MacEachen to MacDonald when he lived in France.

How Neil was selected to be sent away for education, at the Scots College in Paris – we do not know. What he did between 1737 and 1746 is also somewhat of a mystery. What we know for sure is that in April 1746, when Charles Edward Stuart landed in Benbecula, Neil took direct responsibility for the Prince's safety, guiding him through the remotest parts of the Uists and eventually sailing with him 'Over the sea to Skye'.

There are Prince's hiding places galore in the Highlands of Scotland, but the Uists can pride themselves with some *bona fide* hideouts. The main ones were the cave at Glen Corrodale, and a hut in the Roisinis peninsula, whose remnants can still be observed.

Neil – now officially 'Neil Etienne MacDonald' – joined the French army's Scottish Regiments, married a French wife, and had two children (a boy, the future Marshal, and a girl). Etienne Jacques Josef Alexandre (MacEachen's son), was keen on a military career. When the Revolution of 1789 saw the vast majority of the officer's corps flee into exile or lose their heads at the guillotine, Alexandre MacDonald rose within two years from the rank of Lieutenant to that of General. Campaigns took him to Holland, Italy (where he was Governor of Rome), and Switzerland.

MacDonald supported Napoleon's rise to power, helped the Emperor to a decisive French victory at Wagram and was made a Marshal of France on the battlefield. Years later he was sent to accept the Emperor's surrender.

Finally, after the death of his third wife, Marshal MacDonald decided to visit the land of his ancestors:

HMS *Swift* anchored in Loch Skipport, and an open boat took the Marshal to the North Ford. From thence, he went by cart to Howbeg where he met a crowd of a few hundred MacDonalds who had gathered for the occasion. According to evidence gathered at the time he recognised '*the river my father told me he used for a trout fishing*' and visited the ruins of his father's house, collecting some earth, which he brought back to France to be put in his grave.

It's easy to read too much into a story. But I wonder how distinguished Marshal MacDonald's career would have been in the British Army with a publicly Jacobite father. There is a very happy balance about the fact that this story of an exiled islander is brought to us by a semi-exiled Parisian.

Jean Didier Hache's first visit to Benbecula was accidental, but he's become a familiar island figure over the years. He found the full story of Marshal MacDonald's visit to Uist in the French archives, translated it, and *The French MacDonald: Journey of a Marshal of Napoleon in the Highlands and Islands of Scotland* is to be published by the Islands Book Trust this year.

Meantime, I have a tired and emotional Maxwell MacLeod on my hands. During the interview with Lachlainn Morrison, Max had been unable to contain his curiosity about rowing songs and suddenly appeared on tape as a mystery voice, causing my number one interviewee to detour onto slightly obscure avenues of thought. Visualising a night of heavy editing to excise his voice, or recording another introduction to Grimsay to introduce the hitherto silent support man, I must have shot a look of extreme bad temper. This did shut him up – eventually. But as we sit down for an *al fresco* picnic, I can tell we need to clear the air.

'Lesley, you know that your happiness is my only concern as your butler, Sherpa, doormat or whatever I am. Do you know my favorite Gaelic proverb, *The most slippery place on earth is the doorstep of the big hoose*?'

'And you feel that in this relationship, I am the big house?'

Maxwell laughs despite himself.

'I wouldn't dream of calling you *Taigh Mhòr*.'

'Even though I have absolutely no interest in wooden boats.'

'Even though my interest in wooden boats should be the highlight of this entire trip.'

Now I think we're getting to the heart of the matter.

'So that'll be why you interrupted every other sentence of my interview with Lachlainn Morrison.'

'Ach, what you were asking him was boring. Do you know that man can sing rowing songs that probably date back four centuries? He can tell who built a local wooden boat just by examining its planking.'

I sense what is about to follow is a long damned-up speech that must be heard. Assembling a wedge of white bread, cheese and (merciful heavens) Branston Pickle, I lean back on the heather, survey the fabulous white beaches nibbling at the narrow causeway connecting Grimsay to North Uist and attempt to listen.

Eyes wide shut cycling back from Sunamul

'Okay, I may be a one-trick pony but I can't help thinking that even fifty years ago, in every little inlet, a small wooden boat would be drawn up. Built by a local crofter, it would be an expression of the shape and strength of the waves, the economic health of the area, everything. Further up, near Berneray, for example, you'd need much tougher boats – boats that could withstand the force of the Atlantic swell, but light enough to be pulled up because there are no harbours.'

This is getting perilously close to my own private obsession with the absence of decent Hebridean harbours, but I manage to maintain an air of disdainful cheese and pickle sandwich priority. There is no point encouraging him.

'I thought the trouble these days is that causeways and barriers mean the Atlantic swell *isn't* getting through.'

Maxwell looks at me with some exasperation.

'Lesley, I *am* the Atlantic swell.'

I have no idea if this was the standard of chat-up line he'd been employing lately, but the conversation dissolves into some hilarity.

'In fact, the last time I hit the Atlantic swell off Bernerary I put two great companions onto a rock at 1am out there. There were two girls…'

He catches my expression.

'Okay – there were two adult human beings and they turned to me and said you're just about to hit two whales. And I thought, how ridiculous. And of course, they were trying to tell me we were about to hit large rocks, which we did. And it was on what we call a "foul tide", which means you hit the rock and the tide is peeling away so the boat is going to fall over and you are all going to die.'

This is fairly impressive.

'So I went and looked at the map and saw the rock was called the Drowning Rock, which wasn't a good start. But we landed on the rock in a dinghy, pulled the boat over and managed to get off.'

Archie McCorquondale and I relive mis-spent youths on the Lochmaddy pool table

'Well, it's nice to know that even in tranquil situations like this there's always at least the memory of danger for you.'

Max laughs self-effacingly – almost. 'Well, that's the thing. To me the sea offers such adventure and danger that I find it frustrating today's island culture is no longer engaging with that dangerous environment, because it was so inspirational. If all you're doing now is getting on a CalMac ferry, the most dangerous thing you'll encounter is the food.'

This is a bit rich, coming from a Quartermaster who makes butter-free sandwiches from doorsteps of white bread, and has never been known to turn down a CalMac fish supper.

'Max, have a sandwich and calm down.'

He is unquestionably the ideal Hebridean companion.

Thanks to all these pleasant diversions, we are once again hopelessly late – so the bike is thrown in the back of the transit and we drive through a fabulous open terrain towards Lochmaddy. Cycling through sand with bike wheels stuffed full of marram grass and clover has taken its toll. I'm almost on my knees by the time we stumble into Lochmaddy to meet Neil Johnston from the Uist Outdoor Centre. He's just returned from a crossing to St Kilda on his modern rib – and he looks considerably more shell-shocked than I am. And a bit like a cross between Captain Nemo and the Michelin man in his full protective diving wet suit.

'It's forty-five miles offshore, but we had ideal sailing conditions and saw whales, dolphins, seals and of course all the birds out there.'

I can believe it. Neil's face is still covered in sand with flecks of seaweed.

'One of the women who went out today had an ambition for forty years to get to St Kilda – so she's delighted. The rib takes one hour forty minutes in good conditions, so ten-hour journeys only to find you cannot land, or can land but cannot get off again – those days are over.'

'Do the passengers have to be strapped down and swathed in rubber too?'

'Yes, they do – with survival suits and life jackets, because even on a hot day travelling at thirty knots creates an artificial wind and people can get quite cold and tired if they aren't equipped properly.'

'So is St Kilda your main destination now?'

'No, it's still the Monach Islands. Even though you don't get the full contingent of seals till September when they're breeding, there are a few thousand of them there all year round. And it's a fabulous experience. Today at St Kilda, it was a bit like Piccadilly Circus with six or eight boats trying to land thirty or forty visitors. Some of the army buildings look a bit tatty and it can be a real shock for people who've visualised this place of ultimate remoteness if a cruise ship pulls up and starts disgorging people onto the shore. We try giving gentle warnings...'

It occurs to me that one of Neil's harshest warnings would fail to register on the typical mainland mindset.

'But the seascapes are fabulous, the cliffs are always utterly inspiring and the buildings and people are only a small part of it. I think for most people it is still a life-changing experience – but if you want guaranteed solitude and a feeling of remoteness, you can't beat the Monach Islands. Most of the time you have the place to yourself, apart from the seals.'

Crossing to climb
Eabhal

So do the seals threaten the prosperity of the hundreds of jobs connected to fish farms? Neil's adamant that the Atlantic Grey Seals stay out west where there are no fish farms. It's the Common Seals that are the fishermen's problem and he says the two species don't mix.

Later in the Lochmaddy Hotel pub, Marine Harvest man Archie McCorquondale disagrees. He reckons both types of seal kill thousands of farmed fish every year. Uncharacteristically, I don't quite have the energy to argue.

I should go off to quiz the super-fit men and women cyclists of the Hebridean Challenge – contestants in an annual race to canoe, abseil, run, and mostly cycle their way up the island chain from Barra. They've covered my four-day journey in just one afternoon. I'm sure there's a lot I could learn from them about technique, tyres, trauma and tread. But after Neil insists on paying for a sticky toffee pudding (my preferred rocket fuel) I let Archie beat me on the pool table instead.

I think they've both been practising.

Lochmaddy to Berneray North Uist

Thatching, seal oil, goose hunting and Dun spotting

Taigh Chearsabhagh is an award-winning arts centre in Lochmaddy – it's also a triumph of island myth over mainland 'fact'. *Cearsabhagh* (the loch's name changes in Gaelic if it's used without the *Taigh*) is so called because Norse invaders arrived in fog looking for Lochmaddy and sailed into the neighbouring bay by mistake.

IS BEAG A CHEARAINEAS SINN, GE MOR A DH'FHUILINGEAS SINN

CEARRADH NA H-AIRNE

LITTLE WE COMPLAIN THOUGH WE SUFFER MUCH
SEAN-FHACAL GAELIC PROVERB

'Jings' they shouted in early Norse. 'It's the wrong bay.' And that's what the Gaelic name means. Wrong bay. This of course is complete makey-uppey, a name devised to support a story locals liked. And why not? On islands where 'proper' history was often written by incomers, local names often carry more descriptive force.

Take *Taigh Dearg*, Lochmaddy's newest hotel. Built to a Norwegian design by a local consortium, planners were apparently taken aback when the building was finally unveiled – painted bright red.

As *Taigh Chearsabhagh* manager Norman MacLeod notes, the intention might have been clear if the council employed more Gaelic-speaking staff. *Taigh* means house. *Dearg* means red.

Visitors should never underestimate the superior savvy of local craftsmen either. Norman shows me round artworks installed on the rocky foreshore. One is a large, shiny, white igloo shape – begun by a London artist who took weeks to paste individual rock chips onto a lump of concrete to represent a massive pile of salt, and completed by a local builder who harled the lump in an afternoon – 'She'd have been at it till Doomsday.'

With its Outdoor Centre, two hotels and Arts Centre, Lochmaddy is a far busier hub than Lochboisdale further south. The village straddles several bays with a shoreline forty-three miles long. Virtually the first mention anywhere of Lochmaddy is a complaint of 'piracie and murder' in a report dated 1616: 'Lochmaldie on the coast of Uist is a rendezvous for pirates.' The coves and inlets around the village were ideal hiding places for ships intercepting fine goods bound for clan chiefs, and contraband activity persisted until the nineteenth century. But life is more civilised (or tame) today. Protected from the prevailing wind, there are trees, bushes – even gardens. And,

Norman MacLeod with 'salt art' in Lochmaddy

Neil Nicholson, the designer thatcher

in the opinion of Norman, just enough visitors. I ask if locals would prefer their ferry to shift to Mallaig from Uig on Skye – making the Lochaber port the main terminal for all the Uists, north and south.

'Well, if journey times were shorter and we got more visitors, where would we put them?'

'Er, you could expand?'

'Why would we want to do that? Things are grand just as they are.'

Maybe. The most difficult type of tourist industry to scale up is the one the Hebrideans currently have – a lot of visitors over a tiny summer season. It hardly makes sense to make a year-round investment for eight weeks of occupancy. Or does it?

Thatching

We leave Lochmaddy along the fabulous, lochan-studded, single track road towards Berneray. The first stop is at Clachan Sanda, to meet a young man who's managed to buck the tourist trend the traditional way – thirty-three-year-old Neil Nicholson. He grew up at the northern end of North Uist in a family croft house which overlooked two stone ruins – shells of the homes built by his great-grandfather, who moved there from the island of Boreray in the 1920s.

'It's funny. From the top of the roof when I'm thatching you can actually see Boreray. Sometimes I wonder if that's why he picked this site.'

These old houses were 'white houses' with chimneys – unlike 'black houses', which had fires in the middle of the floor and smoke escaping from small holes in the roof.

'You can tell the fireplace was in the south end. Those beams and raf-

A Clachan Sanda thatched cottage

ters remained intact when the building collapsed, because the peat smoke from the fire actually preserved them.'

The young Nicholson went off to college in Aberdeen to study design without any great intention of returning home. But when he did come back to start a design business ten years ago, he stayed for a while in a cottage overlooking the other stone ruin. Eventually, the condition of the buildings began to depress him. And when part of the roof finally caved in, he consulted the neighbour who had originally thatched them. First, he had to cut turfs 2ft square, to act as the underpinning material and the main insulation for the house. First time round, Neil cut the slabs by hand from an adjacent field. It took a month. So the thatching apprentice converted a plough into a makeshift turf slab-cutting machine.

'You have to be careful which turf you cut. Heathery peat is best because the roots of the plant bind it together, but it's almost impossible to cut. Sandy turf is easy to cut but can crumble on the roof, so a mix between the two is best.'

Each turf slab goes on the framework of the wooden beams, grass-side in, soil-side out. It's placed like a diamond, with the top hanging over the beam so it clings 'like a stale piece of bread when it's gone hard'.

On steep parts of the roof, around the chimneys for example, wooden pegs are used to keep the turfs together. Finally it's time for the marram grass. And though the Western Isles are flanked by the longest beaches in Britain, most marram is not suitable for thatching because it's been nibbled and weakened by the sheep or cattle traditionally allowed to graze there. That has led to an exchange of views with Scottish Natural Heritage, which has worries about the use of brush cutters to harvest the marram on the animal-excluded acres around Balivanich airport on Benbecula.

Brush cutters do sound a lot less romantic than scythes. But Neil insists electrical power gives a cleaner cut, which is better for the marram grass. I'd imagine the finished results might be damp and drafty.

But the cottages are so well insulated they are like mini saunas inside. Careful construction helps. Round-cornered and low-lying, they avoid the worst of the wind. In fact, during the hurricane force winds of 2005, Neil's houses hardly had a grass or turf out of place. The thatch, which is never removed, can accumulate to a thickness of thirty inches on

Map 6

a century-old house. It dries quickly and provides ideal insulation – warm in the winter, dry and cool in the summer. Even when it rains – and it does rain – the thatch dries out very fast. In summer, the grass attracts its own share of wildlife. Flies find it an ideal home in high winds and the birds are apparently fascinated by the flies and the netting which they use to sharpen their beaks.

Sitting inside, it sounds as if the roof, somewhat distant above a conventional plasterboard ceiling, has a life of its own. Leaning into the deep window recess to see out from under straggling strands of thatch, I'm reminded of peering out from underneath a long childish fringe. From outside, the wide-set windows resemble a shy, smiling face. Neil reassures me this isn't sentimental nonsense.

'I've often felt the thatch is a bit like your own hair. Really it has the same function.'

And it does. Not just providing insulation but also attracting attention – and trade. Despite the notoriously short season of Hebridean tourism, and against local trends, these thatched croft-houses were occupied for thirty weeks of last year. So could Neil's business expand? Yes it could. Is this the kind of eco-friendly tourism Uist needs? Yes it is. But does Neil have the energy to confront the authorities again over the marram he needs to thatch or the broadband he needs to offer online bookings? Well… tomorrow is another day. But let's face it. If life in a black house had been this good 200 years ago, no one would ever have left.

Discovering Duns

Life down this side road is so good we decide to spend the rest of the morning looping back for a tour of the small roads we've had to whip past. I'm fascinated by the road heading off east just above Lochmaddy, into a hopscotch of lochans, peat bogs and low glinting sun. Loch Portain is just two miles from Lochmaddy by sea – seven miles by land. But what a journey. Every other lochan (and there are many, since North Uist has fifteen per cent of the UK's total freshwater) has a Dun or ancient dwelling built on an island in the centre. One in particular looks like a lost location from the tales of King Arthur – round as a crown with tall stones poking out like abandoned gravestones. I walk across the heather to see if the stepping stones to the Crannog are still intact. They are. I sit for a while, transfixed. The partly submerged stones seem like a bridge to another time – a bit like the wardrobe in the tales of Narnia. I finally leave with a new obsession. Duns.

From about 400 BC, people on the Hebrides began to build Brochs, complex dwellings reaching a height of over ten metres. They were the most sophisticated prehistoric buildings in northern Europe – and unique to Scotland. Most are now reduced to low mounds – and many were built in freshwater lochs. With hundreds of lochs, North Uist has hundreds of loch-dwellings. And, happily, Kate MacDonald tells me I'm not the only one confused about the terminology. The difference between Brochs, Duns and Crannogs is still a matter of fierce archaeological debate – which is maybe why there's been little progress in understanding the people who lived in them. Crannogs are found all over Ireland and Scotland, and are dwellings built on artificial islets, often accessed by a stone-built causeway (rather than a bridge), and usually Iron Age. Dun is a west coast name, widely applied to the ruins of fort-like structures, which includes Brochs and Crannogs. Got it?

Margaret Fenton and her Dun exhibition

Back at *Taigh Chearsabhagh* in Lochmaddy, coincidence takes another mighty leap forward as I bump into Margaret Fenton, who happens to be dismantling her exhibition about the 108 Duns of North Uist.

This is always the sign of a good obsession – a happy coincidence and a fellow traveller. Especially a fellow traveller dogged enough to have photographed every single Dun, but modest enough to admit she still has absolutely no idea why they're there.

'No one has found weapons on any of the sites, so the idea of a defensive location doesn't seem right.'

I must say the idea of being stuck on a tiny island surrounded by marauding Vikings wouldn't seem like a great defensive move anyway.

'I think they were like bus stops.'

Huh?

'Well, when you plot the Duns on a map there are only a few places where they're inaccessible by water. The lochs all linked up into one long natural canal with a few places where the boats could've been dragged. Basically, this whole inland lochscape was a big bus route for small boats

A mystery Dun near Lochportain

and the Duns were settlements where it was easy and safe to stop.'

This conjured up such a fabulous romantic vision of Hebridean gondola-like traffic jams, you'd think I could just leave it. But oh no.

'They could still have built the Duns at the lochside. A lot of these islands look artificial. Wasn't that a helluva lot more work?'

I must say, if I had just shared my pet theory on the sacred Duns and been greeted by niggling doubt, I would've pouted all the way to the pub.

Margaret just shrugs.

So here it is. On the basis of no research whatsoever, I'd like to think prehistoric Hebrideans built Duns in lochs – for the *cráic*. Why not? Are we the only generation of humans to build and locate for aesthetic reasons? And after the first house in a loch was built, might the others not have copied it to keep up with the prehistoric MacJoneses? In addition to which, an island home might have offered more – how shall we say – sanitation solutions, than a home surrounded by earth.

Anyway, I tell Max I now want to personally visit and photograph as many Dun sites as possible. Max points out that given the vast amount of time I've spent trotting about pretending to be Guinevere of the Lake, we probably only have time for another one. Shame. The landscape of North Uist that day was dreamlike. The oval peat stacks between houses looked like Duns. Old turf-topped cottage ruins looked like Duns. *Heavens ter Betsy*, even the transit looked like a Dun. Finally, Max loses patience and drives to the Dun-free coastline at *Caolas na Hearadh* (the Sound of Harris) and Hoebeg – once the Hebrides biggest kelp-cutting ground.

Nothing much to see now apart from living proof that if the Gaels do indeed have five words for the colour blue, it probably isn't enough.

Kelp

Kelp is the missing link in the Hebridean story and landscape. It became valuable because it produced an alkali used in the manufacture

A seal on the beach near Sollas

of soap, glass, sodium and iodine. It caused people to move to the coast before clearances or sheep farms and its value to landowners prompted the Ships' Passengers Act of 1802, making emigration prohibitively expensive for local people.

But why would emigration be an option for locals whilst the kelp industry was booming? I'm to meet Bill Lawson, tomorrow and have been flicking through his book *North Uist*:

> The tenants had enough foresight to see that the bubble could not last forever. More foresight than the landlords who were spending as if the boom would never end. In 1814 the crofting system was introduced into North Uist to maximise the number of people and ensure their holdings were too small to be viable without kelp working. After Waterloo, continental sources (of the kelp substitute barilla) became open again. The islands – proprietors and tenants

alike – were ruined. And owners, who a few years earlier had been trying to prevent their tenants leaving, now could not get rid of them quickly enough.

The rest, as they say, has become Clearance history. The kelp trade never became important again – though I'm told a new seaweed factory has opened in Stornoway. And good luck to them. We retrace our steps and head west towards Sollas on the north coast, where the extraordinary tidal reach of the Hebrides (the difference between high and low tide) creates another coastal world at low tide. Islands like Vallay can be reached on foot – though Bill Lawson quotes this 1944 account, by Richard Perry, who came to work as a shepherd on *Bhalaigh* (Vallay) and clearly hated every isolated minute of it.

Wildish Eriksay pony

> Not only did every visit to the peat banks entail a six-mile double crossing of the strand, but we also had to wait upon the tide, that we might go safely through the fords with the five big Clydesdale horses. Sometimes we would be wading through water most of the way, climbing onto the carts when the water was up to the horses' bellies, and it was more like midwinter than August so we were perished with the cold. Three loads to each cart in the day was our limit, and that meant going at it without a break from noon until nine at night, when the horses would be dropping their heads low in their collars.

At high tide Vallay looks decidedly inaccessible and anyway I have one more Dun spotting opportunity left. So we head on towards Loch Olabhat and the Dun on *Eilean Dhomhnaill*. This is slightly underwhelming (see amateur obsessives – see fickle.) So I drag the valiant Maxwell along the coast, where we encounter a fabulous herd of Eriskay ponies (which I like to think were running wild but Max points out were evidently owned and fed by the local farm), and some washed up seals who were definitely not owned by anyone and were also running wild in their own limited way. I mention later on the phone to Mary Schmoller that these tiny, possibly ailing pups had an astonishing air of defiance about them. A 'c'mon, if you think you're big enough' sort of snarl if you went anywhere near.

'Aye, small man syndrome,' says Mary, knowingly.

Berneray

Time to head off to Berneray – a small island with a bigger challenge than snarling seals. You would think there could be no bigger animal problem than the hedgehog invasion of South Uist. It seems four hogs released in the early seventies managed to reproduce their way quickly into a population of 5,000. And though their diet is mostly slugs, they will also devour any birds' eggs that come their way. Big mistake. Scottish Natural Heritage (SNH) – the conservation controllers – have been engaged in a war to the death on South Uist. Poisoning and trapping the hedgehogs began in 1995 but was recently suspended to allow their repatriation to the mainland by charities like the Tiggywinkles who managed to prove the Spiny Normans could actually survive the journey and adjust to their new homes. The whole episode has provided some locals with cash but – more importantly for the maintenance of island humour – given everyone the chance for a sly laugh at the ill-natured clash between clip-board wielding bird lovers and Beatrice Potteresque hedgehog fanciers.

On the mainland, flora and fauna sit happily in the same sentence. Not on the Uists. Listening to locals, you get the strong impression that flora keeps the island economy going whilst fauna generally stops it. Flora employs locals. Fauna employs earnest young incomers. These of course are generalisations. Conservation employs hundreds of locals the length of the island chain.

Anyway Berneray has a new bit of unwanted fauna to contend with – rabbits.

Since the causeway to North Uist was built six years ago, the bunny-free status of the island where Prince Charles once planted tatties has been in danger. So far, only four bunnies have been spotted – but in the opinion of local crofters that's four too many and they've formed a Rabbit Committee to protect Berneray's machair – the most abundant and productive in the Hebrides. If it's a toss-up between Thumper and over 200 species of flowers, there's no contest here. Rabbits will be shot. A limited number of geese will be shot. And if crofting brothers Splash and John MacKillop have anything to do with it, hundreds more geese will bite the dust – and a few seals too.

The prospect of meeting Splash MacKillop on Berneray was making me twitchy. Maxwell had told several amusing stories of Splash's legendary hostility to journalists during Prince Charles's sojurn at the MacKillop residence during the prince's turnip-talking period in the mid-eighties.

The turf house, Berneray

Boat at Berneray

All journalists live with the fear of being found out, of finally meeting that person with the longest memory in the world, the most comprehensive knowledge of grammar or a Holy Grail-like mission to correct an apostrophe wrongly placed twenty years ago. I was building Splash MacKillop into just that man. He might resent past jibes I'd made at royalty. He might hate land reform. All of this was rattling through my mind as we rattled over the causeway. And then it all just disappeared.

Berneray is a wonderful assault on the senses. On the west side, miles of white sandy beaches are concealed behind a half mile band of machair. Such a wild, colourful profusion of flowers, interrupted by the memorial patch of Royal potatoes, that you feel sure someone must have planted it. On the east side, long ledges of rock probe the bay like stone fingers. Houses sit like rings, close to the knuckle. Front doors are perhaps just six feet from the high tide mark in a hugging fit between land and sea.

There's something almost exciting about this engineered confrontation with the elements. No safety net for these islanders in a storm, no decorous distance from nature. As I cycle I glance seaward, I can see waves breaking through the momentarily synchronised front and back windows of each house. The road winds in and out around the bay. And beyond, there are fabulous silhouettes of mountain ranges unfamiliar from this angle. Rounding the corner towards the Gatliff Hostel where we might stay tonight, I spot two stunning houses with green turf roofs. I know I am late, I know I am on the wrong road and I know Max will be on the other single track road looking for me. But there is no more delicious expedition than the one crammed into no available space. So I freewheel down the short hill and stand surveying a house that could have come straight out of prehistoric Scotland – if it were not for the nappies on the washing line. Within minutes, a woman carrying a baby, with a toddler at her heels, emerges.

**Gloria and Splash
MacKillop**

I suppose she must weary of the endless interest her novel home excites amongst camera-wielding tourists. She shrugs. Obviously the answer is yes. But though she is not native, her skills of diplomacy certainly are. Yes the house is dry, yes the turf must be replaced every year, yes it's warm in the winter and no they don't grow beans, sprouts or wear open-toed sandals. Her husband is a local fisherman. They just fancied living in something a little different.

I'm aware of the transit's engine.

'They're waiting for you – he's got his brother John there. And there are Australians. And they're all going out to clip the sheep if we don't get there soon. Hello…'

Max had finally clocked the turf lady.

So the time had come to encounter Splash MacKillop. I heaved up the hill to find Max waiting at the porch door of the modern bungalow, almost hopping from foot to foot with excitement, though in retrospect, that could have been an early attack of major sciatic back pain.

'Come with me – they're all waiting.'

And I walked into a sunny, cluttered kitchen and a howl of recognition from four people I had never met before. Of course I forget the wireless often precedes me. And whatever crimes against royalty I may have committed, close-armed combat with sundry bosses over the years had clearly stood me in good stead. Splash hugged me like a long lost daughter and proceeded, with his brother John, to give the most fabulously entertaining account of Berneray life.

Geese and the Brahan Seer

'With the numbers of geese, the prophecy of the Brahan Seer will soon come true,' announces John. 'He prophesied in the seventeenth century that Berneray would be laid waste by geese and people would disappear so the only sound left would be the clacking of the beaks.' John's lilting voice, direct gaze and portentous language inject the conversation with a sudden air of gravity. 'There used to be dozens of us down on the machair making hay – now there are just two boys doing it. The young ones aren't as interested in sheep and potatoes. It's not enough for them. That's why the prediction will come true. The only sound on Bernerary will be the honking of the geese. That's what the Seer predicted and we are watching it happen.'

I'm reminded of Lachie Morrison saying the world's second largest grey seal colony on the Monach Islands didn't exist until the people had gone. It's as if the animals gang up when they sense human society is weak.

I recount this and the brothers, clearly contemporaries of Lachie, nod gravely.

'Don't get me wrong. The goose is a beautiful bird but it's as if they are laughing at us. The whole balance of nature is completely out of control.'

Little we complain, though we suffer much. The MacKillops could have coined the old Gaelic proverb.

Back in the nineties on Islay, naturalist David Bellamy left many Scots with the impression geese numbers were teetering on the brink. This year alone, SNH have shot 1,000 geese on the Uists to bring numbers under control. Heid bummer David McLennan acknowledges some species are out of control.

Kate and John MacKillop

But the MacKillops see the whole thing more urgently and emotionally.

'The geese are destroying our livelihood and waiting for us to go. Not only do geese eat the machair, they take the grass out by the roots. So in a couple of years you've got moss. And that's the end of crofting.'

Why doesn't SNH agree?

John's voice rises ten decibels and he knocks over a tea cup.

'Because they know better.'

Whatever SNH are doing right, it isn't PR or community relations.

The general impression from locals is that the conservation quango believes it *must* stick up for birds and habitat because crofters will shoot anything that moves for target practice, dig up peat bogs, and hack down fledgling forests for bonfires after denuding every available river of passing salmon.

In fact, the small farmers and crofters of the West Coast have maintained unique habitats like the machair of the Hebrides, without help, for centuries. They are the real custodians of Scottish Natural Heritage. Custodians who resent having their ancient rights and responsibilities rewritten by what they perceive to be city-based, clipboard-wielding youngsters with the unassailable authority of working for a quango.

Now of course, this is a sweeping generalisation. SNH staff are hard-working and well-meaning. And sometimes, crofters are just plain wrong or happily collecting subsidies for what used to come naturally (like building *Cruachan* or haystacks instead of making silage to provide autumn food for birds). But the words I hear applied to SNH are unusually consistent: slow, arrogant, bureaucratic and frustrating.

The only consolation for SNH is that they're not the only bit of government making the *Uibhistich* see red.

The Scottish Executive has started to consult on the possibility of creating a Marine National Park to include the Sound of Harris, the waters of the Minch and weirdly, the entire land mass of North Uist. Given the state of hostility between many crofters and the conservation bodies, it's no wonder this is currently a goose that isn't flying.

Astonishing, then, that the Executive managed to aggravate the situation by conducting their only consultation to date on South Uist (wrong island) in the back of a van in the Co-op car park.

Mind you, Western Isles Council don't seem to have done much better. They want to build a causeway across the Sound of Harris to link the Uists with Harris and finally create one 'Long Island' that will offer dramatic improvements in services and transport.

It's a massive, ambitious proposal and the council hope to include turbines so that tidal energy can offset some of the cost. Initial studies suggest the tides would have to be channelled into narrow spaces beneath bridges to achieve the force needed to drive the turbines, and that worries the hell out of some Berneray folk. Some fear such a long causeway – Europe's longest – would be unsafe. A Uist family died in 2005 after being swept away from just such an inundated stretch of road. Some believe the causeways will change tidal patterns and strip away parts of the sandy coastline.

Others worry that after centuries the upgraded road links alone would change island life completely. And it would be sad for Berneray, the only inhabited island in the watery chaos that is the Sound of Harris, if its reward for survival was to become a giant stepping stone for everyone else travelling north and south.

It doesn't take a PR guru to spot that the people of Berneray might need sensitive handling if they are not to veto the causeway project. Aston-

Gatliff Hostel, Berneray

ishing then, that Western Isles Council scheduled no consultation meeting for Berneray and held the neighbouring Lochmaddy event at 5pm (awkward for locals) so that the travelling suits from Stornoway could race down the road afterwards and hold a second meeting on South Uist at 8pm. Presumably the council saved one night's expenses. And once again, the islanders most affected by change are consulted least.

'Exactly,' says John as I give the MacKillop brothers the edited highlights. 'Other people think they know best about everything these days.'

I'm about to switch off the recorder lest I encourage another bout of savage goose talk, when John mentions seal oil.

Sunset over Baleshare

'Ah yes. We used to kill a seal every year. Just one. And we used the blubber for the horses – they had beautiful coats afterwards. We just forced the blubber into their mouths. And then we boiled down the seal oil for ourselves. It cured everything.'

'…and more.' Splash has a splendid disdain for the infinite. 'It cured my pleurisy in two weeks and my wife's arthritis. Of course it gave you TB if you took too much.'

'Tuberculosis?'

'Yes. TB.'

'Well maybe that's why doctors didn't want you to use it?'

'Ah, but we always knew when we had had enough.'

By now I am on the edge of my seat.

John leans forward and opened the palm of his big hand.

'When the oil gathered in a pool in the centre of your palm, then you knew you had taken enough seal oil.'

'Yes, that was enough. Then you would be cured.'

I look long and hard at the two brothers for any hint of mischief making. They were absolutely serious.

'Now we have seals everywhere but no seal oil, geese everywhere and we can hardly shoot them and even rabbits across the causeway. And what can we do to get balance? Nothing.'

The tea cup wobbles again.

But not as badly as SNH. They've brought so few of these key local people with them, it's not a case of shooting the messenger – islanders are queuing up to shoot the whole conservation message.

Leaving Splash MacKillop's house, and realising I didn't mention royal vegetables once, we detour for a quick look at the Gatliff Hostel. Established in the sixties by Herbert Gatliff, the string of remote, basic hostels is

93

RABBITS

There have been sightings of rabbits on Berneray. If you do see any on Berneray, please inform any member of the community council. SNH have been informed about the issue.

**Berneray
Community Council
rabbit alert**

designed for independent travellers, with no booking ahead, to encourage a spirit of adventure and unpredictability. Small parties must share space with the folk who've turned up on the night. When we arrive, absolutely no one will speak to us on tape except a reluctant hostel manager.

Keen to avoid invading any more of their space – we are breathing, for example – we ditch plans to stay without exchanging more than a glance.

Outside we run back to the transit, like giggling teenagers excused from a night with adults. The night is young, the bikes are slung in the back and we hightail it back to North Uist and, just to satisfy my curiosity, across the island to Baleshare – a long thin sandy island parallel to the mainland and connected by bridges. As we arrive, Baleshare is suddenly cast into fabulous silhouette by the sunset. I love this about setting out 'too late' – you can have the world to yourselves, in all its glorious sun-setting clarity.

Back finally to Lochmaddy and the welcoming B&B of Alina Morrison – a woman whose establishment is so popular she doesn't advertise and relies on word of mouth for business. There isn't even a sign outside her house ('in case we get too many people').

Hey – who am I to argue anymore. Maybe small is beautiful. Either way, tomorrow we'll be leaving the traditional heart of this island chain for the bigger, brasher ways of Lewis and Harris. Wait a minute. Rodel, population seventy, bigger and brasher? I'm still coming back to Benbecula from tiny Sunamul, perspective shot.

Max tells me I've gone native. Maybe.

But given the slightest encouragement, I go native almost anywhere.

Leverburgh to Rodel South Harris

The MacLeod mystery and the failed fishing

Great men with great ideas. It seems South Harris has had more than its fair share. After Lord Leverhulme bought the island, the village of *An-t-Ob* (tidal bay) was duly renamed Leverburgh in his honour. Three piers were built for fifty herring drifters to supply his Lordship's new MacFisheries chain of fish shops across the UK. But local people wanted land, not boats, and warned that the shallow channels of the Sound of Harris made for extremely dodgy navigation and fishing.

After one year of fish landings, the Great Man died and the project was scrapped. The land he'd paid £36,000 to acquire was sold for just £900. And though fish is now plentiful on South Harris, it's delivered by a nice man from Buckie, who travels over from the east coast each week. Lord Leverhulme must be turning in his London grave.

IS MÒID I SID, MU'N DUBHAIRT AN DREACHAN-DONN, 'N UAIR A RINN E DHILEAG 'S A' MHUIR MHÒIR

"IT'S THE BIGGER FOR THAT," AS THE WREN SAID WHEN IT PEED IN THE SEA

SEAN-FHACAL GAELIC PROVERB

Meanwhile, five miles east, another group of Great Men appear to be lying somewhat easier in theirs. In 1528 Alasdair Crotach MacLeod (Alexander the Humpbacked) built St Clements Church in Rodel and prepared a magnificent tomb with carvings, clever features and unexplained mysteries. This was about the time the powerful Lordship of the Isles collapsed and many clan chiefs were making their own arrangements rather than depend on burial with their predecessors in the Lordship graveyard on Iona.

The church and his tomb are considered two of the finest monuments in the Hebrides. No wonder. The Crotach had a flair for the dramatic, which even enabled him to win a wager with King James V. This was no mean feat, since James at the time was having other island chiefs imprisoned or dispossessed. The chief was said to have been challenged at the royal court to accept that its grandeur could not be equalled by anything on the Isles. Alasdair replied that he had a finer table and candlesticks than any the court could provide. When James V came to visit Dunvegan he found that MacLeod had set out a feast on one of the high, flat hills, now known as 'MacLeod's Tables', facing Dunvegan, and the whole scene was lit by clansmen in all their Celtic finery, holding aloft flaming torches. The king conceded defeat.

It's raining as Max and I totter off the ferry, so an indoor tour of St Clements Church seems like a good idea – and not one but three local guides volunteer. We make our various ways to the church, which looks neat from the outside, but not exactly impressive. Within seconds I stand corrected by guide number one, local boat builder, John MacAulay.

St Clements Church

'This was the powerhouse of the MacLeods. A huge symbol. At the time when it was being constructed, people were living in thatched houses and had a very poor existence, and to have this placed in their midst must've been like having the Millennium Dome erected on St Kilda or something. Alistair Crotach was the eighth chief of the Clan MacLeod. And he lies here with his armour and mail and claymore, with religious carvings around him and above him the birlinn – the traditional ship of the Lords of the Isles and the means of everyday travel. These were the Cal Mac ferries of

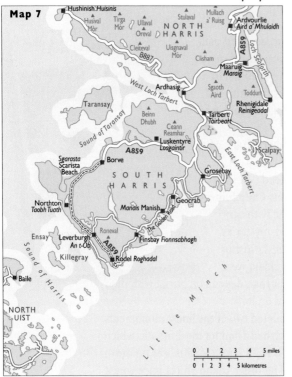

their day. The chapel was restored by Captain Alexander MacLeod as part of a model village, along with a hotel, harbour and houses in the 1700s. His dad, Donald the Trojan from Berneray, Harris, was quite a character. When he was seventy he married a girl of sixteen – he was doing pretty well.'

'His wives weren't.' (John stolidly ignores this.)

'To prove he was up to the task he had to perform a leap from lying on his back to standing on his feet – impossible even for a trained athlete.'

'Maybe the world's first break dancer!'

Despite himself, John laughs. 'I find this place fascinating. I come here when it's quite dark and yet it feels safe and comfortable. There is something about it. Most people feel something spiritual.'

I was sorry to lower the tone, but with another two guides due to appear anytime, I needed to capture the highlights fast – and the next were outside. I called them gargoyles. John corrected me.

'They are fertility symbols. On the tower there's a male figure who appears to be wearing a very short kilt and exposing his private parts.'

'He's holding them.'

'Well, he was. Until Lady Dunmore took a dislike to what she was seeing and ordered her ghillie to shoot off the offending part.'

'And her ghillie was evidently a reasonable shot.'

'Evidently.'

'Actually it isn't a gargoyle. It's a well-made figure of a man – almost floating up the tower wall.'

Rodel Church and
the 'incomplete'
statue

'On the next wall there's a female figure squatting and exposing her parts.'

'Politely we could say it's like she's in childbirth minus the child. And looks like she's had the shotgun treatment as well.'

'May have been.' (You wonder if men realise there's actually something down there.) 'Did these figures cause offence or was it just target practice? There are things we don't understand about this place.'

I'm intrigued about John's first love – boats. And without Maxwell around, I may even enquire. I'm impressed to hear he is building a replica of Joshua Slocomb's *Spray* – Slocomb was the first man to sail solo round the world and John's been building the replica between sailing round the world himself.

Maxwell had briefed me on the dos and don'ts of conversing with a top boat builder. The biggest bit of advice: don't mention fibreglass.

'So what do you think of fibreglass boats?'

(Long pause.)

'Fibreglass boats are good for fibreglass people.'

Silence.

I make a mental note to listen to Max in future.

'So is it easy to find the wood you need to build?'

'It was a bit difficult to get good quality oak in Scotland a few years ago, simply because during the building of the Scottish Parliament every little scrap of oak in the country was being swallowed up. I use what has always been used in boat building in Scotland, and that is larch for the planking and oak for the framing. Every boat builder has his individual style. Looking at an old wooden boat, you can tell which coast the boat was made for, what kind of wave pattern, and who built it.'

'But the next generation doesn't seem to have your skills, or maybe even value them.'

'There's a different outlook these days. The world has found our islands and our islands are becoming more like the rest of the world. Our young people are part of that world. A fibreglass world. Give it its due, fibreglass

A birlinn on the Crotach's Rodel tomb

produces boats quickly – but I haven't seen an *old* fibreglass boat yet. I wonder what happens to them. You don't see them rotting on a beach, and yet they disappear. Where to, I don't know.'

'And would Lingerabay [the proposed super quarry] have been more fibreglass or real jobs?'

'Well, there was the promise of jobs but then it was maybe a bit too big.'

I know I'm meant to be impartial and I wouldn't fancy a job at a quarry myself. But this objection is not about the dirt, or the possible pollution – just the size. This is the story of these islands. Everything's too big. The Lewis windfarm's too big, fixing a harbour's too big, even extending a B&B is getting too big. Or to quote another Gaelic proverb, *As the wren said*, hugely impressed by its own tiny contribution to the vast ocean after an airborne 'leak', *it's the bigger for that.*

'You're not big on big.'

'We do like to be in control of our own destiny. That's ingrained in all island people.'

'Yes, but look at the Shetlanders. They don't see getting big as becoming dependent. Quite the opposite.'

'Maybe, but we value control – not becoming beholden to someone or some power from outwith the islands.'

'But has no one here got cash or assets? Does expansion have to involve non-islanders? And are there no mainlanders you can trust?"

I can see this boat builder is not for turning.

But I can also see why he's preoccupied by St Clements. Not many churches easily combine bold displays of sexuality and humour with the business of death – and self defence. St Clements was part of an elaborate medieval lookout system. The window in the tower allowed locals to monitor a bonfire warning chain that stretched across hillocks and islands from Harris to Uist. And yet despite, or perhaps because of these practical, earthly functions, St Clements has become a spiritual sanctuary for people. Electricity hasn't been connected, so for most of the year the church sits fully open and accessible in a state of calm semi darkness. Illuminated occasionally by the lamps and candles of local musicians but not, in general, by the voice of any Minister. Perhaps that is the source of St Clements' power – it's a place for unmediated spirituality in an overly-mediated island chain.

According to Bill Lawson, 'One singer said she could see her voice travelling along the walls.'

Bill is a man whose reputation precedes him.

He's written over fifty books on the history and genealogy of the islands and established *Seallam* – a family history centre, in Northton, just beyond Leverburgh. He's a walking encyclopaedia on matters Hebridean, a human bridge. He and his wife Chris have pieced together every family tree in the Outer Isles – a neverending Forth Bridge kind of task – and have connected families divided by the Atlantic since the Clearances. Doubtless through his devotion to oral history, Bill knows good stories communicate volumes. So tour number two with ex-postie Donald MacRae (nicknamed Noy) starts with a grave that contains the remains of all the MacLeod chief's flag-bearers. Each body was laid on a grille, which was riddled, like the grate on a fire, to let the previous dusty remains fall through into a pit below. The last time the neighbouring casket was opened there were fourteen skulls inside. In another corner, a bardess lies buried upside down, at her own request – 'lest her lying tongue should point to heaven'.

I look at Noy for reassurance Bill isn't making all of this up.

'It's true. Captain Alexander MacLeod did repairs in the eighteenth century several times – first time round, the masons and carpenters had a party, set fire to the place and burned it down.'

After an hour inside this fabulous, mischievous building, I'm starting to warm to the MacLeods. Especially the sandy-haired one, who's booked us in for fish and chips in the Anchorage Restaurant back at Leverburgh.

We split up over lunch. Max drags John off to a separate table and talks about boats (again?). I drag Bill and Noy back to the subject that's really baffling me. Fish. And where better to try and solve the mystery of Banffshire fish deliveries on Harris than here, in the port that baffled Lord Leverhulme a century before.

'Bill, what I'm about to say feels like heresy.'

'Fire away – Noy, would you pass the salt.'

John MacAulay amidst his replica of Slocomb's *Spray*

'I'm seeing evidence of inactivity all around on the fishing front and I don't understand it. We are surrounded by fish but no one's fishing. You get deliveries from Buckie.'

'And he's a very nice man.'

'But he's not a local man. Why not? Why are harbours here non-existent, dodgy, hard to get into or impossible to moor at? Why are they empty? I've heard guys on East Coast trawlers mocking the Western Isles boys for the small scale of their fishing ambitions. They say Hebrideans are scared of losing sight of land and use the Sabbath as an excuse. Which is nonsense when you look at the number of islanders decorated for bravery in the wars. But why was none of that skill used to set up their own boats here? Why does everyone today complain about the Swedish, Spanish and East Coast trawlers coming round to hoover up fish. Why haven't local fishermen been out hoovering up fish themselves? Because they are more ecologically minded? Or because the prospect of building harbours, maneouvering large, expensive boats and taking out scary-sized loans stopped them in their tracks? What is it?'

'Your chips are getting cold, you know.'

I could see I would have to raise the emotional temperature of this challenge to get an answer.

'Okay, I can see that with expansion comes debt. With that comes dependency on the opinions of a mainland banker. And with that comes endless worry. Better to have no development than to be beholden. But that won't work any more. These days family members *are* beholden – to a building society. The days of waiting to inherit the croft are over. Family businesses need to expand to pay wages to pay mortgages to keep their children here.'

'You could be right.'

Boy, this man can resist an argument when he's having fish and chips. 'Bill – why are the Western Isles not fish heaven?'

'Ask Duncan McInnes.'

Fishermen – where are they?

This is sound advice. An unguarded outburst like that in front of the skippers of Scalpay could have been deadly.

Duncan McInnes has been the head of the Western Isles Fishermen's Association for almost twenty years. He's based on Great Bernera on the west side of Lewis and, amazingly, when I phone him at home I get him first time.

'Duncan, why is there no large scale fishing industry here on the Western Isles?

'Western Isles' boats have always been distinctive. They are short, shallow drafted vessels, designed to be hauled up on slipways rather than anchored. Slipways were a cheaper solution than stone harbours. And

At the boat shed

remember, the rise and fall of the tides around the Hebrides is substantial, twice the height of the seas around Shetland, for example. That makes harbours much more difficult to construct. At low tide the boats are lying on the harbour floor, so there's a lot of movement and friction.'

'Fair enough, but then there would be no harbours at all in Ireland or southern England – isn't their tidal reach even bigger? Surely lack of cash and Sunday observance must have been factors – no point in travelling too far from home every weekend, and therefore no point in having large boats and therefore no drive to invest in piers.'

'Well, maybe up to a point that's true. But remember, island men *were* sailing on the Sabbath. At any one time, half the able-bodied men on these islands were away on trawlers, merchant ships or the Navy. Fishermen who stayed here always had to make do and mend. In the old days at Carloway on the west coast of Lewis, they salted fish rather than trying to sell it direct and fresh into the Scottish market – you'll see salting sheds right down at slipways all over the islands. Same with the shellfish. There were no fancy storage techniques for prawns or lobsters, so the men built holding ponds at the shore with stone dykes to let salt water in, but stop the creatures getting out. You can still see the old ponds on Great Bernera in Lewis. And as for sending them on to the fish markets in Billingsgate in London, the lobsters were simply packed in tea chests with straw; quite often the message would come back, "dead on arrival" – with a bill for the transport. Whether the lobsters really died or survived, who knows?'

But that's my point – why were the transport methods so... antique?

'There has been a reluctance amongst fishermen to adapt to new systems. In some ways, that may have saved our bacon. In the sixties boats on islands like Scalpay were as modern as any in the rest of the Scottish fleet. Then came the herring ban in the late seventies and changes in netting systems. Local boats had to scale up considerably to chase mackerel – the only plentiful fish stock on the go. Quite a lot of them didn't want to do that. It would mean big loans to get big boats, and big journeys, which would mean breaking the Sabbath. But then something else happened. Britain joined the EU and fishermen here realised there was another way – and diversified into shellfish. As a result, we now have 320 vessels registered in the Western Isles, more than any other region of Scotland. Our live storage is the best in Europe. Before Christmas, we had 50 tonnes of lobster stored here worth £1 million. We don't flood the market.

By managing stock we've added £2k per tonne to prices. You can see live storage for brown crab and scallops at Kallin pier near Grimsay.'

'So you guys have landed on your feet, compared to the fishermen of Peterhead and Fraserburgh – thanks to the Sabbath?'

'They were over-dependent on whitefish, so they have taken the big hit. For the Western Isles the biggest problem now is the weather. You know, in the 1700s they had much calmer weather. That's how open boats managed to sail to the Flannan Isles in the summer. Now it can be wild or flat calm at any time of year.'

Bill Lawson and Donald (Noy) MacRae in the Anchorage, Leverburgh

But I'm still puzzled.

'Wouldn't your lives be easier now if you had decent harbours like they have had for centuries in Caithness?'

'Well, it could have been political. Until the Western Isles Council was created in the seventies, the islands were all divided between mainland county councils and had to compete with their mainland fishing communities for investment. Having said that, many east coast harbours are closed in bad weather. They may be well built but can the boats actually use them? Our tie-ups are less permanent, but safer. We have a pontoon system which means the boats rise and fall with the tide, instead of being tied to a static concrete pier that might look more substantial but in practice offers less protection. We've built four pontoons in ten years – modified from designs used in the Shetlands and Faroes. If we had been stuck building old-fashioned piers, we could only have afforded one. Take Stockinish, a tiny creek on the Golden Road in Harris. With the barrage there, twenty vessels now tie up in a remote community which had no activity at all.'

'So the action's all off the beaten track now – not in the big empty harbours we've been noticing.'

'Mostly. But there is also a deep-seated antipathy to big investors here. Look at Lingerabay – the row over that quarry proposal went on for nine years. Look at the windfarms in Lewis. It's the biggest potential source of income in our lifetime. And look at Shetland. They aren't arguing. They have just gone for it.'

Duncan is a pro windfarm, canny, entrepreneurial fisherman. But as Lord Leverhulme discovered ninety years ago, before quotas, herring bans or Spanish trawlers had even entered the argument, thinking small and thinking about local land is far more common.

Lord Leverhulme and the big fishing failure

In *The Soap Man*, Roger Hutchinson tells the story of how the eminent Lancashire industrialist tried to transform the lives of 30,000 people on Lewis (and later Harris) by a massive expansion of fishing. He wanted them to forsake their crofts and come to live near Stornoway in a Hebridean version of Port Sunlight, his model village near Liverpool.

His attempt to win crofters over to live in bungalows as employees of MacFisheries failed miserably.

The turning point may well have been the moment he believed he'd converted an angry crowd, swelled by men just back from the ravages of the First World War at Gress Bridge near Stornoway:

> Do you realise that Stornoway is right in the centre of the richest fishing grounds in the whole world? The fishing which is being carried on in an old fashioned, happy go lucky way is now to be prosecuted on scientific lines. Recently at Stornoway I saw half of the fishing boats without a single herring. I have a plan for putting an end to that sort of thing. I am prepared to supply a fleet of airplanes and trained observers who will daily scan the sea in circles around the island. An observer from one of these planes cannot fail to notice any shoal of herring over which he passes. Immediately he does so he sends a wireless message to the Harbour Master at Stornoway. Every time a message of that kind comes in there is a loudspeaker announcement so all skippers at the pier get the exact location of the shoal. The boats are headed for that spot – and next morning they steam back to port loaded with herrings to the gunwales. Hitherto the return to port has been with light boats and heavy hearts. In future it will be with light hearts and heavy boats!

Leverhulme intended to spend £5 million on Lewis. In addition to the great fleet of fishing and cargo boats, there would be a huge fish canning factory, railways, an electricity power station and substantial, well equipped houses.

But that day standing before the crowd, Leverhulme faced eloquent opposition from one local man, John MacLeod – who would surely have become a Scottish people's hero after this speech, had it not been conducted in the relative obscurity of rural Lewis:

'It is not your fault but your misfortune that your upbringing, your experience, and your outlook are such that a proper understanding of our point of view is outwith your comprehension. You have spoken of steady work and steady pay in tones of veneration. I have no doubt that in your view and in the view of those unfortunate people who are compelled to live their lives in smoky towns, steady work and steady pay are very desirable things. But in Lewis we have never been accustomed to either – and strange though it must seem to your lordship we do not greatly desire them. We attend to our crofts in seed time and harvest and we follow the fishing in its season and when neither requires our attention we are free to rest and contemplate. You have referred to our houses as hovels – but they are our homes and I will venture to say my Lord that poor though these homes may be, you will find more real human happiness in them then you'll find in your castles throughout the land. We are not in opposition to your schemes of work: we only oppose you when you say you cannot give us the land and on that point we will oppose you with all our strength. You have bought this island. But you have not bought us, and we refuse to be the bond slaves of any man. We want to live our own lives in our own way, poor in material things but at least clear of the factory bell: free and independent.'

Leverhulme responded, 'Give my schemes a chance – give me a period of ten years and… if there are still some who prefer life on the land they can have two, three, four crofts apiece.' Roger Hutchinson remarks: 'They cheered him, of course. They cheered him because they were good natured people, because they were amused by the prospect of being offered four crofts apiece, because they appreciated the performance if not the message and because a landowner who was prepared to engage in open debate was a rarity and they did not want the courageous little Soap Man to leave Gress thinking that in coming to talk to them he had wasted his time.'

This last insightful remark reminds me of a joke told by Angus Peter

Marram grass

Campbell – 'Did you hear the one about the Lewisman who loved his wife so much he almost told her?'

I realise it's quite possible to cause massive offence – or even massive delight – on the Western Isles and know nothing of the true impact. It might just be best to assume all is well and relax.

But back at the fish conundrum. It seems, in the end, the argument was settled by events, dear boy, events. The Stornoway fleet was slow to mechanise after the First World War and when restrictions were lifted, fish was suddenly competing with other more 'exotic' foodstuffs. Britain had imposed a trade embargo on the new Soviet Union which caused a virtual collapse in the valuable east European herring trade. Prohibition in American also played a part – salted herring had been used in saloons as salted peanuts are used now. Even that was over. The wholesale price of fish collapsed. And such was the enduring desire for land, not bungalows, that four years later, in 1923, 260 young men and women from Lewis set sail on the *Metagama* to Ontario, where they were promised smallholdings on the Canadian prairie. 'These isles are now being emptied,' announced one Canadian journal. 'Only the old are left behind.'

Leverhulme died in 1925 without admitting his mistake of overvaluing the possible bounty of the sea. The port installations at Leverburgh were bought and scrapped by a demolition company, Harris was divided into several estates, the country areas of Lewis became a jigsaw of different tenures and only Stornoway gained by accepting Leverhulme's offer of community ownership, enshrining the town's assets in the Stornoway Trust, which still exists today. After all his effort and argument, it seems there is very little Hebridean affection for Leverhulme. The Northern Ireland poet Louis MacNiece wrote:

To the island of Harris he turned his eyes
As more adapted to enterprise
He introduced his commercial cult
Leverburgh is the sole result
Leverburgh was meant to be
The hub of the fishing industry
All that remained at Lever's death
Was a waste of money and a waste of breath
All that remained of Lever's plans
Were some half built piers and some empty cans.

So that was the problem with fishing.

Having one foot in the croft ruled out the possibility of saving money (because crofts were designed to be unprofitable), and of spending unlimited time on deep sea fishing. There were always competitors with bigger, better-equipped boats. Islanders weren't trying to make massive profits. Customs like not fishing on the Sabbath mattered to them. Leaving some of the catch on the shore for widows to collect mattered too. The expansion deal offered by Leverhulme not only coincided with a European collapse in fish sales and fish prices, it had strings attached that were unacceptable to free-spirited people.

Fish explained at last… almost.

I have a feeling that islanders are basically uncertain players in the cash economy and very uncertain borrowers. In the old days, crofters put years of their time and labour into making improvements in houses or land, only to be evicted so the next tenant could be charged more. The discovery of the kelp market, for many, resulted only in hard labour and higher rents. The long campaign for land reform resulted in security of tenure for the few and no new crofts – and since the family had always been the principal form of human currency on the islands, that simply meant overcrowding.

Why would islanders invest beyond that which they could touch and trust? And where would they find the cash anyway?

Many of those who went searching overseas found cash, and never came back. Many of those who remained found no cash – until the advent of crofting subsidies in the seventies – and developed a chronic fear of indebtedness, bankruptcy and failure. Big has come to mean greedy, even though small is coming to mean unviable. Combine all of that with a religious imperative to keep life as simple and uncomplicated as possible, and it's hard to create an enterprise culture.

The Soap Man was facing impossible odds last century. And I wonder if those odds have really changed.

Rodel to Scalpay Harris

The big Gaelic music argument, tweed and rain

Why is Gaelic music so melancholy? It wasn't the two-hour argument I was expecting when I slung the bike against the harled wall of the *Seallam* Genealogy Centre in Northton. This modest building is like a Hebridean Tardis. Inside, Bill and his wife Chris Lawson have squeezed a bookshop, a publishing empire (currently celebrating the arrival of its fiftieth book), a Learn Direct computer room and a genealogy centre containing the history of virtually every household in the Western Isles for the last two centuries. That's 27,500 family trees. Bill pulls a folder from the wall of history – the recent history of a family of ten from Point in Lewis.

B'FHEARR A BHI SÀMHACH NA DROCH DHÀN A GHABHAIL

BETTER BE SILENT THAN SING A BAD SONG

SEAN-FHACAL
GAELIC PROVERB

'Donald went to St Catherine's in Ontario, William went to Thunder Bay, John was in Alaska, Murdo was in Buffalo, Norman was lost in the war, Katy-Ann went to Thunder Bay, George went to Canada but came back, Etta taught in the school next door, a young boy died in infancy... and Mary-Ann was Chris's mother.'

No wonder Chris Lawson thinks she has cousins everywhere. She does. She and Bill have spent decades cataloguing the relentless drift of local people.

Bill has a sense of mission and an uncommon outspokenness.

'When I first came here fifty years ago, people asked who you had met and who they were related to. Family was all that mattered. Oral sources depended on memory, written sources on the translator's grasp of Gaelic. Both were prone to error. So we decided to check everything – starting with the 1851 census.'

And those big family trees explain everything. If families of nine were hard to sustain in industrial Glasgow, they were almost impossible to sustain here. On the islands, loss and the grief surrounding departure were always going to be bigger themes than arrival and the pleasure of reunion.

Which brings us to the delicate subject of song.

Taking my life in my hands, I explain that the radio series I'm making, *On the*

Bill and Chris Lawson, *Seallam*

Bike, is accompanied by music from an Orcadian band, Saltfishforty, be-cause… their music is more upbeat and cheery than anything I could find in the Hebridean repertoire.

There's a sharp intake of breath from Chris.

'Have you listened to this?' she asks, and whacks the latest selection from the all-woman group *Bannal* onto the *Seallam* CD player.

Mouth Music

It is certainly feisty stuff. Vigorous 'mouth music' once accompanied every physical task from spinning and rowing to waulking (finishing tweed cloth).

Martin Martin – whose *Description of the Western Isles of Scotland* accompanied Johnson and Boswell on their Hebridean Tour – complained in 1703 of hearing a madhouse of women, so raucous and raw was the unaccompanied sound to 'refined' mainland ears. As ever, Margaret Fay Shaw has a more sympathetic account of a *luadhadh* or waulking, 'which is when the cloth is shrunk and made ready for the tailor'.

> My first *luadhadh* was held in Peigi's byre. Planks that served as a bridge across the burn were made to serve as the table. A lantern hung from the rafters and shone down on the singers in their rough aprons, their heads tied in handkerchiefs, their sleeves rolled high. The air was potent with the smell of hot urine, but no substitute will give the softness of texture nor set the colour, especially of indigo. When finished, the tweed was thoroughly washed in a running stream and dried on the heather, exposed to the sun and wind for several days until perfectly clean. The women kneaded and pushed the cloth around and around the table with song after song. The one who sang the verse line would give turns and grace notes to take in all the syllables, always in absolute time and with a rhythm that was marvellous to me. When ready at last it was rolled up tightly and two women would face across it and clapping the roll would sing the clapping song called in Glendale the *coileach* in quicktime which finished the *luadhadh*. The company would shout, 'give them the *coileach*' for the words of these last songs are to a great extent extemporised and consist of witty and ribald remarks about the people present with reference to their actual or possible love affairs. The singers then washed and changed, to gather with the other members of the party in the kitchen, where a dram was passed and tea with scones and cake. Then began the singing and dancing with great hilarity.

With a song tradition as feisty and female as this, why couldn't I find any Gaelic music to suit? Well, some of the words that flew through my brain when I first imagined cycling up the Western Isles were, light, fast, nimble, optimistic, freewheeling, and cheery. Admittedly, I didn't make an absolutely forensic search for Gaelic music that evoked these qualities. But I found several options fast in the Orcadian repertoire.

Chris is still just looking at me.

I can see this discussion isn't going to be a short one. Why should it be? She is in her world – I doubtless appear to be taking ill-judged pot shots at it. What do I know about Gaelic music except the very little I hear? Except that, to my mind, the very little is melancholic and wistful at best – mournful and despairing at worst. And the Gaels I've been meeting aren't.

Now don't get me wrong. I quite understand that the default setting for Scot is more than a little introspective and prone to gloom. I am not a relentlessly cheery person. I would have painted the whole house Wedgewood Blue (ie grey) if my Canadian-bred, sunshine-yellow-loving husband hadn't stopped me. And my idea of fun is mooching around isolated island chains, without shops. I like sad, atmospheric music in bursts, but I also like variety. And if a night of entertainment is going to major on just one emotion, 'grief' wouldn't be my first choice. I don't understand the Gaelic attachment to mournfulness. It's as if singing anything cheery is letting the side down.

But why do I get the impression all is gloom – albeit often beautiful, poignant, heart-rending gloom – in the world of Gaelic song?

Is it to do with me, the songs I've heard, the songs I haven't heard, or the oddly matter-of-fact explanations of misery given in English before a single note has been sung? Questioning an artform that evidently delights and animates the majority of people around me feels positively shameful.

So I run my 'Gaelic introduction theory' past Gaeldom's unofficial musical supremo, Arthur Cormack of the band *Cliar* and the *Fèisean* Movement. He was not very amused…

'Singers like Michael Marra, Dick Gaughan or Tony McManus do long introductions to their songs in English – I take it they're okay?'

Good point. When these storyteller/songwriters are on stage they weave long, imaginative universes around the songs they're about to sing. The English introductions I've heard to Gaelic songs, by contrast, seem perfunctory, even embarrassed, something that just needs to be got out of the way. I'm sure uneasiness about the attention span of non-Gaels in the audience is a factor – but I also suspect a deep uneasiness about the business of performance lurking not far behind. And yet, on stage everything must be about performance. From the first hello to the last verse. In English or in Gaelic. In speech or in song. That doesn't mean faking things or being inauthentic. It does mean being bold and self-confident enough to make sure your entire act reaches, touches and alters the mood of the audience. Performance is the reason singers are on the stage and we are in the audience. Just delivering songs like a musical postie is not enough. For instance, the incredible popularity of Runrig's mainland gigs seems to have owed less to an understanding of content and context than to the sense of confidence and urgency their 'big sound' created amongst the crowd. The music was the message. Capercaillie have also crossed the language divide with finely pitched vocals, brilliant instrumentals and a variety of song types in Gaelic and English. Their appeal for non-Gaels is not entirely based on meaning either.

Listeners bring meaning to music and traditional music relies heavily on association with sounds, instruments or melodies. My own sixteen childhood summers attending Highland Games mean I can actually smell cut grass when I hear the sound of bagpipes being tuned. The signature tune for Robbie Shepherd's *Take the Floor* fills me with happiness – even though dance band music isn't my preferred type of musical listening – because the Riddoch family outpost in Belfast tuned in to Robbie every Saturday teatime, and it brings back strong associations of warmth and intimacy. That means I can cheerfully waltz round the kitchen to 'Take the Floor' to this day, whilst my husband and step-daughters run screaming from the room, appalled at the schmaltzy sentimentality of it all. Gaelic music will have that same emotional 'surround' for people who've been brought up hearing it and singing it. But without those wider associations, non-Gaels may struggle to get from Gaelic music what Gaels are getting. Well, let me be honest – I'm struggling. A lot of the very 'mannered' Gaelic songs I'm hearing *en passant* in shops, on *Radio nan Gàidheal*, or in the Mod highlights on TV, leave me unmoved.

I know how much music defines identity. But much of what I'm hearing is not defining who Gaels are today – it's defining who their forebears were. Or more precisely, one aspect of their forebears' experience – loss. When I pass on, I hope my most despairing moments do not become my epitaph, no matter how much anyone enjoys the wake. I'm sure ancient Gaels like Donald the Trojan would be delighted with the creation of some new cheery, upbeat, satirical or plain silly songs to encompass all the emotions they felt and all of the boisterous life they loved.

Happily, the future of Gaelic music doesn't depend on winning over sceptics like me. It does depend, though, on engaging local youngsters.

And if the playful sounds of Billy Matheson aka Mac a noonoo are anything to go by, tradition may have to learn to share the stage with

Droukit near Luskentyre

experimentation. Billy's a comedy sketch writer and performer and his third album *Beyond the Balaclava,* includes original tracks and some satirical cover versions that are either hilarious or sacrilegious according to your point of view. My favourite is 'I Don't Like Sundays', an impish version of the Boomtown Rats' 'I Don't Like Mondays'. Billy writes and sings in English, not Gaelic. Is there room for a non-Gaelic speaking Gael singing about present-day life in the Hebridean music scene right now? There must be.

Better be silent than sing a bad song. No one could disagree with the proverb. But the big question is, who decides what constitutes a bad song? Surely it ought to be the audience?

Gaeldom is crying out for youth, mirth, absurdity, humour and unrestrained cheek – they generally get it at *Fèisean* festivals. But the most talented young musicians on the Outer Isles are still encouraged to aspire towards the role of tradition bearers – and although that's seen as an honour, I can feel the sore young backs from here.

And suddenly I realise I've said this – aloud. To a Gael with a cup of very hot coffee in her hand!

In fact, after her very long listen, Chris generously concedes that Ishbel MacAskill's introduction to a recent Uist night of Gaelic song was indeed 'about the dumped, desperate and deid'.

'But,' she adds, 'you can hear a pin drop when she's singing. She's lost in the emotion and so are we.'

And I don't doubt it.

But Gaelic has five words for the colour blue – and nature poems described by James Hunter, historian of the crofting community, as utterly euphoric? Why not get lost in songs about them as well? In short, when can we all cheer up?

I sense I've been verging on sacrilege. And I'm grateful to the broad-minded Lawsons for letting me give voice to it all. I also suspect they go and lie down in a darkened room when I finally leave.

DJ the Weaver

Outside *Seallam*, rain starts, and I become aware of a few small problems. Half-mast plastic over-trousers drip rainwater into trendy cutaway trainer socks I must have 'borrowed' from a step-daughter. Serves me right. My recently washed jacket has clearly lost its waterproofness and the decision to wear lip-gloss in the fairly substantial headwind has caused me to be cycling with two wands of hair permanently plaited across my sodden face.

And then… in the rolling waves of the beach at Luskentyre, I spot company. A group of people are swimming in the surf – some fully clothed. One woman wearing a swimsuit is caked with white sand – it's just 10 degrees. I shimmy down to the beach and almost get dragged in.

This is hardy. I ask if they are locals. They laugh.

'No. We're from Scotland.'

The answer says it all. The mainland does feel like another country.

'Friends think we're crazy – especially when they realise we only take twenty pounds spending money – there's nowhere to spend it. We just go out when we want, swim when we want, and go walking wherever. It's great.'

And they're right. There's something about this coast that keeps your attention riveted on the ever-changing colours of the sea. The long ex-

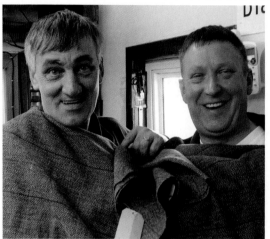

DJ the Weaver and DJ the Postie

panse of Scarista beach is fabulous – but it's the offshore islands framing each view that makes Luskentyre hard to beat. The beach and island views have prompted a minor rash of four and five star self-catering accommodation here – following where the Martins of Scarista House began. But tempting as it is to drop in for a wee diversionary coffee, I'm aware that I'm late (again!) to see a weaver and have to weave in and out of every sandy bay at Luskentyre to get there. It's tiring on the bike, but it is this involvement with the sea, these constant brushes with the coast, that make west coast Harris feel both eventful and approachable. There are very few houses, because almost everyone was cleared from the fertile machair land. So you don't feel 'watched' as you frolic. Unfortunate reason – wonderful outcome.

But if locals are thin on the ground on the west side, some larger than life characters almost make up for it.

Like Donald John MacKay. I've hardly put the bike down when DJ strides out of his weaving shed, strides purposefully towards me and pumps my arm like a loom.

Needing a few seconds to gather myself, and struck forcibly by the wolf-like quality in his grey eyes, I mutter something inconsequential.

'Nice day.'

'Yes it *is*,' says DJ, 'Yes it *is*. Come in here and see *everything*.'

Meeting DJ is like having an energy transplant.

The ebullient weaver won part of the contract to supply Harris Tweed for Nike trainers a few years back – and orders have been flowing in ever since.

DJ the Weaver (as he's known locally) stands beside DJ the Postie in his airy croft shed beside a fabulous white beach, absentmindedly patting the loom like a farmer pats his collie.

'I'm struggling to cope with demand, but then there's only myself able to weave.' DJ's wife Maureen does all the administration behind the Luskentyre Harris Tweed Company. The weaving must be done in the weaver's home, which doesn't make for easy expansion beyond individual cottage industries, although this strict rule has helped make and maintain the brand. In many eyes, one-off Nike contracts apart, they're also the reason Harris Tweed is struggling. Competitors like Donegal Tweed use angora and other luxury fibres, and sell tweed goods by the shipload in Donegal itself. By comparison, Harris is a tweed desert. And there are fears that the recent purchase of the Stornoway mills by a Yorkshireman may result in local asset-stripping and closure with the machinery moved elsewhere – it's already resulted in a controversial decision to cut the number of designs from 8,000 to just five, and to restrict output almost exclusively to the production of traditional men's jackets. Few are convinced this is the right way to go. And despite DJ's energy, I'm struck by an underlying feeling of impotence and hopelessness. Just like the Vatersay folk facing coastal erosion, the South Uist folk facing Lochboisdale pier, Lachie facing the hard-faced hauliers of times past, the Berneray crofters facing the nature quangos today and Neil facing the 'call later' mainland-based broadband companies every other day of the week. Whoever is right or wrong about decisions taken or investment withheld, the deadening local impact of this lost control across big tranches of life, is palpable.

'Yes, tweed was always exported off the island in bales to be made into garments elsewhere. So we've very little here to sell visitors. Just bags and caps.'

DJ has put his finger on it. It's not just tweed. Island products aren't available on the islands because they're manufactured, processed and made more profitable elsewhere. Like a Third World economy, the Western Isles is packing tweed, fish and seaweed into boxes to send to mainland operators – along with the potential for making money. I ask if anyone has advertised for designers to move to Harris, experience the Good Life and start producing really valuable and profitable locally finished goods.

'It's true. We need someone to help us manufacture jackets here, someone with commercial tailoring skills. It's far easier to sell something made up in Harris Tweed than a length of the material. If we had designers here, we could make our own trainers, upholstery, and soft furnishings.'

Donald John Morrison, postie and Scarista Golf Club Vice Captain

Too right. Earlier I'd been looking for a selection of Harris Tweed bags and had phoned one bag-maker who lives near Stornoway to find the location of any Harris-based outlets. There are none. She is the mother of four children, including a baby. She distributes her very nifty bags as far as a car journey will take her before the weans make too much of a fuss. As with so many small businesses the one word that terrifies her is success. Another two words are pretty scary – new orders. She says she doesn't want to become that busy. As things

stand, each person is working to the limits of their own personal circumstances. Unless someone thinks bigger and outside the family group, these businesses will only just survive.

'So, DJ, have you advertised for a designer?'

'Well, no.'

'Have you tried to find an apprentice?'

'If I had an apprentice I'd be standing over that person and while I'm doing that I'm not earning. And there's nothing to stop that apprentice learning the trade and taking his skills elsewhere.'

'But how were you taught?'

'I wasn't taught. I grew up with it – my father was a weaver.'

'So you were taught!'

'No, I wasn't. I just learned.'

It makes you want to scream.

DJ's an energetic, imaginative man, who currently has no successor in a business that should be sweeping the board in a world craving authenticity. But none of his nephews or nieces are interested in joining the business. Why not?

'Peaks and troughs. You can have good months, and in bad months you fall back on the croft. Now the croft doesn't seem worth the bother to young folk and they want certainty and a steady wage.'

The need to service a monthly mortgage payment is maybe the biggest single driver of change on the islands. The fear of not meeting those large, regular, monthly payments for the rest of their adult life is turning young folk away from every venture that involves 'peaks and troughs'. And yet, without the means and perhaps the will to control production locally, no traditional island trade (except perhaps construction) is without them. Perhaps older incomers are needed behind the loom – or perhaps it's time to challenge the rules that govern tweed production.

The problem is not lack of demand – Harris Tweed is still a high value product and with designers like Vivienne Westwood, Alexander McQueen, Paul Smith and Ralph Lauren using it, the textile's profile has constantly risen. But with the constraints of a cottage industry, tweed can neither scale up nor settle down.

After the broadcast of this interview, I was contacted by the Harris Development Trust – horrified to hear the story of the last Harris-based, Harris Tweed weaver – which is what DJ could easily become.

They had a bit of a truth session about the skills needed to keep tweed alive and have applied for funds to set up an entrepreneurship – not just an apprenticeship – scheme. It'll train a young weaver in marketing, investing, publicity, business – all the non-weaving skills a modern craftsman needs to survive in this precarious world.

It has taken 160 years to tackle the weakness in the original creation of Harris Tweed – established in 1844 by Catherine, Countess of Dunmore.

She was keen to support her tenants by introducing new industries and, at the height of production, tweed on Harris provided employment for hundreds of people. But where was the control? Who had contact with mainland markets? In 1996 there were just seven *Hearaich* (Harris folk) in full-time production. Today there are only two. One is DJ MacKay.

Let's hope it's not too late.

Meantime people have been trying to think creatively to raise tweed's profile. The local golf course is the fabulous Isle of Harris Golf Club at Scarista. Tournament winners at their Open Competition in August receive made to measure Harris Tweed jackets, in a special Scarista Golf Tweed produced by DJ and co-sponsored by Isle of Harris Knitwear.

According to DJ the postie – otherwise known as Donald John Morrison, the Scarista Club Vice Captain – 'We've gone three better than the American Masters in Augusta. They hand out one green jacket – we hand out four on the day.'

The Harris Open is a sell-out – just like the special run of Nike Trainers. But after all the special events are over, the long slog for everyday trade begins all over again.

It's still raining heavily, and despite instructions to leave me to my fate, Maxwell has back-tracked with our new vehicle – more an estate car than a transit – and finds me gamely peching up the long slow slope that runs from the sandy west coast of Harris towards Tarbert and the East. The great thing about hills in the mind of an unfit, amateur and frankly hill-phobic cyclist like myself, is that they stick so prominently in the mind, they eclipse all else. Thus I think the journey to Tarbert ends at the top of this hill and the remaining couple of hundred uneventful metres will take about ten minutes. My wilful inability to give miles of non-hilly terrain their energy-sapping due is probably the only reason I can manage longish cycle journeys in the first place.

I attempt to persuade Maxwell that once up the hill, I'll be freewheeling all the way to Tarbert. Maxwell assures me that having just come from Tarbert this is seriously delusional and given the weather I will be knackered, wet, tired and – far more serious than all of these for his own well-being – very grumpy. I can see a certain logic to this argument

Cycling past Scarista Beach

and we pile the bike in the back of the car. Reaching the top, and realising there are indeed eight more miles to Tarbert, I suggest a detour. I've heard very enthusiastic reports of an arts café called Skoon in a place called Geocrab. Without doubt the Gaelic pronunciation of the village will not sound as the English speaker would deliver it – Geo crab – and I'm intrigued to hear what's right. I'm even more intrigued, as a coffee dependent tee-totaller, about the promise of strong, home-brewed coffee and the possibility of buns. I'm pleased to see Maxwell has given up his earlier determination to produce picnic lunches consisting of doorsteps

**The Skoon Team –
Andrew and Emma
Craig and baby Lena**

of white bread with great lumps of processed cheese. Having succeeded in persuading my quartermaster that cheese is only edible in sandwiches with Branston Pickle, I was distraught to discover the half-finished jar must have been left by someone in the transit we hastily abandoned with the keys above the sun visor as instructed in the ferry car park on Berneray.

Psychologically, I cannot come to terms with the loss of so much perfectly good pickle and am now stuck between a rock and a hard place when faced with Maxwell's picnic offerings.

'Let's go to Skoon and I'll buy you a late lunch.'

This works perfectly and off we go, winding up and down the inlets of the Golden Road. I had thought this fabulous single track road along the east coast of Harris got its name from the current display of weather conditions. Rain on the mica-studded rocks makes the landscape glint so brightly in the broadening shafts of sunlight we have to wear sunglasses to drive. But no. Apparently it's an ironic name given by mainlanders shocked at the price of connecting mere crofters to the outside world. I prefer my version.

Andrew and Emma Craig took a bold decision to open Skoon three years ago. They converted the old crofthouse themselves, started serving delicious food and soups – and in quiet moments Andrew has been able to indulge his first love, painting. His vibrant and moody seascapes cover the whitewashed walls. Painting, catering and coping with a new baby, the couple are run off their feet.

'In the summer there's no time to go anywhere else – in the winter there's time but nowhere open to go to!' At least it means Andrew gets a lot of painting done and the baby is getting plenty of off-season quality time with her parents. Outside, the rain has stopped, rainbows are darting everywhere and Tarbert awaits.

**The bright lights of
Tarbert**

Scalpay to Uig Lewis

Treasure Island and the crofting wind millionaires

Scalpay, six short but arduous miles off the beaten track, was not part of the original game plan.

Locals call it Treasure Island because of its posh homes and fishing wealth. But, like any hive of activity and affluence, the island has its detractors. Some South Harris folk tried to warn me off a visit.

'Scalpay? We went all the way up there for a wedding, sailed up in a boat and spent the night completely ignored. They're so clannish they've no time for anyone but themselves. But they're almost in Lewis – what can you expect?'

My reservations are a lot more mundane. The road is an exhausting series of hump-backed hills, which certainly teach respect for the logic of boat-based travel.

I'd begun to realise local Hebridean rivalry is a highly developed art-form. Everyone wants to hear their island is best. For the broadcasts, I'd tried to spot points of local distinction that made each island best at something – that way I wouldn't have to lie or start World War Three, if cornered. Barra unquestionably has the most talkative people. South Uist folk are the most musical. North Uist has the most spectacular scenery. Harris folk are the most entrepreneurial, and Lewis… is Lewis. For the *Leodhasach* (Lewis folk), their island is everything. For inhabitants of the South-

ern Isles, it is a place of unattractive bogs, wide roads, fast cars, white elephants, self-perpetuating mafias hogging Gaelic language cash and uncaring quango workers who rarely venture south of the Clisham – and the place they are forced to visit if they want to shop at a supermarket and see their children.

Thanks to a week of daily encounters with outspoken, independent-minded characters, I was definitely getting attuned to the southern view.

Indeed, words and phrases were starting to haunt me. I spent the day after Luskentyre muttering, 'Peaks and troughs. Peaks and troughs.' Interspersed with, 'Yes it *is*. Yes it *is*.' Pedalling along from Luskentyre, it occurred to me that just as pets grow like their owners (or vice versa), weavers grow like their looms. DJ spoke with a repeat pattern here, an extra emphasis there. A syllable held till a new thought was grabbed and played into the conversation like thread from a fresh bobbin.

I had started to find some handholds in this culture and didn't want to move to an unfamiliar and possibly hostile cliff-face. But Maxwell felt differently.

Scalpay, he maintained, was an island studded with examples of Hebridean prowess. The key to the chest of what makes Hebrideans tick. He related a number of hard to repeat highlights from a supposedly recent trip. Scalpay sweaters knitted with a traditional design to let strangers as far away as Ireland know the origins of any sailor washed up on their distant shores. Sweaters so tough, they could withstand being torn apart by steam engines. Men so tough, every other one was a qualified sea captain. Religious adherence so strict, everyone attended Free Church twice a week to hear the best precentor-led singing on the islands. A restaurant so well stocked with fish it would unquestionably eliminate every memory of the flat Mars Bars I had been forced to consume in lieu of dinner on a previous trip.

After spending the best part of two hours' cycling Scalpay's octopus-like length and breadth, Maxwell had to accept that times have changed. The restaurant has closed and though one woman is knitting angora sweaters, they lack the sturdiness of the classic design.

Sea captains are hard to find. Some suggest that's due to the switch from shares to wages. Traditionally crewmen were paid quarterly, not weekly. And during bad times they got potatoes and grain, or just fish, not cash. Others suggest the fish farm and creel fishing offer an easier life – home every evening. One wag suggests even consummate sailors lacked the confidence to sit exams for captains' licences when the regulations changed, in case they failed and shamed their families. Another maintains island men wouldn't lower themselves to sweat for a piece of paperwork that would only confirm skills they already patently possessed.

The precentor singing tradition has been hit by the slow decline in Gaelic (psalm singing at the breakfast or dinner table used to be commonplace), and the Free Church schism has seen the Free Church Continuing make off with the best singers. According to local livewire, Health Board member and B&B owner Margaret MacKenzie, 'the only time we all come together and hear these great old men singing is at funerals'.

She thinks that the change from island to bridge-connected promontory in 1995 has also distanced neighbours.

'When we were an island, you had to use the ferry. On the crossings you talked to people. Now we wave at each other like the rest of the world, but we don't share our day. We don't talk. And then at the end of the week we go to different churches. We have proximity not community, just like everyone else.'

To a mainlander, the standard of what constitutes community on Scalpay has always been pretty high. In the 1990s Van Morrison visited, shortly after his joint recording venture with the Chieftains, to see if he could collaborate with their psalm-singing Free Church congregation. By all accounts the man from Orangefield was awestruck by the emotionalism of the powerful waves of voice and concluded, 'It's fine as it is.'

But then, the Scalpay folk have had plenty of singing practice.

Alastair MacLeod, a former fisherman, recalls psalm singing at sea: 'When the nets were shot, one person would take over the wheelhouse and we would have worship in the foc'sle. In my father's day, on a summer's evening you could hear the men singing from one boat to another.'

Their exacting, evangelical focus on worship probably cemented the reputation of Scalpay seamen as impossibly clannish. The island has been a hard world for outsiders to penetrate, though some have managed and seem very happy. In the village of Maaruig (near by sea but an hour's drive by land), it's the same story. The village hugs the Harris/Lewis border on an inlet of Loch Seaforth, and it's completely full of Morrisons. A local phone book of nicknames is the only way to find anyone.

I stayed on Scalpay twenty years ago. After exchanging nods with the elderly gentleman working in the field next to my holiday cottage, we finally had a conversation. It transpired that the cottage I was staying in had been bought by a wealthy man from a well-known construction firm who had been attracted to Maaruig because of its perfect stillness and adherence to old ways.

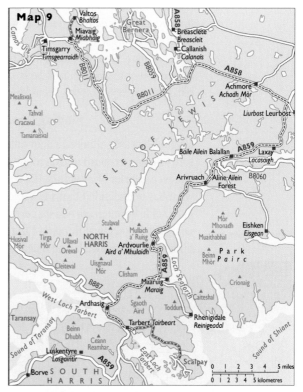

Imagine his horror when he arrived to find roadsides covered with rusting cars, fields covered with chemical fertiliser (not old-fashioned seaweed), and a shore-line ringed with rubbish.

After comradely complaints, the disgruntled Englishman began to realise he was on his own. He tried to organise a beach clear up. By all accounts, no one turned up. He tried to close the fish farm and after that few local people spoke to him. He kept a daily log of otter movements for almost two years, to try and prove the fish farm was disturbing them. The animals must have gone native, because despite the daily outboard motor and disturbance, they just kept on swimming. Eventually, one day he approached the crofter I was now talking to.

'Why don't you use seaweed on this land instead of fertiliser? Do you know it was used here traditionally?'

Even in the retelling, this mild-mannered, slightly stooped gentlemen straightened, as if facing his critic anew.

'That seaweed broke the back of my grandmother and her mother and all the women who lived here. Don't you dare lecture me.'

Walking round the litter-strewn loch on the long walk to Rhenigidale, the last Harris village without a road at that time, I could literally see both sides. Maaruig in the morning light was like an MC Escher picture cleverly constructed to offer two completely different images – rubbish or loch, depending entirely on the perspective of the viewer. Incomers like the otter-lover couldn't see the loch for the litter. Locals couldn't see the litter for the loch.

Perspective may seem like a small thing. But the clash of perspectives explains everything from World War Two to disputes over the height of Leylandi hedges. Perhaps the test of any incomer is how they cope with having a minority perspective, perhaps for the first time in their lives. And the test of island communities is how they get beyond the proverb *Put out the Englishman and bring in the dog* every time an existing perspective is challenged.

Chairman Mao once said, but doubtless didn't mean, 'Let a thousand flowers bloom.' On the hard soils of North Harris the survival of any blossom, native or import, should be a cause for quiet celebration.

Finding Donald Morrison

Maxwell has long admired a man called Donald (nicknamed Dolly) Morrison, who has written a weekly column from Scalpay for the *Oban Times* for almost a quarter of a century. His column matter of factly communicates what has been landed that week and according to Maxwell uses the language of fishermen, not newspapermen – which explains its longevity and near-cult following with men of the sea, as Maxwell has decided to style

Sheep shearing on Scalpay

himself again today. Having failed to find anyone actively performing the

craft skills he believed Scalpay to possess, I had cruelly vetoed trying to find his hero in preference for some elusive members of the younger generation. Or an early start on the long schlep that is Clisham (800 metres high) and the possibility we might get to our next interview in Lewis on time.

Maxwell informs me he has tracked down a young *Scalpaigh* hand shearing sheep in a fank at the end of the island. They will be shearing for some time – and we are going past Dolly's house, so perhaps we could simply stop and say hello.

I would have to be the queen of meanness not to give this one a try.

Max adjusts his casually chosen tweed outfit of the day, smooths his hair into shape (Dolly is clearly a top rank hero) and knocks on the door. Nothing happens for some time, then dogs bark, there's a shuffling sound and the door opens. A smiling, white-haired elderly man beams out.

Maxwell takes a very deep breath, as if reading an Oscar nomination.

'My name is Maxwell MacLeod. I just want to thank you for your services to fishing, the islands and your community over these last twenty-five years. I have read your columns in the *Oban Times,* as many of us do, brought up on the islands – I grew up on Iona and am now exiled on the mainland. It is a privilege to meet you, sir, and I'd like to shake your hand.'

'What?'

Maxwell embarks on the full, formal introduction all over again – at louder volume. This time the old man is leaning towards him, concentrating hard.

'Who did you say you are again?'

'Maxwell MacLeod – we met when I was last on the island ten years ago.'

No sign of recognition.

'My father was the Reverend George MacLeod who set up the Iona Community.'

'Ah.'

'Well, we just stopped to say thanks for your columns. They were a delight to read and they brought the *cráic* of the men at the fishing to life.'

'Ach well, great that you enjoyed them.'

'I certainly did, sir. And I'm delighted to meet you again.'

'Ach, I've been getting on alright except for losing my leg some time ago.'

He bangs his wooden leg against the doorpost for effect.

Maxwell looks puzzled.

'What happened?'

'Ach, just one of those things. Makes it harder to get around, though.'

'Is that why you stopped doing your columns for the paper?'

'I didn't write for the *Oban Times.*'

Maxwell looks suddenly baffled.

'Was it the *Oban Gazette*? I thought it was the *Oban Times.*'

'No, you want Dolly.'

'Aren't you Dolly?'

'No, no. He lives over there in the sheltered housing.'

The door closes and we both explode with laughter. Unintentionally, Maxwell has delivered exactly what he promised about Scalpay. Traditional *cráic.* Why would anyone interrupt a man in full flight? Maxwell was clearly having fun and an interruption would just be rude and bad form. If the wooden leg hadn't come into the conversation, we would have been allowed to leave the island quite convinced we had just met Dolly of *Oban Times* fame.

Regaining his composure, Maxwell marches across the road to the small group of sheltered houses and after banging very loudly on the door to be heard above the television, he finally delivers his words of thanks to the right man and comes out mightily relieved.

'Now for the fank.'

After this I wonder if we should expect sheep, goats or wild boar in the fank. But sure enough, a group of four island men is busily shearing away. Including 'young' William Morrison, twenty-one, who has the perfect life – two weeks on the rigs in the North Sea, two weeks back on the croft.

'I do the croft work with the men here – they keep me right on the Gaelic as well as the shearing.'

'Don't people your age speak Gaelic?'

'Well, we all learned it, but we don't speak it. It's not…'

'Cool?'

'No. Not really. But I want to keep speaking it and I want to keep working outdoors. It's a great life.'

While I'm recording, Maxwell discovers he has lost his coat with my digital camera in the pocket. He manfully coaxes his old SLR into life for a few pictures of the fank before scurrying off to stand on one leg at Scalpay pier for mobile phone reception. Thus he discovers he left the coat at the coffee and bun heaven that was Skoon Café.

But happily for our shot-to-pieces schedule, the valiant Andrew is about to leave for Tarbert, and will bring coat and camera with him.

Finding Margaret MacKenzie

One sheep fank, one meeting with Andrew and one emotional reunion with his coat later, Maxwell and I are trying to find Margaret MacKenzie to rectify the photo-free nature of our Scalpay stay. Her mobile and home phone are not answering, so we stop at the local health centre to establish where her district nurse rounds might have taken her. The Health Service being what it is, I have low expectations of help without signing several forms in triplicate, producing my NHS number and finding my driving licence. But this is Harris, not home. I ask at Reception if anyone knows where Margaret is and three heads simultaneously turn to the window.

'Well it depends which car she's taken. If it's the Mercedes she's planning to drive to Stornoway later, in which case she'll be leaving at half past three.'

The three heads crane to scan the furthest extremity of the car park.

'No – she's driving the red Polo, so she must have an afternoon surgery. I think she'll be at the old folks' home.'

'So I'll give them a phone and we'll find her for you.'

And simple as that, she was found. Margaret spoke earlier about the loss of community and yet we located her in just two phone calls. If this is distance, the old days must have offered a degree of intimacy bordering on suffocation. I comment on the marvel of their people-locating service to the reception staff, who laugh.

'People here use the phone the way they used to use their own tongues. The old people aren't isolated, they're on the phone to each other all the time. I'll bet the biggest chunk of a *Hearach*'s (Harris person's) phone bill is the local call section. There's a lot going on here, you know.'

Thus encouraged, I wonder if there's an internet café so I can send some editing scripts.

'Well, there's an internet terminal in the school.' (Which looks harder to enter than Fort Knox.) 'The car park looks busy so there might be some people on the computers already, but I'm sure you wouldn't have long to wait.'

Wait? I may be going native in many other respects, but after a morning like this morning, and an afternoon like this afternoon where we're once again touch and go to meet a group of people on time, at a sheep grid in a mobile phone blackout zone, I don't think I could handle the stress.

This is a delightfully and maddeningly topsy-turvy place. Private whereabouts are public knowledge. And public services are sometimes in schools, which many people now feel reluctant to enter. Life on the mainland has tended to privatise people – we want leaflets or internet access so we can find things out at unreasonable hours and without human contact. Our private homes have become inviolable and sacrosanct, even

Margaret MacKenzie with the former owner of the Harris Hotel

first-footing at Hogmanay is on the way out. Here, it's different. Homes double as shop fronts because of a past full of cottage industries.

Every other house used to sell tweed. Now they sell paintings, tweed, caps, bags or eggs. I recall Bill Lawson's take on the big difference between Lewis and Harris, 'On Lewis if they see a stranger on the road outside, they pull the curtains. On Harris, they come out to see who you are.' That's not just out of curiosity or civility. It's also the only way home-based commerce works. Without the luxury of local shops to sell goods, homes have had to become workplaces and shop fronts too.

I photograph the irrepressible Margaret, who pulls the only slightly reluctant former owner of the neighbouring Harris Hotel into the picture.

The weather's improving – and I ask where she's off to this afternoon.
'Ach, we might go for a picnic.'

'Luskentyre beach?'

'No – that's a beach of death for us.' Margaret has such a fabulously dramatic way of putting things. 'The graveyard there and the strength of family ties mean we have to go and visit all our dead relations. It fairly wrecks the picnic mood, so we go to Huishinish – the beach beside the island of Scarp.'

I'm never sure if Margaret is joking or not.

She is easily the most outspoken islander around, and as Vice Chair of the Western Isles Health Board, even the row over the appointment of controversial journalist John MacLeod as press spokesman doesn't upset her unduly.

'People ask if it's stressful attending Health Board meetings. I tell them I've managed the Scalpay Bus Group, and nothing could be more stressful than that. We couldn't even agree about the colour of the new bus. Some wanted green because it was eco-friendly, others thought that was a touch Papish, blue was an offence to Celtic supporters – in the end I suggested metallic grey, because it doesn't show the dirt.'

And right on cue the metallic grey community bus drives past.

I am definitely warming to Scalpay. Its folk are struggling with the loss of old ways. Perhaps they had so much, it's hard for them to see their resource base is still far bigger than most of their Hebridean neighbours.

I cycle a bit and then cheat and chum Maxwell in the van up a bit of the Hebrides' highest hill, Clisham – winding up on time but quickly knee-deep in bog at the other side.

Bog paths at Erisort

Bogs and miles of scraggy flag pole pine. That's how the Aline Forest is now, but if locals can raise £4 million, they'll transform Scotland's biggest community-owned woodland into a paradise of dry, sheltered paths, competition level mountain bike tracks and five star lodges, complete with webcams showing seals, herons and eagles at play in hard to reach coastal parts of the forest.

The hi-tech stuff sounds interesting, but paths – on Lewis? I start out feeling sceptical, but within minutes I'm a convert. The supposed walking paradise we see from the road is actually a boggy nightmare the second you leave it. Without trees, a strong wind can take your ears off, even in summer. And without wellies, trying to follow Kenny Mackay (Erisort Community Co-ordinator), Marion Ferguson (Aline Woodland Development Officer) and Ian McLeod (Erisort Trust Director) into the forest is a total mistake. I'm up beyond my ankles in seconds and quickly see their point. Walking in a bog isn't much fun. Walking beside an 'A' road with cars thumping past at 70 mph isn't much fun either. It seems bizarre, but the descendants of people who spent much of their lives bent double with outdoor activity now need paths to walk on, just like everyone else. I suppose as Johnson exhorted, islanders are finally attending to their 'small wants' but I still find the barefaced convenience of it all a little hard to accept, and recount an incident at a B&B some days earlier, where two seven-year-old girls desperate to get onto the beach were straining with frustration at adults slowly finishing their breakfasts.

'Why can't you just go without the grown-ups?' I asked.

'They're not allowed on the beach by themselves without an adult,' came the reply from the next room.

What! The beach was a pristine, three-mile long, highly visible wonderland, accessible by crossing a road upon which I had counted approximately five cars all morning. Of course, you never know what bad experiences might lie behind such caution, but...

'Seven! What were you doing when you were seven? I'll bet you were sailing boats.'

Embarrassed smiles all round.

'Sailing at five, actually.'

'So what are you guys doing with your youngsters? It's no wonder they don't want outdoor jobs anymore. You're taking all the excitement out of it!'

The group exchanged glances as if to say, this woman doesn't realise how complicated it all is – does anyone have the energy to argue with her?

Nobody did. And as I recount the tale in the Aline Forest, there's no clamour to tackle the subject either. But Ian (a new dad) and Marion (a new mum) have a go.

'I think you're right, we do try to take the risk out of everything. I can remember, as a child, taking a fishing rod out and disappearing onto the moors for hours on end and getting a row when I came back late. Why don't we let our own kids do the same? It would take a psychologist to explain whether we've changed as parents or they've changed as children.'

Marion chips in.

'A lot of fishermen wouldn't recommend young people taking up their job. Lone shellfish fishermen have one of the highest death rates on the islands.'

Ian doesn't think danger is the real problem.

'At least fishing earns a decent income – crofting doesn't. The kids are surfing the internet like everyone else and watching the television like everyone else. There's no reason they wouldn't want to become IT consultants like everyone else as well.'

'It's true. The young have choices. My grandparents didn't. They weren't going outside to enjoy themselves. People saw outdoors as work. So why would you go out for a walk after your day? They didn't encourage us to do it.'

From the heat of the reaction there's a raw nerve here and I think Marion has put her finger on it. The decision by this generation to get 'proper' 9–5 jobs has turned the Great Outdoors into the same optional extra mainlanders experience at weekends and on special occasions only. Lewis folk are working like us, commuting in cars sealed from the environment like us and coming home brain-dead to children watching *The Simpsons* like us. The only difference is the niggling guilt they carry about the abandonment of the hard, nature-focused lives of their forebears, because they are far closer to those times than mainlanders. But what else can they do? Attend boat-building classes to teach their own kids skills they never used themselves?

Perhaps this first generation of salaried employee needs to fight harder for a modern 'crofting compromise'. It's as if the stark choice facing Lord Leverhulme's piper all those years ago (keep your job or lose it to sow tatties) is still facing islanders today. You can become a full time mortgage slave and lose contact with nature. Or you can plug away at the old cottage industries – peaks, troughs and all – and be at the mercy of markets you cannot control. If anyone can forge some new terms of trade in the way we work, it should be the Gaels.

We are all suddenly distracted by a curious sight: pine beauty moths covering a tree. Strangely, given that these moths stripped half the forest bare in the eighties, the Erisort team seem strangely calm. Especially Ian, who's about to start work for SNH in a few days.

'Two or three bucketfuls of these caterpillars would fall from the trees at the height of the infestation. As you walked you could hear this "rain" – the sound of caterpillar droppings falling as they were eating.'

Yuk.

'So just seeing a few like this is not a problem. There'll always be some. It's part of the natural ecosystem and most of the forest is beyond the young stage where the trees are at threat.'

Well, good luck to them. This group have analysed the problems of boggy Lewis thoroughly, overcome all the guilt-tripping stereotypes I have tried to throw their way – and had the vision and courage to buy a 'worthless' bit of half-dead forest from the Forestry Commission in the first place. They need to find a wealthy benefactor to make the project work in full, but I've a feeling they've a few Get Out of Jail Cards up their sleeves too.

If they only had B&Bs that would accept visitors on the Sabbath, they'd be laughing. And I wouldn't be facing a day's cycle across country to Uig in wet trainers. But it's Saturday night and two days of phoning months beforehand found no B&B on the Pairc Peninsula willing to take us in. Community coordinator Kenny Mackay finds this almost impossible to believe until I start reeling off the list of names.

'It's strange, I know quite a few of these people don't observe a Free

Church type of Sabbath themselves. I suppose they must still be worried about appearing to break ranks.'

'Fine, but that leaves me with a massive cycle across the island and, I have to say, no warm and fuzzy feeling about the Pairc peninsula.'

This was completely unfair, but also true. And at least in part caused by something else. My own mistake in hiring two support vans for the trip instead of one. Call me mean, call me someone who likes the small adventure of a new hired car every time we take a ferry, or just call me plain stupid. I'm sure Maxwell has managed all three. But transit number one, left at the pier on North Uist, was replaced by a strange looking estate car upon arrival in Harris. Arguably it did fulfil the criteria – that three bikes could be put in the back. Mind you, I'd assumed that would be possible without removing all front wheels and saddles. Several key bits of kit had already been lost because bags wedged under the mountain of bicycle parts were impossible to check.

One of the side-doors was jammed, making back strain inevitable and the temptation not to use the bikes was almost irresistable.

The effort of packing and unpacking editing equipment every morning and night made departures late. And that then piled pressure on the cycling, thanks to the selection of outdoor meeting venues in areas without mo-

The Clisham climb

bile phone reception. Thus any change of plan was proving impossible to communicate, and uncertainties about cycling pace combined with the absolute certainty of a bad mood amongst stood-up interviewees, meant the car was being used as often as the bike.

I realised this had to stop and had sent Maxwell to Stornoway to find a proper van.

'Don't worry about me,' I muttered stoically. 'A bit of hard cycling will do me no harm.'

'Even into the prevailing wind? You realise you'll be heading west most of the way?'

'No worries. Done this before remember? Just don't come back with anything weird. We need a transit not a campervan, sports car, lorry or pickup truck, okay?'

A nightmarish vision of Max and the Beanstalk had suddenly flashed through my mind.

And so, about to be marooned at the Aline Forest late in the afternoon

VWs have hugely capacious boots

with a gargantuan cycle ahead, I am absolutely appalled at the offer of a lift across to Uig by Kenny Mackay.

'How could you think I'd give up a three-hour cycle for a lift … will the bike fit in the back?'

'You know how they say there is no such thing as a free lunch? Well there's no such thing as a free ride either. We're not just trying to build this recreation centre on Erisort, we're about to build the biggest community-owned windfarm in Britain. And no one knows about it. And that's not helping us and I've been told to bend your ear.'

I do love a man who comes straight to the point.

'Will one hour be enough?'

'We'll make a stab at it.'

And the story is roughly as follows…

The wind revolution at Eishken

The Eishken windfarm could change the face of Scotland. It could turn one of the poorest parts of the Western Isles into a mini Shetland, trigger other developments that will justify a subsea connector and ensure Scotland achieves its future goals for energy largely by renewable means.

And there are no discernible downsides – because this is not the controversial Lewis windfarm proposal in north Lewis. It's the Eishken proposal on the border of Lewis and Harris.

And to date, everyone has got the two schemes mixed up.

The Lewis windfarm proposal was shifted from its original preferred site on moorland in the very north of the island because of EU habitat and wildlife designations. Many now believe that designation should have been challenged – because the resulting compromise includes a twenty-mile strip of turbines along the populated coast which doesn't allow any real escape from the visual intrusion.

The clump on the dreich Barvas Moor is more acceptable to many, though the scale of AMEC's proposal has rekindled traditional suspicion of large-scale development, commercialism and landowner-led schemes. The SNP Executive elected in May 2007 has promised to stand by the outcome of a local windfarm referendum. And so after six years of planning and argument the Lewis windfarm looks set to fail.

Eishken, on the other hand, is as near a dream large windfarm proposal as it's possible to get. And that's mostly because locals thrust themselves into the planning process of landowner Nicholas Oppenheim early on.

Using the cautionary example of developments further north, a local trust bargained with Oppenheim for a share of ownership – not just the usual one per cent income from the turbines he owned. After pondering the prospect of grinding local opposition, the landowner agreed and raised the total number of turbines from 100 to 133 to give ownership of thirty-three to the *Muaithabhal* Trust (named after a local mountain).

That gives an eye-watering projected income of £10 million a year for the communities of Kinloch, Pairc and the 'Loch Seaforth' villages of North Harris.

It takes a few minutes for those figures to sink in. I look at Kenny, gamely driving his weather-beaten car along the single track road to Uig. He is an unlikely Chris Tarrant.

'So, over time, each person in the area could effectively become a millionaire?'

'Well, they could, but that's not the way we've decided to spend the cash. It's for the community, not for individuals directly.'

How many people are there in Pairc?'

'Maybe a thousand souls in all.'

'And they'd receive roughly £10 million a year.'

'Yip.'

'You're sure you haven't got a decimal point wrong?'

'Nope.'

Later I discover that this is equivalent to the annual income of Western Isles Enterprise. It is perhaps not far off the community benefit total negotiated by the wily Shetlanders at the height of Scotland's oil production industry. And it's a sum equal to the entire fuel bill of the Western Isles.

If the Development Fund set up by the Council chose to spend their thirty per cent share of Eishken's income on paying that bill, this single windfarm could give free energy to every islander from Barra to the Butt. From these 133 turbines the Western Isles could be transformed in five years from the place with Europe's highest fuel bills to the place with the lowest.

'Even after the council takes its 30 per cent for the wider community, we'll still have about £7 million a year. We want to build a causeway across Loch Erisort with tidal energy turbines to take forty minutes of the round trip to Stornoway. That would encourage more people working in Stornoway to live on Pairc. We'll build a state of the art, community-owned old folks' home, so elderly people don't need to leave the area to get care as they do now. We'll support existing businesses, and pay off loans for students who come home and start up new enterprises.'

It's as well I'm not driving – by now I'd be off the road.

'This is as near perfect as any community project I've ever come across. Tell me there's no catch.'

'There's a catch. It's not going to happen.'

'What!'

'Eagles and SNH.'

It's a great tribute to islanders that although animals have been accorded higher status than humans since sheep displaced their ancestors in the nineteenth century, very few vent the anger they must feel on the sheep, deer, fish, hedgehogs, geese, seals – or in this case eagles in their midst. But thanks to an unproven threat to a number of eagles, this windfarm will not happen fast – or even at all. Scottish Natural Heritage objected to the full Eishken proposal, claiming eagles might be injured by the blades. As a result, a scaled down plan for just fifty-two turbines (six locally owned) has landed on Ministers' desks, with community income cut from ten to two million pounds a year and with generating capacity halved.

For remote Pairc, almost empty because of Clearances 120 years ago, that means eagles may thrive but people may not. Massive transformation will take decades, if it happens at all.

'Could you not compromise?'

'Oppenheim and ourselves have offered a five-year study, because we believe it will prove bird strike to be a negligible concern. At that point we hope phase two of Eishken will finally get the go-ahead.'

I salute their patience, but wonder if turbine-making in Scotland, or the local population base, or indeed the planet has the time. It'll take three years from final approval to construction of phase one. That means a decade before Eishken's full generating capacity is reached, even though the energy is available and needed right now. And even though ten public meetings and three months of consultation provoked only fifteen objections.

If such a loss of income and energy was sustained anywhere else because of birds – even eagles – I'd like to think there would be a public outcry. But then the clout of our nature regulators makes outcry difficult here. Offending the Nature quangos is like offending a landowner in days gone past. With almost half the population employed in the public sector, it doesn't pay to make a fuss. But that's why we have politicians.

At Eishken not a penny of public money need be spent outside the subsidy for the 'green energy' the windfarm will produce – the developers will pay for road improvements or a local deepwater port. All the Executive needs do is act to support the plan – and subsea cable the energy to the south of Scotland.

All in all, it's been a fabulous day. I'm bowled over by the vision and good-humoured single-mindedness of local people. And the smiling face of Elma Morrison makes me feel I've arrived at a long-lost Lewis home, rather than a guest house. Maxwell will doubtless put in an appearance soon with a Winnebago or HGV lorry or whatever other unstraightforward vehicle he has sourced in Stornoway. I am going to sleep.

Uig to Callanish Lewis

Storytelling, beaches, and midnight hippies at Callanish

Uig is a startling surprise. Causeways run beside thin inland lochs towards a coastline bulging with beaches. It's a tumbling paradise of white sand after a sea of inland bog, sandwiched between the Atlantic and a run of Marilyns (hills with a drop of at least 150 metres on all sides). The area has long been remote, even by Lewis standards. People had to make their own amusement, and ceilidhs or gatherings were not optional extras, but the only means of meeting anyone. Storytelling was a big feature of any visit, and so every aspect of the land and people became known, named and incorporated into folklore. Maybe even 'super known'.

Not a large stone, bay or promontory here is without a story, actual or mythical, and the Gaelic Storytelling Project has adapted technology to let visitors hear the best of them. I meet Malcolm MacLean, heid bummer of the Gaelic Arts Agency and Chrisella Ross at the Uig shop which hires out their e-storytelling devices. The Gaels bravely tackle bikes for the first time in decades and wobble down the single track road to Uig Beach. We pass the fabulously eccentric *Baile-na-Cille* Hotel – where a succulent dinner of local produce is served at 7pm precisely, whether diners are on time or not – and hit the GPS co-ordinates that prompt the 'i-pack' into life. Selecting English, I hear Dr Finlay MacLeod relate the tale of the Brahan Seer as we stand above the very spot where the 'prophet' supposedly found his gift. In fact his mum found

it for him. Isn't it always the way? The story, roughly paraphrased, goes like this...

The mother of the young Kenneth MacKenzie saw a beautiful young woman appear in the graveyard over an open grave – her own. The next morning she left it again for the entire day and returned at nightfall. The *cailleach* put her staff across the grave – the woman could not enter. In conversation it transpired she was a Norwegian Princess, shipwrecked here and therefore destined to lie in a Lewis grave by night, but able to travel back to her own people by day. A double life after death – if you follow – that could only continue if she could enter the grave. In exchange for the *cailleach* removing her staff, the princess said her son would find a pebble on the beach, and through it he would see the future. He found it, looked through and became the Brahan Seer, who prophesied, amongst other things, that the Isle of Lewis would sink

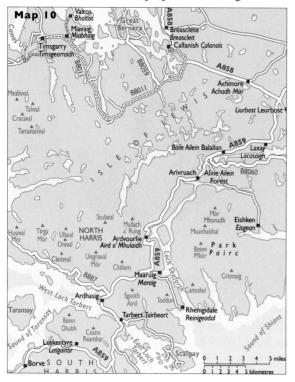

(causing huge anxiety when the new Ullapool ferry was launched with the same name) and that the Isle of Berneray would finally echo to the sound of clacking geese when the people had all been driven out.

We wander on a few feet and the i-pack kicks into life again with the story of the Lewis Chessmen – yards from the dune where a lad reportedly found the pieces in 1831. The pieces, crafted from walrus ivory and whales' teeth, are described by the British Museum as the fifth most important homeland artefact in their collection.

They belong to at least four different sets found on Uig Beach in the 1830s. Amazingly, the chances are that most Scottish kids will have seen them. Not because of their century-long display at the British Museum, but because of their year-long presence in *Harry Potter and the Philosopher's Stone* – JK Rowling's box office hit – which featured replicas of the forlorn bishops, brooding queens and soldiers biting their shields.

In reality, eleven of the Chessmen are permanently housed in Edinburgh, eighty-two are in the British Museum and none are on Lewis.

Does this matter?

Well, the British Museum gets five million visitors a year – equivalent to the entire population of Scotland. Far more people will see the Chessmen there than amidst the sand and stones of the windswept Western Isles.

Never mind that for those unable to fire their imaginations, the tiny figures lose almost all of their power to inspire or perplex. Never mind that out of context those artefacts appear quite unremarkable. And never mind that for those prepared to make the physical journey across the Minch, their presence *in situ* might be unforgettable. Maybe life-changing.

Such is the restorative power of the past.

If the spinal route that's been created actually means anything, it needs to knit these ancient islands together to create the archaeological island trail from heaven. The great thing about Orkney is the proximity of key sites. Maes Howe, Skara Brae and the Rings of Brodgar and Stenness are only half an hour's drive apart. Sea crossings mean the Western Isles treasures will never be quite so compactly displayed.

But the biggest obstacle isn't logistical. Islanders aren't yet thinking 'long island'. Division into separate county councils until the seventies didn't help. And although better roads, causeways, an island-wide radio station, and a single council all help, hearts and minds do not belong to 'the Western Isles' – however they are named – but to the home patch. Plans are small-scale and local. The boys from Scarista golf course have visited Askernish – once. The Askernish boys haven't yet returned the visit. And in many ways, why should they? If a change is as good as a rest, why would an islander spend valuable time visiting other islands?

As an island friend memorably said, 'You head west – we're off to Glasgow for a curry.'

Maybe this is why islanders who'd never travelled to the mainland felt able to set off for the New World. Once home was lost, nothing close to it was ever as attractive. Elma's B&B is fast becoming our home from home. The traditional croft house is so relaxed, we chat, plan and eat together. I persuade her husband Angus to haul a table up the tight stairs so I can survey Valtos beach whilst editing on my laptop. Maxwell forsakes his booked room and pitches a tent instead. He borrows a fishing rod and gets

Carved replica of a Lewis Chessman piece at Ardroil Bay

a sympathetic welcome when he finally turns up for breakfast the next morning, empty-handed and late.

Elma takes me on a quick spin in her car, on a fabulous circular tour of beaches – and suddenly, past the singer Dougie MacLean. A familiar figure for me back in Perthshire, I'm amazed to see Dougie standing outside an old crofthouse. It turns out he bought it twelve years ago and has fixed it up to become a spiritual home for himself, the family and – at Hogmanay particularly – half the musicians of the Outer Isles. The back section of the house has been kept as it was found, with tilly lamps, candles and crates. The ideal place for extensive musical sessions. I mention that we may be heading to Callanish the following night to spot hippies

At Uig Beach with
Malcolm MacLean
and Chrisella Ross
– shown below holding
the i-pack storytelling
device

at the lunar standstill in the wee small hours – the MacLeans seem quite game, though I can imagine at 3am it may be a different story.

Later I cycle off at Elma's suggestion to meet the local historian of the parish, Donald MacAulay, who does rope access work on oil rigs, railways, bridges, masts and tunnels all over the world. He's keen to establish we've managed to relax in Uig after the hectic week that must have passed. Indeed, almost everywhere Elma sends us, the same calm, solicitous atmosphere prevails. It's as if living in an epic, mythic, story-dominated landscape soothes adults, just as bedtime stories soothe children.

Donald's pressurised off-island work maintains his relaxed on-island living, and allows him to explore the physical legacy of his clan background and its famous sixteenth century chief, Donald Cam MacAulay. Pointing out the Hill of Evil Counsel and the Stack of Donald Cam, Donald describes how he's walked and camped at all the evocatively named locations that shaped the life of his violent and revolutionary forebear – one of the last island chiefs to stand against James VI.

It's a short cycle back from Donald's house to Valtos for dinner, and it's worth it. Elma has made a salad with fresh crab from one of Angus's boats.

Angus speaks lightly about adventures past; the sea has been a large part of his life and the whole wall behind him is studded with pictures of fishing boats in all kinds of weather.

He was a weaver too. Elma digs out the copybook from 1963 and I can hardly believe how little he earned.

'I got basically a fiver a yard.'

That sounds okay.

'Except a weaver's yard is thirteen feet long. And I'd do thirty-five lengths.'

'So you'd get thirty-five fivers for thirteen times more work than I first thought?'

'No – one fiver for thirty-five lengths of thirteen feet.'

'What?'

'The mill would provide the bobbins and we'd send back the cloth which they'd finish off.'

'And then?'

'No idea. We don't know where it went.'

Again I'm speechless at the bad deal island craftsmen and women have had to settle for. The phrase 'divide and conquer' springs to mind along with the slogan 'the workers, united will never be defeated'.

Is this the opposite? The workers, divided (into individual cottage industries) – will always be defeated? But, approaching the midnight hour, this is no time for Marxist introspection.

Hippies and Free Kirk choirs at Callanish

My friend Douglas Scott has calculated the precise time the moon will be at its lowest point in the heavens for eighteen years. If we get to the Callanish stones at 3.45am tomorrow, and if it's a cloudless night, we'll see the moon 'walk' across hills shaped like a woman lying on her back before setting into the middle of the stone circle.

Many archaeo-astronomers like Douglas believe Scotland's key stone circles are set out like calendars to mark the lowest and highest orbits of

Breathing space

the sun and the moon. He thinks our forebears believed the sun and moon 'impregnated' Mother Earth with energy, bringing forth crops and new life. Seems fair enough to me, but has apparently caused fury amongst 'proper' archaeologists, who say no such inferences can be drawn, even though so many of the sites are oriented precisely to these key positions of the sun two thousand years ago.

Hey ho. The pagan nature of the event guarantees an entertaining evening – as long as we are all aiming for the same 'moon-walking' time. But a quick moment of mobile phone reception throws a spanner into the works. Douglas has texted to say he may have made a small mistake about the time. It could be 1am, not 3.45am. And it is tonight not tomorrow night. Great.

A one-hour drive across country would be all very well if I was wasting only my own time in the wee small hours. But the valiant Maxwell is determined to drive despite having developed sciatic pain which has been building up into agonising cramps relieved only by

stopping the van and stamping around outside for several minutes. Since
I am also experiencing twinges of lower back pain relieved only by sitting
sideways in the passenger's seat, we're quite a combination. Add to this
the responsibility of dragging Dougie MacLean and his wife Jenny out of
their bolthole at the wrong time, on a possible wild goose chase, and the
pressure surrounding this midnight drive to Callanish is mounting.

Even if Douglas has now got the right time, we will see the walking moon
but not the assembled masses if they still think it's 3.45am tomorrow night.

'Let's just go,' says Max at midnight.

He is the ideal companion.

So we do – and with the MacLeans in their Land Rover behind (and
then in front after a few stops for sciatic stamping and sideways stretching),
we head for Callanish, with some clouds building and a growing feeling of
excitement.

At the stone circle car park there are only seven cars. Fearing the worst,
we wander up the path and suddenly hear ethereal chanting. Sure enough,
silhouetted against an iridescent sky is the unmistakable shape of druid-
like gowns. Seconds later, the reassuring sound of drums floats across
from the stones on a wave of incense that tells the old hippies present we
are in good company.

'Great,' mutters Dougie as the incense floats over. 'This is going to be
fab.'

I have had the tape recorder running in case our own remarks are the
only sound I manage to record – which is just as well. Out of the darkness,
we bump into a Jethro Tull lookalike carrying a set of bagpipes.

We ask if the big moon moment has happened.

'Something happened half an hour ago and all the pagans started
howling – you know that ululating stuff. Then this Free Church choir
started singing something in Gaelic, and for a crazy moment they seemed

**Jenny and Dougie
MacLean and a
shivery bite**

to be trying to outdo one another. I mean it's nothing to me, eh. I'm fae Fife. But I thought, this is crap. If this moon thing means something, then don't fight over it – just let it happen. But they were all still singing at each other, so I thought the pipes will sort this out and started playing "Amazing Grace". It was so loud it kind of drowned them out and they all sang along. Magic.'

'So is that you away home now?'

'Aye, that's enough. I've been here for the past two nights as well. Time to get back to Cumbernauld.'

'I thought you said you are from Fife?'

'I am – my God, I'm not from Cumbernauld. I just stay there. But I'm in it, not of it. Know what I mean? In it, not of it.'

He disappears into the night, and another face looms out of it.

'Welcome to Callanish on behalf of Jesus Christ.'

The young face is smiling and playful.

'Thanks – I didn't realise this was His kinda place.'

'God created the rocks and the stones and the moon – and Jesus.'

'Aye, fair enough.'

'We're here as a group of Free Church worshipping Christians to sing the praises of God out here in the open air on this special night.'

'But what's special about it for Christians?'

'Well God created the rocks and the stones and the moon – and…'

'I'm not trying to be funny, but we've got that. What I mean is, that pagans believe tonight sees the moon penetrate the earth in an ancient pre-Christian fertility ritual. So what precisely can that mean for Christians?'

'It means… ach, I don't know really.'

This sudden outburst of good-natured honesty is incredibly endearing. The lad reaches for his mobile phone and says, 'I can get the Gaelic choir back for you if you want to record them. They've gone off to someone's house for tea.' This is priceless.

'Absolutely, if it's not too much trouble, by all means get them back.'

Meantime, my attention is drawn to silver reflective sheets around the base of the two massive stones at the centre of the circle. As we draw

nearer, I can see four or five women's faces peering out from those insulating tin-foil sheets marathon runners use to prevent heat loss. With thermal bonnets and gloves, these gals are clearly professional stone circle groupies.

'We're shamanic astrologers from Louisiana.'

I try to keep a straight face.

'I was here in 1977 for the summer solstice because Callanish has a great

The Gaelic choir

calling for me. Actually I was here in 1992 as well, with some witches.'

Fine.

'Then when I found out the moon was actually walking on my birthday – my seventieth birthday – I knew I had to come here again.'

For seventy, she's wearing pretty well.

'What are shamanic astrologers?'

'People who believe the moon will come out of all these clouds and walk into the centre of this circle.'

Right. I can see exactly why the Free Church choir have been unable to shift them – if indeed they have even tried. What the hell, I thought.

'What's your name?'

'Linda from Santa Fe.'

'Okay. On three ladies. One, two, three.'

And off we go with a beautifully harmonised verse of 'Happy Birthday'. When we finish, Linda is (almost) over the moon and amidst the whooping noises which only Americans can make without sounding self-conscious, she shouts, 'Hey you guys, I'm seventy and I'm at Callanish – wooooooooaaaaaaaaaaaahhhhhhhhhhh!'

And off they all go.

'Woooooooooooaaaaaaaaaaaaaahhhhhhhhhhhhh!'

I feel a gentle tap on my shoulder – the Free Church choir back from tea.

'C'mon,' says a suddenly enlivened Linda, 'sing us "Amazing Grace".'

Determined not to be outdone or to appear churlish, the choir, who technically aren't a choir and can't sing anything but psalms, gamely apply the words of Psalm 23, 'The Lord's My Shepherd', to the tune of 'Amazing Grace'. It is absolutely beautiful and I find myself singing along.

After this they sing an even more haunting Gaelic song, led by Anna, a young woman who asks me not to name her in case her parents 'get annoyed'.

'Do they think you're out at 1am drinking?'

'They don't know I'm out at all.'

Anna's high, clear tones soar above the deeper voices around her – I have a strong impression of the Young Mermaid statue in Denmark with the waves swirling around but never quite overwhelming her. The effect is electrifying – and strangely, a more fitting tribute for the natural phenomenon happening above us than all the earlier pagan ululations. Ironic, although not as ironic as the subsequent discovery that Anna was permitted to lead the singing outdoors like this, but not in Church – unless no men were available.

I don't want to spoil the moment, but...

'What are you stifling her for? She's fantastic.'

'We aren't stifling her. She's singing now.'

'Alright, but it's a shame she can't do it in a proper church.'

'But this is a proper church. This is God's church.'

'You're quick on your feet, I'll give you that.'

Shamanic flame-thrower

The singers gamely take a few pictures and go back to someone's house for more tea.

But the night is not quite over. Beyond the stones and the shamanic astrologers, Free Church choir, pipers, druids and bystanders I spot some flame throwing.

Actually, I can feel it. Even from fifty yards away the paraffin fumes are eye-watering.

A tiny young American woman is swinging flaming sticks around (those shamanic astrologers can fairly perform), and I start speaking to a bemused young man with carefully beaded dreadlocks, who is gazing at her intently.

'Serendipity man, we were meant to be here. Though we didn't know this moon thing would happen. She's using my firestaff actually – this is cool.'

In fact the young flame-throwing woman is beyond cool.

She'd come all the way from Louisiana to sit under some stones with her mum, and was wearing a star-spangled leotard in case she got the

Clouds over Uig

chance of borrowing someone's fire-staff. Impressive.

'Yeah, she's great, but I was almost shocked to see the competition up there tonight.' He points up at the stone circle. 'The old Celtic belief group was up there with their drums and then the moon came out and the Christians started singing at it. It was a bit strange. But I didn't see it as totally hostile. It was like a really pleasant battle of wills as to who would get the loudest call. It was semi-defeated by the guy with the bagpipes.'

'He's from Fife.'

'Aye – but he did them the honour of playing "Amazing Grace" and that to me spoke volumes about how this pettiness doesn't matter. In any case, the slight aggression toned out when the darkness set in. People were getting tired of it. And I mean tired by the time of night and tired of the competitiveness. In the end, Callanish won.'

Silhouetted against the flames, this young man – I never got his name – looks like Edward Scissorhands but talks more sense than everyone else put together. Apart from Jenny MacLean, who's got the wee stove going in the back of her Land Rover.

'Time for tea.'

I can hardly see the tape recorder.

And I hardly want to, in case somehow I've failed to record the most remarkable mixture of voices and views I've heard in one evening.

But it was all on tape.

There's a Gaelic proverb – *The first story from the host and the tales till morning from the guest.*

Tonight Callanish stone circle was the host.

And humanity was the guest.

And for all our competing tales till dawn, we were left with the mystery.

What story has Callanish been trying to tell?

Callanish to Ness Lewis

Bungalows, war memorials, windy arguments and Pygmy Island

After the late finish and the moonset at Callanish, we head for a big snooze at the next night's B&B. It is in fact a guest house empire in a land without hotels. Neil MacArthur owns a large modern house; his son Donald bought the big house next door and they operate Loch Roag and Eshcol guest houses between them – double and twins with Neil – families, singles and all meals with Donald. Amazingly father and son are still speaking to one another. But though it may be the source of more than half his business, Neil's not keen on Callanish.

'It's true Callanish is a magnet. In the season, May to September, we could double or treble the amount of accommodation. But people make too much of the stones. It amazes me. People believe in energy from the stones and energy from the moon and Mother Earth, as they call it – but they can't believe in energy from the gospel.'

Fair point I suppose – it's just as improbable.

'The circle has no meaning for Christians, even though it was laid out in a cross, long before the time of Christ. That's intriguing, I'll grant you.'

Clever old circle – it seems to have a story for everyone.

'I've lived here all my life and it's so ordinary to me, it takes guys like you to point it out again. We had guests here about ten years ago and they went for a walk and they met an old gentleman and were talking to him about the stones. And he said, "I've never been there". And he was a local!'

'You know a lot about stones you're not interested in. Methinks you doth protest too much, Neil – I'll bet you were up there last night.'

'*No* – I was *not*! I like my sleep. Anyway, it's not my kind of place. One night in June, they were hugging the stones.'

'How do you know?'

'I just heard. I said, "Why are you doing that?" ."Oh we want to drink in the energy," they said. "Energy," I said, "I could be doing with some of that."'

Malky MacLean (or Calum as I should correctly call him) said the last time the lunar standstill happened, in 1987, people from Japan arrived off a jet having made a tour of all the other significant sites with lunar orientation, taking pocketfuls of earth to swap around them: they took

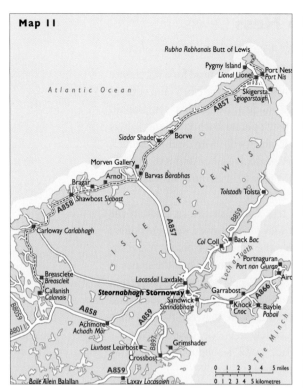

Map 11

earth from Callanish to bury in the Arizona desert. Naturally, Neil can top that one.

'There were people from South Africa planting precious stones at Callanish. And I was saying, whoever will excavate them in fifty years time will be confused.'

I'm confused now.

The Orcadians seem genuinely fond of their prehistoric sites. At the winter solstice there's a queue to get into Maes Howe and watch the incredible moment the sun creeps up the chamber and hits the back wall for a fleeting few seconds. And local farmers proudly manage independent sites like Mine Howe or the Tomb of the Eagles. And further south on the Uists, locals want council cash to interpret their special places.

But at Callanish, the Mamma of them all, villagers are lukewarm or even slightly hostile to their famous formation.

The experts who've spent their lives unravelling the site are incomers – Ronald and Margaret Curtis. The woman who's mounted a webcam to let others glimpse significant lunar and solar alignments is another incomer – Emma Mitchell. Her tearoom closed recently – amongst other things, it was apparently tough to compete with the official Visitor Centre.

Which is slightly ironic.

Emma is mesmerised by the stones. The staff at the Visitor Centre hardly seem to notice them.

Maybe it's always like that when you have a 'Natural Wonder' in your backyard. But local people – probably brought up in the Free Church to shun pagan, pre-Christian values – feel no real connection to the Callanish site.

For me, that local frostiness seems to rub off on Callanish. The shamanic astrologers from Louisiana may have felt at ease in the circle – Maxwell definitely did. I didn't.

But love them or loathe them, Callanish is year-round business. And when Neil MacArthur's son Donald lost his job at a nearby pharmaceutical plant, he learned an important lesson.

'If a place like that folds out here you have to move away. So now with the B&B I've got another string to my bow. I'm a research chemist by day, chef by night. Cooking's like chemistry really. Just mixing things together and timing.'

Donald, like his dad, is far too modest. Dinner is exceptionally good.

Wars, loss and emigrating fishermen

The next morning, leaving Callanish, I stop by the War Memorial at East Loch Roag at the suggestion of a man who has become a regular correspondent by post – Donald John MacLeod. He was incensed at a radio programme I presented years ago, which suggested the Outer Hebrides were the poor relations of Scotland's larger islands. I had asked if the key difference might not be the Orcadians' firm grip upon the means of production. Nothing leaves the Northern Isles without value added. They export ice cream and cheese – not milk. They export pickled rollmop herring – not raw fish. They export Orkney beef at premium rates, and their jewellery industry is the second largest outside Birmingham. You get my drift. Donald got it and was incensed at the implication that Hebrideans somehow had themselves to blame for lagging behind:

Stone hugger at Callanish

Here's a response to your story about the 'backward Hebrideans' and the east coast fishermen taunting islanders about their fear of losing sight of land.

Do you know why Hebrideans are such good seamen? When the Vikings sailed west they put the farmers and all those who were seasick ashore in Orkney and Shetland and the Vikings seafarers sailed on for the Western Isles. Here's where the real fishermen went.

Hundreds of them were evicted during the Clearances – take my native parish of Uig on Lewis. In 1795 the Reverend Hugh Munro stated there were 275 net makers. I doubt if there are 275 people in the entire parish today. If this was the number of net makers there must have been many hundreds of fishermen.

Indeed, the McIvers who developed the port of Liverpool and helped found the Cunard Line, are probable descendants of Iver MacIver after whom rocks near the Isle of Pabbay in the Sound of Harris are named. His ship foundered with a cargo

Tolsta beach

of salt fish en route to Liverpool – a formidable, brave and long haul in a small craft.

But the heavy loss of life in the two wars left the greatest void. Skippers took their fishing knowledge with them to the bottom of the sea, so their experience was not passed on to island youngsters keen to enter the fishing industry. It only takes one generation to lose local skills.

It's true.

The *Iolaire* disaster – the worst ferry disaster in British waters – was a further catastrophe for the Lewis fleet in 1914. Nearly all those aboard who drowned as the ship hit rocks within sight of Stornoway were fishermen returning from the horrors of war. Typical of the villages affected was Sheshader in Point on the east coast of Lewis. In 1914 the village had twenty-six houses with able-bodied men. In World War One, nineteen were killed or badly wounded. Ten more were lost on the *Iolaire*. The loss of twenty-nine from this village meant they were unable to man fishing boats thereafter. Among the dead were five sets of brothers and thirty-nine Macleods – a European record for the number of people with the same surname dying on the same ship. Instead of sympathy the authorities' first act, apparently, was to tell widows without children they were not entitled to a pension. Neither were elderly parents who lost their bread-winning sons.

Surviving sailors, soldiers and airmen had been promised 'a land fit for heroes'. This did not materialise. So, hundreds from the Western Isles emigrated – many of them fishermen. In 1920, a group of young men from North Tolsta started inshore fishing with a cutter registered as *Clan Murray*. Her crew averaged seventeen years of age. Four years later, almost all emigrated on board the *Marloch* to Canada. It is reckoned that 2,000 Lewis men died in both wars and over 3,000 – mostly ex-servicemen – left for Canada shortly afterwards as a result of the government's emigration drive. More islanders emigrated than were killed in the war.

In their absence the big steam trawlers from Grimsby, Hull and Fleetwood invaded the fishing grounds around the Western Isles, putting the final nail in the coffin of the open boats from Lewis that fished with long lines. The trawlers often carried away the lines as they hoovered up small fish, big fish and breeding fish – eventually destroying inshore fishing

Travellers' site at Callanish

grounds such as Broad Bay, east of Lewis, which was one of the major fish breeding grounds in Britain, where for centuries hundreds of locals had fished with long lines and drift nets.

As Donald observed in another letter:

After thirty years of steam trawlers and seine net boats from the East Coast the fishing in Broad Bay was finally destroyed. Many of the English trawlers fished illegally inside the three mile limit – they used to put sacks over their names and locals could not identify them. When the English trawlers left, the French and Spanish trawlers came from the 1960s onwards and killed every fish that was left. One of my friends counted thirteen French trawlers fishing line abreast between the Flannan Isles and St Kilda without a fishery protection vessel in sight.

Many Western Isles villages are now derelict. In Uig there were five schools when I was young – today there is one. In 1891 the population of the Western Isles was 44,987 and that of Iceland 70,927. Today the population of the Western Isles is around 25,000 and declining fast, while Iceland has increased to nearly 280,000. The Icelanders have not suffered losses in two World Wars and their government has fought to preserve their fishing industry. Today Lewis would be better off if it was under Norwegian jurisdiction, as it was hundreds of years ago. A Norwegian government would not allow fishermen to land at Stornoway and then pay a fortune to transport fish by car ferry across the Minch.

All of this has resulted in Lewis men losing the knowledge needed to fish deep waters for white fish. The old fishermen with the skills are dead and the young ones are clueless.

Read the war memorial at East Loch Roag and weep. Callanish, Breasclete and Garynahine – you are reading the names in death of three crofting/fishing villages. forty-nine villagers died in the two wars. Another twenty-five were crippled – taking the war casualty list to seventy-four. There were only eighty-nine homes with able bodied men. This must be one of the highest war losses per head sustained by any area in the UK. Brothers and cousins were killed including eleven MacLeans, nine

*An Gearrannan
restored blackhouse
near Barvas*

MacAulays and nine MacIvers. Medals for bravery were awarded including – two Distinguished Conduct Medals (next to the VC), one Distinguished Service Cross, two Military Crosses, one Military Medal and three Croix de Guerre from the French government. For such a sparsely populated community this shows the high degree of bravery and loss during those war years. How could the islands ever recover?

The statistics of Donald's patient research are impressive. The personal stories behind them are astonishing. Donald MacKinnon, who served with the Royal Navy and was the survivor of a Russian convoy – plucked unconscious from the freezing sea – was born in 1921, the eldest of a family of ten at Cluer on the Island of Harris. He was clever, but left school at fourteen to build roads and earn money to support his mother, who ran the croft while his father, James, was away in the merchant navy. Because crofts were designed to be unsustainable – especially for a family of ten – almost half the men of the islands were thought to be working off the island at any one time. Many of them worked in the merchant fleet, others on trawlers and whalers. They would plant crops in spring, go away for a couple of long voyages, return home in the autumn to lift the crops and then go back to sea in the winter, until spring and crop time again.

But in June 1940 that pattern was interrupted when James MacKinnon – too old for conscription – signed up as a carpenter to support the war effort. MacKinnon senior served in the Royal Naval Volunteer Reserve (RNVR) as a volunteer and worked on armed trawlers, rescue ships and supply ships loaded with food and ammunition to service tankers and troopships. After completing one voyage he planned to go home on leave, but the captain of the MV *Pizarro* asked him to make one more trip, to Gibraltar. The ship was torpedoed by an Italian submarine 700 miles west of the Scilly Isles. Unbelievably, his widow was left to bring up nine children with no financial assistance from the British state. The pay of merchant seamen was stopped when their ships were sunk and the authorities would not grant her a war widow's pension, stating her husband was only 'missing presumed lost'. Despite such harsh treatment, men continued to join the RNVR. Sea skills learned as youngsters enabled islanders to handle boats in any conditions under oar or sail. This could have contributed to the disproportionately heavy losses suffered by island sailors: unlike lads recruited from cities, the Stornowegians, as they were called, were deployed immediately to the front line. As writer James Shaw Grant put it, this was 'not courage for a cause but courage for its own sake – the courage of the Vikings'.

Donald Macleod from Ranish survived the sinking of the SS *Empire Florizel* and a plane crash en route to hospital in North Africa on the same day. Earlier he had been a survivor of the SS *Ulea* – along with his brother Neil, who had survived the sinking of his first ship, the SS *Cyprian Prince*.

Donald MacKenzie from Sheshader was one of only three survivors after HMS *Esk* hit a mine. After his lifeboat capsized he was picked up by HMS *Ivanhoe*, which also hit a mine and exploded. He swam all night, through burning oil and mines, before being rescued. He went straight back to serve on the Russian convoys.

John MacIver from North Tolsta and Angus Murray from Shawbost were both awarded British Empire Medals for 'skill and resource in bringing survivors to safety in circumstances that would have daunted the bravest'. They each navigated a lifeboat after MV *Richmond Castle* was torpedoed southeast of Cape Farewell. It was the only time neighbours were decorated for bravery in charge of different lifeboats from the same ship.

Donald M Maclean from Stornoway survived a night in the sea off Rockall after his boat, the *Transylvania,* was sunk. He later helped capture the German cargo ship *Bianca* and was awarded the Distinguished Service Cross for helping sink a U-Boat.

John MacMillan of North Tolsta was commended posthumously when his merchant ship was mined and sunk off Cape Race. Though badly burned, he gave his life belt to a seaman who could not swim. **MacMillan** died from his injuries. Earlier he had survived the sinking of SS *Empire Ability* off the Canary Islands.

Chief Petty Officer Donald MacLeod from Bayble was commended posthumously after trying to cut adrift two burning craft that were endangering a fuel barge in the harbour at Malta. His Commanding Officer wrote, 'the craft exploded and he met his death instantly. He well knew the risk he ran and did his duty unhesitatingly, despite that knowledge.'

Dun Carloway and a mad biker

So many islanders served and died, a Western Isles seaman was selected to be the model for a statue in the Merchant Navy Garden of Remembrance in London.

I can see why this level of un- acknowledged sacrifice and bravery haunts Donald John MacLeod. Not only did the Western Isles lose their bravest and most skilled seamen in two wars, one tragic shipwreck and subsequent emigration, outsiders like me are unaware of the loss and ignorant of its impact on the vitality of island communities.

Standing before the forest of names on the East Loch Roag memorial, I am now very much the wiser.

But unable to think of any more good reasons to delay today's long haul to the Butt.

Painting of crofthouse by Moira MacLean

North of Callanish the road is inland and the coastline hidden. With bog to the right, clouds overhead and only glimpses of sea to the left, the going suddenly gets very slow.

After a detour to Dun Carloway, and a shameful attempt to emulate *The Italian Job* on its carefully constructed steps, I decide to make this a people kind of day. Especially people who own tearooms and pubs. At the Doune Braes Hotel in Carloway, I meet the owner, Eileen MacDonald. She was one of the first hoteliers to apply for a Sunday licence a decade back, and still has tourists driving twenty-three miles from Stornoway on a Sunday night because they can't get anything to eat in town. Eileen doesn't register much change in the licensing board's attitude to hospitality.

Sometimes I wonder if that problem extends a bit further – to the *Leodhasach* themselves.

Hospitality issues

During the cycle journey, at a place that shall not be named, I discover it is, as women describe it, a time of the month. I head some miles to the nearest shop in search of… provisions. Three women are talking purposefully about deliveries and labelling new stock. I am the only customer. I can't see any… provisions in the usual place beside the toiletries. The customary shame about female functions may mean relevant… stuff is somehow beneath the counter. So I ask and in fact the… stuff is behind a door. As I pay I ask if they have a loo I could use. It doesn't take Einstein to make the connection. Indeed, even a man might understand. I've bought… provisions, and I might be in a hurry to… use them.

The shop assistant looks at me. I'm not her problem.

'There are facilities at a beach a few miles along the road.'

Fabulous. Knowing I'm going to write about this and knowing I have already fallen in love with this bit of the world and therefore expect to be back, I decide to follow this advice without snarling or special pleading. I cycle towards the 'facilities' embroiled in some amateur transactional analysis. My inner adult (who wants to come back) recognises that shops are not public toilets and that shops would be awash with unwanted bladders if they didn't draw the line somewhere (like the door).

My inner child wants to wait till the shop van is broken down in the rain and I am the only car passing for an hour. I would then… actually, I would then stop and offer them a lift. Which is the reason this whole scenario is bothering me. I was brought up by Highland parents to think that helpfulness was the first rule of Highlandness. I then brought myself up to think that helpfulness towards strangers is the first rule of humanness. People are generally wary because they expect wariness. As soon as that unvirtuous circle is broken new things can happen. A temporary mini community of strangers can be formed – based on delight, optimism and co-operation.

It ain't happening here.

The 'facilities' are portakabins, designed to be tucked behind a building – not bunged out on a windy headland. All credit to someone, there is still loo roll and hand towels. And everything works. But the dilapidated, paint-free appearance of the portakabins is dreadful. Apparently they were to have been replaced by a permanent stone building with showers. But island contractors submitted such high prices for the work that locals concluded they had their hands full and didn't really want the work. So the project is on the back burner for another year.

This is the madness that comes with too small an economy. The slightest bit of extra demand sends stress levels, prices and tempers flying. Are people actually happier with decline?

I think yet again of Johnson's remark about ornamentation of the mind mattering more than the relief of small discomforts. I mentioned this a week earlier to Mary Schmoller from South Uist, who took quite a different meaning from Johnson's words: 'Yes, there is a lot more to life than materialism.'

'Actually, I don't think that's what he meant. We're human beings with physical needs and desires for warmth, shelter, sex. I think he's saying that people here attend only to intellectual needs and let the creature comforts go hang.'

'Well, that's not true. You clearly haven't been round to my house for tea.'

Now this is indeed the other side of my miserable rant. Home-based Highland hospitality is a sight to behold. Dr Johnson, for all his keen insight into Highland character, failed to observe during his fortnight travelling the Inner Isles, that neither he nor Boswell appear to have paid for any accommodation anywhere they stayed. Generous hospitality was so commonplace it was unremarkable: 'To enter a habitation without leave, seems to be not considered here as rudeness or intrusion. The old laws of hospitality still give this licence to a stranger.'

Old laws of hospitality have been slightly amended. Instead of accepting a bed for the night, visitors must now eat their weight before trying to leave. On that earlier visit to Harris, I went to visit the 'cousin' of a friend, John. I had spent a week alone, walking, reading and generally becoming a better person, and decided on the last night I had earned a night of sociable *cráic* with people I assumed to be my own age. Although they lived up the Golden Road, I thought I might persuade them out to the pub – after a week of purposeful, solitary clean living, I was ready for it. Weaving along the twisting single track road I finally came to their house, knocked on the door and an old woman answered. Clearly all diplomatic effort had deserted me, because she said 'Ach, John has been telling you I am his cousin again. We use the word quite loosely here. But don't worry, we may be old but we're lots of fun.'

And so it proved. Four filled rolls, two pieces of shortbread and one currant slice later, I insisted I had had enough. The trolley was groaning with food but Ella wheeled it away as if to restock. I followed her through to the kitchen and attempted to put my foot down.

'Look, no more food Ella. My mother is from Caithness. It may not be the Western Isles but she's a Highlander and I know what I'm saying here. I am saying no. Not a Southern no, not an English no, this is a Highland no. No thank you. No.'

This emphatic refusal worked. Ella stopped plying me with food and started trying to marry me to her nephew instead. Later I recounted the story to John, who told me he'd visited Ella the previous year with an English friend whose inability to say 'no' sufficiently firmly prompted a frenzy of Hebridean largesse. The two men were released from over-eating only by Ella's suggestion that the 'boys' might like to go and get some peat for the fire. Outside on the heather, John's friend was violently ill. When he felt better, the two returned to the house with a few sacks of peat.

'Ach, you'll want something after being outside for so long – what about a nice piece of millionaire's shortbread?'

Hospitality on the Western Isles knows no bounds – inside a family home. Outside, I'm afraid the opposite is generally true. I have had so many mean portions, so much offhand service and so many badly presented meals, I've grown quite used to it. It is as if the public realm has little value for Hebridean people. And yet the public realm supports almost every job. The poet Hugh MacDiarmid said he'd 'aye be whaur extremes meet' and went to live on Shetland. I really think he missed a trick.

The Hebridean ethic is all about hospitality, and yet the visitor often experiences a complete lack of it. I've cycled for hours to reach visitor centres that are shut at 4pm – in summer. I've cycled to reach B&Bs with landladies who offer no evening meal and will cheerfully watch as you head for the nearest beach clutching a portable tin-foil BBQ – in the rain. I've seen B&B signs swing 'shut' on Friday nights, in case the tourist wants to stay the whole weekend and will not dematerialise on the Sabbath. And that has happened in

**'Wallpaper pirate'
Moira MacLean at
the Morven Gallery**

places that are not Free Church strongholds. I've been manhandled out of a pub that was serving locals but not 'tourists' on a Sunday, for daring to point out they were open.

On the other hand, I've witnessed acts of kindness and generosity every day we've been on the islands. The difference is crystal clear.

When you're known – you're in. When you're not – you're out.

I don't think this is because of an innate hostility to strangers. It's force of habit. Locals don't need small shops or cafés or pubs or hotels – they've got cousins. Visitors haven't. So there's an inverse relation between the strength of family ties and the level of hospitality a stranger can expect. The stronger the former, the weaker the latter.

That tension between the interior and exterior of Hebridean lives is the raw material for Moira MacLean's paintings – quite literally.

The wallpaper pirate

We stop at the Morven Gallery to meet the 'wallpaper pirate', so named because her hazy, dreamy landscapes incorporate bits of flowery wallpaper 'borrowed' from empty Hebridean homes.

When we arrive around lunchtime she's painting. I see the gallery owner's look of momentary panic as an unexpected busload comes tumbling past us. She's trying to say the gallery doesn't do food. But too late. The cagoule-clad, hunger-crazed Americans have spotted some scones and a coffee machine and are settling in for brunch.

Finally, Moira appears. At long last, a young local woman prepared to be interviewed and to speak her mind.

'When I was young, we used to creep into derelict houses and play. Later on when I went to art college I realised I was really interested in those faded, chintzy rose patterns. I started collecting them.'

'How do you collect bits of wallpaper? Girl, you were desecrating these places!'

'Yes – I call myself the wallpaper pirate. I usually have to make some kind of compromised entrance via a window, head-first with a special tourie [bonnet] so no one will know who I am.'

She'd just given the game away, but never mind.

'People were crazy for decorating in the fifties. It was like a form of optimism – let's make this place feel new again, let's put another layer on. And quite often there are seven layers of wallpaper through the different decades and different styles. I think they used wallpaper as insulation too.'

A detail from
Ravishing Harbours II
by Moira MacLean

Moira has me thinking now. On this trip we've stayed in some houses of almost surreal girly pinkness filled with rose-covered wallpaper, and pictures of lowland flower-swamped gardens. In short, everything that isn't outside the croft window.

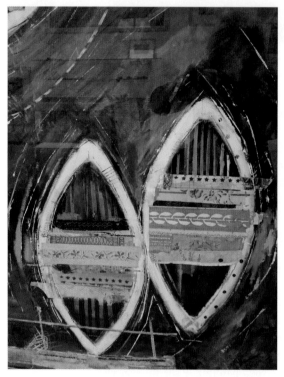

'I think it's a reaction against the long winters. And I must say they did it with much more style long ago. The papers were hand-printed, you can see the suction of the inks. They had mica in them, which makes them glisten slightly. The colours were much more tasteful – candy colours that I like to use – aqua, pink and sunshine yellow. I think the houses were decorated like that to keep people optimistic. But things changed and folk didn't want to be associated with the old days and the poverty. So they got rid of the v-lining [wood-panelling on walls] and the dressers and the rose wallpaper and the old fifties kitchens and even the old sash windows painted the candy colours, and they've gone for the cherry wood and roughcast. They want to untangle themselves from that past and appear more modern and more – wealthy I guess.'

She's right. It's UPVC county here. Everything is harled, everything is a bungalow and my guess is that everyone got a grant in the seventies, and good luck to them. It all looks a bit suburban. I've inadvertently struck upon Ms MacLean's specialist subject.

'I know, and I think it's absolutely horrific. I have a real problem with this kit house thing – off I go on my bike and there's another blue-framed kit house popping up. It's like they're spawning. They don't suit the landscape. But there's something idyllic about the croft house with the two storm windows peeping up from the side of a hill – they just seem to nestle, and sit in the landscape far better.'

Mind you, the 'classic' look has a lot to do with poverty. The small windows were designed to keep heat in and draughts out. People would have loved more light, they just couldn't afford it. Are we lionising an aesthetic that is the product of poverty?

'I can see that for locals it's all too close to their childhood and being compromised for cash and hating draughts and rattly sash windows and it being Baltic all the time. It's the people who move in who want the tradition most.'

'And what's a young gal like you doing in a place like this?'

'I didn't expect to be here – various romances kept me. What I've found is that you can survive up here without too much cash, so that frees up time to do work. If I was in the city I'd be working all the time just to maintain the lifestyle and I wouldn't have time to paint.'

It's hard to describe Moira's pictures. They are warm about nature without being in any way kitschy.

'The thing I like about the wallpaper is that it's like a little surprise or gift. The paint is totally fresh, and then there are these old fragments of wallpaper that have seen generations. It's a duality.'

And it really works. Having spent some time drifting round the gallery – which is a working model of how to let light into an old croft house without destroying the traditional design – it struck me that trips to the seaside remind most people of their own yesterdays. And then, in these paintings, they find little shreds of wallpaper from someone else's yesterdays. When I'm back minus bikes and transits – I'm bagging one of these. But not now. Max and I are ravenous. The Americans have cleaned up, there is not even a scone left, so we head off looking for food.

We retrace our route in the van, thinking we passed a café nearby. Fifteen miles later – travelling in the wrong direction – we have found nothing. Finally we stumble on a wind-turbine powered community café catering for an unexpected deluge of farmers from a nearby sheepdog trial. In a vain attempt to beat the queue, we order a couple of baked potatoes at the counter. We've had so many baked tattie meals I'm starting to pine for Max's sandwiches. But then we'd need a shop to buy the components – and shops are even thinner on the ground than cafés.

It's bizarre. North Lewis sustains the largest population in the Hebrides and has the smallest provision of creature comforts.

The bold wind-lover...

Neil Finlayson aims to change that. He's set up several companies, worked in the States and come home to raise a family, push the case for wind energy, investigate uses for stored hydrogen and apply internet solutions to island life. And if that means becoming unpopular by supporting industrial-scale windfarms like the current controversial AMEC proposal – he's prepared to do it. Standing in the lea of the Morven Gallery for shelter, I ask Neil to mutter something for level and hope that he isn't going to be... 'Supershy?' That is indeed the right word.

There have been whole villages of supershy on this trip – and more in Lewis than anywhere else, I'd have to say. But thankfully supershy doesn't describe Neil, who calmly analyses the current strengths and weaknesses of Lewis life.

'Crofting is an enabler for housing, but not much of a goer agriculturally. Land use has become a very static thing and that's a problem. The layout of the crofts inhibits development in all kinds of ways. The windfarm isn't the first plan to attract hostility, we've tried to get a golf course going at Ness and there was resistance to that too. The crofters who are active come into meetings and are worried about the impact of new plans on what they do. And that's understandable. But Stornoway's getting very lively now – ninety-five students

Robust dialogue with Neil Finlayson

wanted summer employment this year with the council – that's three times the number looking for jobs last year, an indicator young people are seeing opportunities.'

'Really?' I'm not trying to be funny, but if was a business-minded youngster looking for opportunities, the council would be my last stop.

'Fair point – two-thirds couldn't get jobs at the end of the summer. There are probably far too many people employed in the public sector in the Hebrides. But I think there is a mood to be entrepreneurial.'

'No there isn't.'

'What?'

Oh dear, I can feel a gasket blowing.

'A mood to be entrepreneurial – no there isn't.'

'Yes there is.'

This could be better than the Monty Python argument sketch.

'Neil, we can't have a cup of tea inside this gallery because the owner's worried about employing another member of staff. If she was serving any food on a regular basis, she'd be inundated for part of the year with busloads of tourists who can't find anyone else prepared to cater for public demand outside Stornoway. People are sitting in one-person businesses all the way up this island chain, terrified to expand. And I'm not blaming them. We've heard stories of expansion plans foundering over the need to put in £20k worth of disabled access, folk too busy to train apprentices, Lewis-based mums too busy to distribute their Harris Tweed handbags to Harris... I could go on.'

Neil's look suggests he'd rather I didn't.

'Look, I've been an entrepreneur for eight years – built a company back in 2000 with ninety-five people, and we sold it – maybe 120 people are working there now. I had another company with fourteen people...'

'I know – you make businesses work. So what's the solution?'

'The council are switched on. People want things to happen, especially at a musical and cultural level. Stornoway is one of the busiest wee towns on the West Coast – think positive. It's a Scottish, Calvinist thing to say things aren't going so well. You've got to remember we are forty miles out in the Atlantic.'

'But the Shetlanders are 200 miles out in the North Sea.'

'Yes – and what they did was exhibit vision thirty years ago. They took advantage of their energy windfall. That can happen here too. They seized the moment. Wind is our moment – and it's just the start of it. Oil will run out. Wind and sun won't. Hydrogen production and marine power offer big possibilities too.'

'So you'll be happy when the turbines go up?'

'I have had my doubts about the shape and location of the AMEC proposal, but not its size. I'd have been happy with one twice the size...'

'You'll need an armed guard, Neil.'

'Well, maybe. I'm suspicious about the EU habitat designations that blocked off inland locations where the turbines would have been sited in a clump, away from public view. If there had been political will at the time, maybe it could have been different. But renewable energy production on an industrial scale is fine, for jobs and for the planet. The people who are against it should go back to the period before electricity. Life was hard.'

With time against us, the bike is slung into the back of the van for a few miles before I decide I have to cycle the final bit to the Butt.

But I'm still late at the northernmost point of Lewis, where the outspoken Gaelic writer Finlay MacLeod is standing on the cliff like a mythic hero above crashing waves spitting foam and surf flying a hundred feet into the air.

Waves lashing the Butt

And the bold windfarm hater

I have never actually met Finlay before but all niceties of introduction are cast aside as he grabs my arm and pulls me right to the edge shouting, 'Isn't it *marvellous*.'

Full of energy himself, Finlay revels in the released energy of nature.

After surveying the storm-battered Lewisian Gneiss cliffs for a few minutes, I have to ask the big question.

'What's wrong with harnessing wind?'

Dr MacLeod looks at me appraisingly, decides I'm game for yet another mini-adventure, and says he can explain this best elsewhere. Suddenly the man is racing like a youngster across a mile of saltwater-soaked turf to an offshore rock called the Pygmy Isle, believed to have housed a race of tiny people. I can't quite see the wind connection, and though Finlay is a few years older than myself I can't quite keep up with him either. But I like his style. Fifteen minutes later I am tackling the most powerfully articulate critic of island windfarms, on top of a remote cliff. And to shield the microphone from the wind, I have my back to the sea. Hey ho.

Finlay is pointing at the wave-battered rock behind me.

'Now I love enigmas, and the Pygmy Isle – *An Luchraban* in Gaelic – is a true enigma. First mention of it that we know about is around the middle of the 1500s by Archdeacon Dean Munro. He came to the island, saw a building called the Kirk and dug beneath it, because people told him there were little people living on the island in the past. He found bones and shards of pottery and amongst them little skeletons that he called, 'round heids of verie littel quantitie'. Jump to Timothy Pont in 1600, who called it the Island of the Little People – *Ylen Dunibeg* in Gaelic – in Blaeu's *Atlas*. We don't know if Pont was actually here – he drew such a curious map of Lewis. But on a remarkable 1600 Irish map, with very few place-names on it, Pygmy Island is there. A Captain Dymes came in 1630 – he dug down and got bones. Martin Martin was on to it. Then into the nineteenth century comes Dr McCulloch, a geologist and sceptic, who said there was no such island. Finally in the beginning of the twentieth century, a Dr MacKenzie comes and does a dig, finds bones and sends them to the Natural History Museum for analysis.'

I should be waiting for the big wind connection but I'm on the edge of my cliff now about these little people – and bringing to Finlay's story all my own gathered observations about fairy people on Dunvegan and indeed, leprechauns in Ireland.

'So what did they find?'

'He found skulls of sheep, goats, oxen and birds. But none of little people.'

Right. That is some story. I'm wet. There's no punchline and I don't know why we are here. Finlay smiles and enlightens me.

'Why it's interesting is that the named environment, with stories embedded in it, makes the land precious. Even this little island covered in thrift and black-back gulls is embedded in the history that goes back hundreds of years, as do the people who live here – hence our rootedness in the place. The named environment and the physical environment are part of us, too. Fifty miles further along there is Sulasgeir, where the Ness

**Button-holing Finlay
MacLeod**

men go for gannets every autumn, and the exquisite island of North Rona, where my great-grandfather was born because his father was caught distilling whisky in Ness and, rather than go to prison on the mainland, he decided to go to Rona for a year. He took his mother with him the first time and then his wife, and then he stayed five years and had two children there, my great-grandfather Finlay being one of them. And he said he regretted ever leaving it. When he came back here, someone said if he climbed a hill he would see Rona on a nice day. He said, 'I don't think my heart could stand it.'

Fair play. The forebears of the islanders I'm meeting now had a very, very hard life. And a great attachment to the land. But thrawn, stubborn spirit that he is, Finlay won't quite accept that backhanded compliment either.

'Was it really difficult? If these conditions are the centre of your life, they don't seem difficult. It's only when you look at it from a wider perspective that you say, "Oh dear, didn't these people have a hard life, they've had to be migrant workers all over the world." But this was still the centre of their universe. And that's why we mustn't see it damaged. Mustn't see it become, for example, the financial playground for multinationals.'

Aha, the windfarms at last. I decide to take my life in my hands – the cliffs are very close – and suggest that whilst the aesthetic jury might agree that a string of turbines are a blight on the coastal strip, what's wrong with a clump on the bleak curves of the dreich Barvas Moor?

'The moors are the essence of what this small island is. Every poet who's tried to describe what home is, puts the moorland and the hills at the centre of it. To violate the moorlands of Lewis on the scale that's proposed – it would damage the island beyond healing. Contracts have been signed, politicians have been touched with powers, improvers are here aplenty.

The Butt stops here

The people were never asked. But that's enough of that.'

And so saying, Finlay bounds off across the very special, superknown bog (perhaps greeting each tuft and hillock by name), with the gait of a man whose predecessors knew well how to stay close to the edge, but just out of trouble.

Squelching back to the Butt, I feel I now understand Finlay's outlook on the emotional importance of land. I understand it, I think – but I don't entirely trust it.

Andy Wightman's book *Who Owns Scotland* took a snapshot of estate ownership so that calm, factual and economic discussion of Scotland's biggest national asset could begin. But the land debate is still awash with emotion. Much of it male, some of it boarding school in origin, and some built up in response to outbursts from land reformers like – well, me.

As a former Isle of Eigg Trust Director, I used to think ex-owner Keith Schellenberg was cold and mechanical in his approach to the island. I now realise I was wrong. He was the most dangerously emotional person around. A former Gordonstoun pupil, he bought the island, became its paternalistic provider, and believed he would therefore win unquestioning love and respect from its people. It didn't happen.

No wonder the laird became over-attached to the land instead. When he wrote poems about the *Sgurr* of Eigg (a 1,000-feet high basalt cliff face) towering over fields and beaches like 'a lion rampant above its prey', we tittered. When his successor, Maruma, described the Massacre Cave as an inspiring uterus, it was all we could do to keep straight faces. Both men had translated bits of landscape into powerful symbols with meaning in their own emotional lives and then felt threatened to the core when locals saw only land – an asset to be used, not beatified. Mind you, opinion on the other side of the landowning coin is no less emotional.

Crofters living on the breadline feel too guilty to sell land their Clearance-threatened forefathers battled to win. Absentee crofters can't admit they will never return, so their houses become derelict. Planning law protects the landscape of the empty glen by blocking sites for building development. On the plus side, land reform has triggered over a dozen community buyouts, with more on the way. These new possibilities are bound to change island outlooks over time. Meanwhile, the average islander who just wants an extra acre for a shed is stuck, incomers with drive and ambition are often isolated and second-home owners can find themselves shunned.

The Highlands is awash with emotion because it's not awash with affordable land. People are left squabbling over tiny plots in an area bigger than Belgium, with a population half the size of Sheffield.

I'm fast coming to the conclusion that land doesn't need more love. It needs more use.

Free Church critic

Back at the Butt, Finlay starts on his other specialist subject, the impact of the Free Church on Lewis. Again, he doesn't hesitate to set forth controversial views which I feel later I must check are alright to broadcast and print. They are.

'The Calvinist church has dominated thinking on Lewis for two centuries. It took over very confidently, there was no alternative narrative at the time and no alternative voice that ever stood up against it publicly. It was strengthened by Gaelic literacy and by the Gaelic Bible, which was published in 1800. So it fitted into family life and into community life. And when ideas come in like that they are very hard to dislodge in a closed society where there isn't public debate, where there isn't public expression. To this day young people are unable to express their views – they are controlled by shame, so it becomes easier to leave. When I left, I was being controlled as a young citizen not by other citizens but by evangelicalism – and so it continues to this very day, over ferries and the like. Why, as a citizen, should my movements be controlled by evangelical Christians? Civic life should never be controlled by any given faith group and their last effective instrument of control is the Sabbath.'

I wonder if Finlay's ever thought of taking a legal case over the lack of Sunday ferry transport, if he feels that strongly.

'I've enquired what can be done about it, under European legislation. But there isn't enough public debate. Everyone keeps their heads down and even the local authority isn't an open forum. People keep their heads down there too. The people who have written about all of this were usually people who had left – Iain Crichton Smith, for example. It was very hard to stay here and express moderate views – moderate to you and to the outside world, but here apparently extreme, deviant, dangerous and shameful.'

Yeah, Butt

'You say this very openly.'

'Yes.'

'Is that easy? Are you ostracised or do people just say, "That's Finlay"?'

'I tend not to be challenged. People know who you are and what family you come from. They shake their heads and say what a pity you didn't follow your parents and your grandparents. My parents are no longer alive. I don't have an older family to which I must show allegiance. I don't shame an older generation by expressing my views. I see what came here as effectively an ancient Judaic folklore, which was written down, and then belief came into it – we started believing the folklore. Of course, we always had folklore: we believed the stories of Fionn, but we believed them in a different way. This was belief absolute. And it's very, very appealing. Wouldn't you like to go on forever? Everlasting life – who wouldn't leap at that? And then they divide it and say, isn't it wonderful up in the clouds but by golly, it's hot down below. And then they complicate things and say your fate was settled before you were even born. Heady stuff.'

It's a puzzle. The non-negotiable fundamentalism of the Free Church repels Finlay but his response to the wind farmers seems fairly non-negotiable too.

Let me eat, let me drink, let me sleep – if only Lewis life could be as straightforward as the Gaelic proverb.

There is a choice to be made now. The strongest winds south of Orkney have flattened crops, killed fishermen and stunted lives. With technology, those winds could deliver an energy-rich future. Without it, some islanders may feel better able to continue in their traditional ways.

Wind is tearing Lewis apart. Or shaking it awake.

Barra to the Butt – mission accomplished.

Next and final stop – Stornoway itself.

Stornoway and Eye Peninsula Lewis

The Free Church, 'Two Ronnies' and Gaelic

Stornoway is in the grip of road rage. No one screams, no one blares their horn – static traffic in three directions is patient as a weekend driver takes forever to reverse from a much sought-after parking space. Only the gritted teeth give the game away.

This is mid-July, the week the Hebridean Celtic Festival and the new Sail (Boat) Festival coincide. The weather's good, and HebFest's Peter Kane tells me online booking means they can confidently expect 14,000 ticket sales to folk from forty-three countries. Thirty biking leather-clad Norwegians are queuing patiently for Levellers tickets inside the tiny office as we speak. There are queues outside every restaurant, café and fish and chip shop.

My patience is being sorely tested by an erratic mobile phone, which hasn't worked since its cliff-top soaking at the Butt of Lewis.

A shop assistant directs me to a hardware store where I'm handed the mobile number of a man nicknamed Ali Baba. He's on holiday, it seems, but his cousin Murdo McIver turns up in a white van within minutes to the spot on the street where I'm standing. While help is at hand the phone performs perfectly. But the second Murdo drives off, the buttons jam again. I conclude the McIvers truly are mobile magicians.

Free Speech on the Free Church...

We're heading for Back Free Church, eight miles outside Stornoway, where seven members of the congregation are gathering to give me a sample of precentor-led singing.

After yesterday's outspoken anti Free Kirk contribution from Dr Finlay, I feel I ought to explore the 'other side'. But trying to dig deeper into Free Church theology has frustrated far better brains than mine. According to James Hunter:

> While it is certainly hard to warm to the narrowly Sabbatarian, bitterly sectarian, faction-ridden and frequently reactionary Free Church of modern times, it is a mistake to assume that Highlands and Islands evangelicalism always exhibited only those traits. By providing its adherents with a deeply felt sense of personal purpose, (and distributing Gaelic Bibles) the early Free Church helped counter

some of the psychological dislocation produced by the collapse of clanship (after Culloden and the Highland Clearances). Equally important was the supply of leadership. At the centre of much religious revivalism were immensely articulate and hugely charismatic lay preachers, (chief amongst them *na daoine* or 'the men'), who regularly attracted entire communities to enormous, open-air gatherings.

And Calum G Brown says:

It is hard to overstate the role of the Free Church as a social institution in Highland Society for there was very little else. Attracting between 90 and 95 per cent of church adherents (on Lewis and Harris) the social regime of the free church distinguished the 'Godly' crofters from the 'lukewarm' landowners by strict Sabbath observance, distinctive Gaelic Psalm singing, the ministers ranting against backsliding, drink, dancing and immorality, and the annual communion seasons when communicants from several parishes gathered for a week of summer prayer meetings and open air services. Free Church ministers in the early years were vigorous critics of landowners and the Clearances – whilst the Kirk [Church of Scotland] promoted Godly dignity and quiet hostility rather than crofter rebellion.

There is more to the Free Church than meets the eye, and there is far more history than one relatively modern creation could desire.

In 1892 the Free Church of Scotland decided to relax rules on the confessional, to pave the way for unification with the United Presbyterian Church. A few ministers objected and left to form the Free Presbyterian Church of Scotland (FPs). When the Free Church and the United Presbyterians did finally unite to form the United Free Church of Scotland, another minority stayed out, keeping the name Free Church (FCs). You might have thought the two Free churches – FCs (nicknamed the Wee Frees) and FPs (Wee Wee Frees) would merge – but no. The FPs oppose using public transport to get to church on the Sabbath, while the FCs do not, and while the FCs use modern translations of the Bible, the FPs stick to the King James Bible.

With Reverend Iain D Campbell at Back Church

The plot thickened in 2000 with another breakaway from the FCs called the Free Church Continuing (FCC). Each schism has resulted in a wrangle over income, churches and congregations. Amazingly though, overall attendance doesn't seem to have diminished greatly despite all this factionalism. Several churchgoers have said they're alarmed at the number of grey heads in congregations – but then that's a problem for mainland churches too.

Nowadays, it can be hard to remember the Free Church had radical origins in land reform, because what greets the outsider is a list of fairly dour do's and don'ts.

Don't do anything on a Sunday is the best known. Although there's fierce debate about what 'doing something' actually means.

When I worked in hotels in Wester Ross thirty years ago, local Free Church women would prepare cold meals on Saturday night for the Sabbath because food preparation and even heating would constitute 'doing' something.

One girl broke a nail, but waited till Monday morning to straighten it off. Sheets put out to dry on the Sabbath often disappeared.

And a new chef, out to check the creels on his only day off, found his boat slashed.

These were extreme reactions.

More usual on Lewis has been the absence of shops, petrol stations, pubs, restaurants or ferries operating anywhere. Even walking is frowned on by some. But behaviour has recently relaxed, some planes land, and some shops open. Though not uniformly, publicly, consistently or predictably enough to leave a cyclist certain of finding a bed for the night, or any hot food.

On the other hand, some of the Free Kirk's proscriptions – don't sing hymns and don't use church organs – have given the world something very special: the startling emotionalism of unaccompanied Gaelic Psalm singing. The attachment to the Psalms seems to have begun with the English Puritans. Because most of their congregation couldn't read, it became a custom for the minister to 'read the Psalm line by line, before the singing thereof'.

The effect is a continuous sound, because although singers stop for breath, they never stop simultaneously. The result is one long rolling musical phrase, varying in length from about four to fourteen minutes. But statistics don't convey the feeling created by these strait-laced Free Church congregations in full flow.

'The Gaelic Long Tunes' by Australian poet Les Murray comes close:

On Sabbath days, on circuit days,
the Free Church assembled from boats and gigs
and between sermons they would tauten
and, exercising all they allowed of art,
haul on the long lines of the Psalms.

The seated precentor, touching text
would start alone, lifting up his whale-long tune
and at the right quaver, the rest set sail
after him, swaying, through eerie and lorn.
No unison of breaths-in gapped their sound.

In disdain of all theatrics, they raised
straight ahead, from plank rows, their beatless God-paean,
their giving like enduring. And in rise
and undulation, in earth-conquest mourned
as loss, all tragedy drowned, and that weird
music impelled them, singing, like solar wind.

Anyway enough of all this theoretical Free Church-related beard pulling. I was about to meet the Real Thing and felt decidedly nervous.

We were scheduled to meet a small group of the Back congregation, who had taken time off work to gather at the church for a small, recordable sample of their singing. Calum was first to arrive. I'd met him some years earlier when he and the American jazz great and academic Professor Willie Ruff were guests on a programme I presented about the possible connections between American gospel music and precentor-led Psalm singing, and a frank discussion of the Gaels' role in the slave trade of North Carolina. After the programme, the rest of the Scottish production team could hardly believe Calum was a real Free Church luminary (if such are admitted to exist in such a self-consciously level-pegging Kirk).

Despite his open-mindedness then, standing beside the stark outline of Back Free Church I wondered how straight questions about Free Kirk ways would be accepted now. Even the size of the church car park is slightly intimidating to someone from the mainland, where such vast swathes of space would only be filled by those on a supermarket mission. Here, car parks fill for God.

And not just on Sundays.

The faithful arrive, chattering away happily in Gaelic – along with the Minister, Iain D Campbell.

What follows is a demonstration of such easy-going humility – theirs – that it caused a fair bit of subsequent humble pie eating – mine.

I get Iain D's name wrong throughout the entire recording (somehow I thought his Christian name was Campbell) but no one corrects me. It's their church, their names and their tradition, but the church group gamely let the interview continue, mistakes, misunderstandings, wrongly pronounced names and all.

I realise I have criticised the Gaelic tendency to correct small mistakes at the drop of a hat, so this may sound a tad perverse.

People usually have a range of reactions to inaccurate personal information. Putting emphasis on the wrong part of the word might easily be ignored the first couple of times. Getting a name completely wrong on ten occasions would normally be corrected as an issue of basic accuracy. I'm reminded again of that passage in Roger Hutchinson's *The Soap Man*, describing the crowd smiling politely as they listen to a man they believe to be dangerously mistaken.

Happily ignorant of my mistake amongst the pews of Back Church, I discover precentor Calum Martin and Minister Iain D Campbell are a very relaxed double act.

'We're the Two Ronnies of the Free Kirk,' says Calum.

'Would you like a few pictures of me orating from the pulpit? I can wave my hands round, if that helps,' offers Iain D, generously.

These guys are co-operative.

'So you're calling the shots as a Minister and Calum has to work fast choosing the songs as precentor.'

'Well…' This over-crisp and barely reverent way of discussing God's work is clearly taking a bit of getting used to. 'Well… choosing the items of praise is up to the person leading the worship. And then the person leading the singing is given a list of Psalm numbers and verses to sing and he chooses the tune and leads it off.'

'So traditionally the precentor can't plan which tunes to use because he's in the dark, so to speak, until the Minister announces the Psalm.'

'They get a list from me, though, because I'm very generous that way.'

'But Iain D is the only minister who does, I think. Mind you, there is a limited repertoire of tunes and they are all in the same metre. So technically any tune could fit any Gaelic Psalm. But there are different keys and therefore different tunes suiting different moods and different sentiments. So an experienced precentor will be quickly able to match a tune with words.'

'And you only sing Psalms not hymns.'

'Yes. Our whole service is very much Bible-focused and word based.'

'So the hymns are makey-uppeys written by humans and you're not up for them?'

A warmed up Iain D doesn't miss a beat this time.

'Not within our formal structure of worship, we use them in other contexts as we use other books as valid expressions of faith.'

'And you don't use an organ or anything?'

'No. The best music is the music that comes from the heart.'

'So instruments are not creations of the Devil, then?'

'There is nothing wrong with music. We have plenty music, we just don't have musical instrumentation. It can get in the way of the heart music.'

Gosh, he's good.

'It's a unique musical form and the longer we can preserve it the better.'

It's the perfect cue for a song – Iain D could be a broadcaster as well.

I run along the pew and the names are consistently double-barrelled.

Katie-Mary, Catherine-Joan, Isobel-Anne, Donald-Roderick.

All present are flanked, as ever, by their past.

'Why have you all got two names?'

'Two grannies or two grandpas. It could be worse.'

'How?'

'We could be named after all of them.'

A Gaelic proverb says: *One snotty nose will set a whole church sniffing*. Strikes me one nose could set a whole island sniffing because church and family are basically still so interchangeable.

The singing is about to start.

Iain D reads the Psalm in Gaelic (in a fairly matter of fact way) and Calum soars in with the sung version, like an emotional tuning fork. Voices lift around him, eyes close and the huge church is now full of life and 'heart music'. Ordinary people dressed in their workaday clothes are transformed into buoys on a sea of sound.

The singing continues long after my recording finishes.

This is absolutely the acceptable face of Free Presbyterianism – but many islanders still complain of *croc a' mhinisteir* (the claw of the Minister) limiting the joy and the options of everyday life. If I found Iain D and Calum locking up the swings on Sunday, I'd be disappointed.

But can the Free Kirk relax its more controversial strictures without losing the traditions that make it distinctive?

Calum describes a recent trip to an ecumenical event in Belfast, encouraged to come by the organiser's assurance that the singing Gaels couldn't lose. Protestant by faith, they were also using a Celtic tongue denied in Catholic worship to most Irish speakers. In the event, the Gaels were enthusiastically claimed by both 'sides' – impressed that CD sales also benefited the Bethesda Hospice on Lewis.

The big empty

Lobster-creel
gathering with **DR**
and his manager John

'Couldn't you do more of the singing as an artform – outside the Church?'

Everyone suddenly looks very uneasy.

'It's not a form of entertainment, like gospel music – it's part of our faith.'

I'm waiting for a thunderbolt to strike. But 'hung for a sheep as a lamb', as my mother often says. I inch forward.

'Does it worry you that the bulk of people think "Free Church" and then "lock the swings?"'

'That is a perception, I know, that a lot of people have about the Free Church. And like many things, I suppose there might be a small grain of truth in it. But we're out to spread the word and the song. Ireland could really pick up the Psalm singing. Our trip there made me realise how lucky we were to take our Gaelic singing style into the Church whereas the Catholics weren't able to do that until 1963 and Vatican II, when they were finally able to use Gaelic in Mass.'

What strange bedfellows. Ireland is regarded as the classic, Celtic country. But its established church chose not to use Gaelic in its religious ritual. Lewis is regarded as a prim, fundamentalist island. But its (almost) established church has been using Gaelic for centuries in regular worship. And in both Catholic Ireland and Presbyterian Lewis, language has been the cornerstone of a long cultural battle to preserve identity against a secular, British state.

While I'm pondering these weighty matters of religion, Max points tactfully at his watch.

Down at Vatisker pier, local haulier DR MacLeod is waiting to whisk us across to the chapel on the Eye Peninsula in his bright orange rib. The

167

chapel, built by a follower of St Columba, could soon be submerged and locals have patiently fund-raised, form-filled and faced bureaucracy for five years to get the go-ahead for preservation work from Historic Scotland.

Only one snag – the harbour is empty and DR's rib can't be launched for maybe an hour and a half. The next snag – architect Campbell McKenzie is standing at the Eye Chapel waiting for us, minus a mobile.

In the ensuing guddle, we chuck the bikes in the rib, breaking our own cameras, and are driven by DR's headman John to Eye, where I accidentally delete the interview with Campbell after recording it. I do exactly the same after interviewing the redoubtable Iain MacLeod, proprietor of Charley Barley's – probably the most famous black pudding maker in Scotland.

Interrupting this string of bad luck, John calls to say the rib is now ready to go for a spin. We pull out past the boats of the Sail Festival – some built by local children. One project has recorded a master at work with time-lapse pictures taken over a year to capture his technique and personal style. Clear of the harbour, I find myself powering the speed boat round deep blue inlets, slowing down to collect creels of fish, crabs… and one large lobster.

The Gaelic finale

DR asks what I've made of the trip. Well – the *Gàidhealtachd* and Scotland are miles, languages and cultures apart. And I've started to think neither side really cares about the other. Even though the Scots have DNA wrapped up in the Gaels. And *vice versa*. The more Scots see the Gaels as backward-thinking teuchters, the more Scots harm that part of their own cultural make-up. The more Gaels insist an understanding of their language is essential for national identity, the more they annoy Scots.

None of this is fair – it's just human. And it's not a recent phenomenon either. I'm grateful to Ewan MacIntyre for sending me the following extract from *Glencoe and the End of the Highland War* by Paul Hopkins, describing the same linguistic tension in the 1700s:

> The poetry was, of course, in Gaelic; and now that Gaelic had died out in the Lowlands, the difference in language was serious and encouraged a belief in another difference, which had less real basis, that of race. Lowlanders referred to Gaelic (and, by implication, to its speakers) as 'Irish'; the fact that its culture was oral, not written, merely confirmed its barbarousness. Many Highlanders saw the Lowlanders as alien invaders (*Gall*, pl. *Goill*) who had robbed them of fertile plain country – a convenient belief, which justified perpetual cattle-raiding and robbery. On a higher level, linguistic and cultural isolation encouraged the highland elite to give their deeper emotional loyalty to Scottish Gaeldom, whose political and cultural centre until 1493 was the court of the MacDonald Lords of the Isles, and sometimes to the greater Gaelic community including Ireland.

After the boat trip, I feel the need for a massive injection of good coffee and some frank talk about Gaeldom. Half an hour later I'm at the Woodlands Café in the grounds of Lews Castle College, waiting for Malcolm MacLean.

I pore over that week's edition of the *Stornoway Gazette* – like every other person in the café. The great stooshie about John MacLeod's controversial appointment as Press Officer of Western Isles Health Board fills the front page – centred on a document he'd supposedly written, leaked to the paper. One comment, 'The average GP... has an ego the size of the Clisham,' has everyone laughing. Another comment does not.

'Regarding maternity services, ours is a day where a mother to be expects to be consulted and pandered to at every point. Many expect the labour process to be pain free and that, as of God given right, the child will be born alive, immaculate and healthy. Our grandmothers certainly expected childbirth to be arduous and knew its outcome could never be entirely clear of risk. She accepted the risk of antenatal, perinatal or neonatal death and the possibility of hereditary or congenital deformity.'

Although some of the doctors with large egos might agree, women in the café are aghast.

'Is he saying we are pandered to for not wanting to die?'

Campbell MacKenzie at Eye Chapel

I'm absolutely sure he wasn't. But for an executive on an island chain that needs women to become mothers, it's an extraordinary perspective.

Malky (as he's known on the mainland) arrives with his own, well-thumbed copy of the *Gazette*. Malcolm as he should be called, heads up the Gaelic Arts Agency and I've known him for years. But it was only cycling around Uig Beach that I realised his name is properly Calum.

Malky may have three names (that I know of) but the islands have at least half a dozen naming traditions.

Names can be descriptive – eg Catriona Ruadh (red-haired Catherine) or patronymic eg Màiri Sheumais (James's Mary or Mary of James), or occupational, eg Dòmhnall Ciobair (Donald the Shepherd), or occupational and patronymic, eg Màiri a' Ghoba (Mary of the Blacksmith), or residential, eg Ràghnall a' Bhràighe (Ronald of/from Braes), or origin-based, eg Ruairidh Leòdhasach (Roderick of Lewis), or the whole shebang, eg Calum Dubh a' Chlachain (Black haired Calum from Clachan).

All of this is quite effortless to the native speaker – and perhaps it's that very ease that causes native speaker resistance to the 'artifical' arts-

based resurgence of the language today.

According to Malky, 'My grandparents walked from village to village because there was no road, walked to the well because there was no running water and went to bed early because there was no electricity. It was a highly interdependent peasant economy. Families and villages worked together to weave, to croft and to work with sheep in the fank. Gaelic was the common language of work, play – everything. There was no need to put it on a pedestal – it was the *lingua franca*. Perhaps that's the root of its problem today. The older generation don't believe a healthy Gaelic society should need to make a song and dance about something as natural as breathing. But Gaelic is at once more threatened and more widely loved than community leaders will admit.'

Calum will readily admit Gaelic is a tough gig for learners. For instance, his mother still talks about a 'trouser' and a 'scissor', because in Gaelic the objects are not thought to be composed of two parts. It's a different way of conceptualising.

It's been suggested to me that the Scottish practice of pronouncing the word 'film' as 'filum' is because of a Gaelic heritage which commonly inserted a vowel between consonants. There's a possible Gaelic origin too for the glottal stop, which results in Glaswegians pronouncing words like Paterson as Pa-erson. In Gaelic, 't' followed by an 'h' makes it silent. Thus the word for father, *athair*, is pronounced aher – as if no 't' were present.

I don't know if a Gaelic heritage explains the grammar problems of present-day Glaswegians. But if it does, that's important. I have long been amazed by the extent to which Scots are embarrassed by 'uneducated' West of Scotland voices. On his Hebridean tour of 1773 Dr Johnson remarked: 'the clans retain little now of their original character... of what they had before the conquest of their country there remain only their language and their poverty. Their language is attacked on every side.'

It still is.

Nowadays Gaelic has a worse enemy than a proscriptive, twitchy post-Culloden government or a Gaelic-denying Scottish education system. The lazy world of the monoglot English speaker is doing the hatchet-job quite nicely. If kids these days can't be bothered learning French – and they can't – how much less enthusiasm will there be for a language that demands a radically different way of thinking, like Gaelic?

And it is different in one big way. Gaelic is soaked in meaning for the people who use the language in a way that English isn't. Thus Gaels don't say any sentence in Gaelic as straightforwardly as the Scots do in English. Gaelic describes the things it names – it doesn't just use language to point at them. Mispronouncing a place-name – Timsgarry, for example

– will generally prompt a Gael to embark on a long tale about what the name actually means. In fact Timsgarry means the Hill of the Scattering – a reference that dates from the Clearances. An English speaker will generally offer advice about *how* to say the word differently – not *why*. In English, names generally have denotation not connotation. In Gaelic there is connotation, meaning and family connection everywhere.

At Back Church everyone had a middle name. Girls were named after grandmothers on both sides. Boys were named after grandfathers. Never mind if the results have become unwieldy – the child must still be known by its origins.

In many ways this is as corny as the American habit of having Harry Connick Junior or Loudon Wainwright III. In other ways it's as tribal as the Icelandic naming system which results in everyone needing nicknames to be distinguished from fathers, grandfathers and great grandfathers, all of whom have variations of the same name. My own grandfather, Magnus More, is an example of this. His name in Norse and Gaelic means big. So he was Big Big. Just how well that described a delightfully calm man of decidedly medium stature, I don't know.

Much of the Gaelic practice of naming and describing fixes people to a very distant past.

English is not always the worse for freeing individuals from constant reference to their origins. Why should new lives be shackled immediately with the trappings of a bygone age? Unless we believe it's more important to ken the faither than the bairn.

Do we still believe that?

I am called Lesley Anne Riddoch because my mum and dad agreed they would call me after the winner of a beautiful baby competition. Gaels just don't do anything this meaningless with language. Which is why they are as distinctive speaking English as they are speaking Gaelic. And the combination known as Macaronic is often as clever, knowing and ironic as the best modern text language being devised by hipster-clad teenage girls in Central Belt schools. Unfortunately Gaels are not that interested in their experience as English speakers. As a result, monoglot English speakers living on the islands must be the worst served minority group in Scotland. They live in a Gaelic-speaking area – so English-speaking Radio Scotland isn't interested. But they don't speak Gaelic so Gaelic-speaking *Radio nan Gàidheal* isn't interested either. That's what you call equality – or failed multiculturalism.

Here's how strongly one local feels about the priority Gaelic speakers have on the islands:

'Non Gaels, who are still one hundred per cent Hebridean, are excluded from the artistic side of things. It's cultural apartheid. Even though Gaelic ceased to exist years ago. Watch any interview on Gaelic TV and see if they go three words without reverting to Ganglish. I'm not meaning helicopter,

Eye Chapel, ever closer to extinction as the sea closes in

oil rig, etc. The Norwegians and French have all adopted these English words. But when you hear a native speaker who doesn't know the Gaelic for chair, flower, spider etc... you're not hearing the death knell, but a distant echo. It was sounded long ago.

'Gaelic now is run by the same old tired faces taking the Gaelic handout. They are only marginally less well off than those who live the life of crofting. A culture which exists on handouts will never produce greatness. It will aspire to mediocrity at best.

'People would never stand by and watch an animal dying slowly, yet they permit themselves to stand in the midst of their own culture as it draws its last, weak breaths. If Hebridean culture was a dog, I would take it to the back of the barn and put it out of its misery.'

Strong sentiments, rarely expressed in public.

But unless Gaelic's guardians start having fun with their language and accord English speakers some share of the cultural limelight, there will be more angry feelings of exclusion – not fewer. Look at the demographics.

On the other hand, it might help English speakers to realise that Gaelic is not just a language, but also a culture whose values still underpin what's distinctive about Scotland. Across the whole of Scotland clan once mattered. Clan ignored ownership and depended instead on loyalty – the loyalty of each man to rise in defence of his clan chief during times of threat. In the clan, family mattered and afforded equal status. When the rest of Scotland capitulated to feudalism the Highlands and Islands tried to stick to its different conception of life with stubbornly communitarian values.

Across mainland Scotland, the clan dwindled to become the extended family, then the nuclear family, and finally individual family members, watching separate TVs in the same house.

There is only one place where the bonds of the clan have any grip: where family loyalty still governs, and where Scotland has left its old values for an indefinite period in cold storage – it's the *Gàidhealtachd*.

No wonder many 'modern' Glaswegians hate the Gaels. If they could shear off the sentimentality and nostalgia that has crippled their society for generations, the Gaels could yet re-emerge as Scotland's radicals – grasping that crown from their jumped up descendants, on the Clyde.

Radical is not how most Scots see the Gaels. The thing most Scots feel instinctively about the Gaels is not respect, nor guilt about their betrayal, nor shame about their repression. Not empathy because of their poverty, nor anger because of their long period of enforced silence. The thing Scots identify most strongly about the Gaels is their sense of superiority.

Put bluntly, the values Gaels have espoused for centuries make the Scots wrong. Wrong to grab the deal England offered 300 years ago. Wrong to put the removal of small comforts before the ornamentation of the mind, to paraphrase Johnson. Wrong to become materialist, wrong to become secular, wrong to become big, wrong to question the primacy of family and wrong to become remote from nature and the spiritual life.

Gaels know they should have led Scotland in a different direction. They couldn't do it. And the great fear – the elephant in the corner – is that in failing to lead, Gaelic culture has imploded and is stifling the folk that remain and the new culture they want to create.

Amazingly, Calum is still sitting there, rubbing his glasses.

'A lot of people would find all this quite hard to hear. Bits of it are over-stated, and bits of it may even be wrong, but overall you definitely have something. Scotland and Gaelic have a long-term dysfunctional relationship and if we are to progress, as Scots or Gaels, then these issues need to be opened up in new ways. But Gaelic isn't going to go away for a long time to come, despite the best efforts of all its grave-diggers.'

I feel one stone and several years lighter.

And I realise I will put that emotional weight back on as soon as we leave the café unless I do more. I've been trying to provoke others all the way through this journey. When I get home, and finish the radio programmes, it might be time to provoke myself.

'So write a book,' says Calum.

Conclusion

The Western Isles is a traditional, superstitious, nature-focused, God-fearing and family-centred society – it has been for centuries. No wonder.

Fifty miles adrift in the Atlantic and 300 years 'adrift' in its own language, geography and linguistic isolation have helped create and maintain a way of life, once commonplace in Scotland but now unique. This rocky island chain is the exposed, stubbornly resistant core of a bigger social massif now almost totally eroded elsewhere. These are islands with echoes. Where a word or custom can trigger memories about times past and places quite distant from this island chain. The Western Isles are working on the old rules and at the old pace. And their people observe, honour and occasionally deep-freeze the old ways of all of us.

The cultural mainstays of Gaelic, crofting, weaving, fishing and Free Church influence, are all in decline. And if these cornerstones collapse, a way of life developed over generations will end or change within the next decade.

Perhaps like the little boy who cried wolf, occasional visitors to the Isles have already exhausted public patience with their warnings of imminent collapse. Johnson believed the 'true' Highlands were in retreat when he visited Skye hoping to see a fully functioning 'Erse' society, carrying weapons, speaking Gaelic, wearing plaid and playing pipes despite the Act of Proscription in 1747 which outlawed these staples of Highland behaviour. One hundred and fifty years later Lord Leverhulme predicted collapse when he failed to rouse the people of Lewis to leave the land and back his over-optimistic plans for a revitalised fishing industry.

Great men with dire warnings have come and gone. And somehow, against all the odds and despite a series of natural and man-made tragedies, the people of the Western Isles have clung on. Now though, they face a bigger challenge. Abandonment not by mainlanders, politicians, investors, ministers or even neighbours – all those hurts have been experienced and borne. But abandonment by their own children.

The average Hebridean teenager doesn't speak Gaelic beyond primary school, doesn't attend the Free or Catholic Church, doesn't want to become a crofter, fisherman or weaver and believe he or she can combine Gaelic identity with life and a full-time job in Glasgow, Edinburgh or London.

Teenagers are leaving.

But others are arriving. And they will have children. All is not lost, but the future will be different. And beyond the power of islanders to shape if they face backwards now, attending to the loss of times past, rather than the challenge of times present.

From the little I've seen, Hebrideans are believers.

Islanders over centuries have defied the gloomiest predictions with an unshakeable belief that anything is possible.

How else could men have launched twenty-foot, uncovered boats into a sullen Atlantic aiming for Ireland to sell fish?

Why else did families wait so long for the land deal promised by successive governments? And why else did they finally leave for lands no one could describe, on journeys longer than anyone had ever experienced, aboard ships owned by people they had never even met.

A better life was possible.

It still is.

But if islanders are battling feelings of denial, disappointment and even guilt about the loss of old ways, they may not be able to grasp the new possibilities that abound. To commit heresy and pack Mrs Thatcher and the Declaration of Arbroath into one sentence, 'while 100 islanders live there *will* be such a thing as society.'

What will it look like and how much will islanders have shaped it? Those are the questions that matter now.

Change is ahead.

But no one knows what the outcome of change will be.

How can the people of the Western Isles and the wider Scottish community shape the course of the next twenty years? Are Gaelic traditions more robust than we imagine? Or, if you want to hear Gaelic spoken naturally and communally, if you want to hear the hair-raising harmonies of the Free Kirk precentor-led congregations, if you want to see thatching or meet Scottish creel fishermen or speak to the last Harris-based tweed weaver – should you visit the Outer Hebrides fast?

Will the possible loss of human habitats finally interest lovers of wild places? It's a supreme irony. Ecologically-minded mainlanders want space, community and contact with nature in their busy lives. And yet islanders are struggling to keep just such a world safe from the blandishments of the fast-paced, secular and impatient mainland world.

The population of the Western Isles fell by 10 per cent in the nineties – the highest rate of decline in Scotland. It'll fall by a further 20 per cent by 2018. Other island groups also have declining populations but in the Western Isles leavers are disproportionately twenty-somethings, residents are disproportionately fifty-somethings and deaths have been exceeding births for five years. A recent upward blip in numbers is almost entirely due to incomers – English folk, Central Belters and foreign 'good lifers' who've experienced enough bright lights for several lifetimes.

So what's the future?

Will non-Gaelic-speaking, non-crofting, non-church-going incomers reverse population decline but accelerate cultural change? Or will the new arrivals prove keener to learn the language and to accept 'traditional' ways of life than the outgoing, modernity-craving crofters' children? Are the outriders of a world weary of its own destructive pace, set to re-colonise the ageing communities of the Western Isles?

The fate of 26,000 Hebridean islanders in 2006 still attracts less interest than the fate of sixty islanders on St Kilda in 1930. Living behind a veil of Gaelic, the people of the Hebrides are often seen by the rest of Scotland as a world apart. Slow to reveal their thoughts or worries to outsiders, or to one another. Fearful and distrustful of mainland ways. Ancient people in a modern world – with ancient facilities that need modernising at a time when numbers hardly justify the effort.

Central-Belt Scots have long whiled away hours in pubs with Gaelic or Hebridean names – but prefer the Spanish costas, Balearics or even exotic Egypt to those machair-fringed island chains when it comes to spending real chunks of time or cash.

Of course, being overlooked by mainland authorities has its advantages. While no one's been watching, islanders have been driving at the age of eight, rowing at the age of five and probably enjoying their first pint shortly thereafter. With strong community links, direct lines of communication, no red tape and small population bases, islands can embrace new ideas fast. The Northern Isles are set to become pioneers of marine, hydrogen energy and wind – but the Hebrides remain divided over how or whether to extract financial value from the force of nature that has long been the islanders' worst foe.

If islanders can't agree on ways to harvest wind, what can they agree on? If large windfarms aren't built, subsea connectors and less intrusive marine energy projects may also pass by. Though perhaps a bypass from the twenty-first century is exactly what some wind objectors want.

That's not possible. Because one tradition is good and gone. The tradition of powerless bystanding.

The new direction for the Outer Hebrides will be steered by its people. Not by remote landowners, the Scottish state, the Free Church or the fish dealers of Billingsgate.

The people of the Outer Hebrides have endured centuries of poverty, uncertainty and emigration. They've bonded to nature and encircled themselves with family. They have left to work for others and returned to work on land they never owned. They've accepted the rules of the Free Church and the word of the priest. They've learned Gaelic as children and watched as the language left on the tongues of their children. Until very recently, Hebridean life has been both free-spirited and woefully constrained.

Now, with wider ownership of land and other assets, the future is a completely open book and the pen is in the hand of the island population for the first time in centuries. The people of the Western Isles must write their own future.

Perhaps in that great project, it may help to believe that the rest of Scotland cares. In the closing words of *No Great Mischief*: 'All of us are better when we are loved.'

Bibliography

Armit, Ian. *Scotland's Hidden History*. Tempus, 2006

Boswell and Johnson. *Journey to the Hebrides*. Edinburgh: Canongate, 2001

Brown, Callum G. (contrib). *People and Society in Scotland*. Vol 2. Edinburgh: John Donald, 1997

Buxton, Ben. Mingulay: *An Island and its People*. Edinburgh: Birlinn, 1995

—*The Vatersay Raiders* (to be published by Birlinn in 2008)

Campbell, John Lorne. *Tales of Barra Told by the Coddie*. Edinburgh: Birlinn

Daiches, David (ed). *The New Companion to Scottish Culture*. Edinburgh: Polygon, 1993

Grant, I.F. *Highland Folk Ways*. Edinburgh: Birlinn, 1995

Hache, Jean Didier. *Neil MacEachen, Marshal MacDonald the Uists and Alexander Carmichael*. Islands Book Trust, 2007

Haswell-Smith, Hamish. *The Scottish Islands*. Edinburgh: Canongate, 2004

Horsley, Phil. *The Isles and Highlands of Western Scotland: Island Hopping Bike Adventures*. Leicester: Cordee, 1997

Hunter, James. *Last of the Free*. Edinburgh: Mainstream, 2000

—*The Making of the Crofting Community*. Edinburgh: John Donald, 2000

Hutchinson, Roger. *The Soap Man*. Edinburgh: Birlinn, 2003

Lawson, Bill. *North Uist and Harris in History and Legend*. Edinburgh: Birlinn, 2003

MacAulay, John. *Silent Tower*. Pentland Press, 1993

—*Birlinn: Longships of the Hebrides*. White Horse Press, 1996

MacDonald, Donald. *Tales and Traditions of the Lews*. Edinburgh: Birlinn, 2000

MacGregor, Alasdair Alpin. *The Western Isles*. London: Robert Hale, 1952

MacLean, Calum. *The Highlands*. Edinburgh: Mainstream, 2006

MacLean, Malcolm and Christopher Carrell (ed). *As an Fhearann: From the Land*. Edinburgh: Mainstream, 1986

MacLeod, Alistair. *No Great Mischief*. London: Vintage, 2001

Murray, Les. *New Collected Poems*. Manchester: Carcanet, 2003

Rixson, Dennis. *The West Highland Galley*. Edinburgh: Birlinn, 1998

Robertson, Boyd and Taylor, Iain. T*each Yourself Gaelic*. London: Hodder & Stoughton, 2005

Shaw, Margaret Fay. *Folksongs and Folklore of South Uist*. London: Routledge and Kegan Paul, 1955

Thompson, Francis. *The Western Isles*. London: Batsford, 1998

'Island Notes' series, www.theislandsbooktrust.com

Appendix
'Outer Hebrides' v 'Western Isles'

Writing this book, I had a problem – what to call the island chain? The proposed title, *Riddoch on the Western Isles,* fell foul of the council's decision to change the name of the island chain back to the Outer Hebrides.

But was there any agreement on that? Can you herd cats? Here is a selection of responses I got after a letter to the *Stornoway Gazette* appealing for help. If there was easy consensus on a naming issue anywhere in Scotland I'd be surprised. On an island chain with as rich a linguistic heritage as the... Outer Isles/ Outer Hebrides/ Hebrides/ Western Isles/ *Innse Gall* – I'd be disappointed. But lest the Western Isles become like the artist formerly known as Prince – which name should a humble non-islander choose? Or is this just another way strangers can always be wrong?

1. What about trail-blazing a new name – 'The Western Hebrides' or just 'Western Hebrides'??? —*Angus Brendan MacNeil*

2. I would vote for *Riddoch in the Outer Isles* —*Sarah Egan*

3. *Riddoch in the Western Isles* – 'Hebrides' is good, but Skye *et al* could be miffed; 'Outer' is not welcoming and brings up jokey Outer bloody Mongolia; Western Isles is the most familiar —*Finlay MacLeod*

4. I like Outer Hebrides. It feels more remote – like Outer Space, man! —*Marina McSween*

5. I don't mind what you call it but if I had to choose I would go for the Outer Hebrides as this is what we were taught from school —*Mairi Campbell*

6. Straw poll in the office. Maria and I reckon that *Riddoch: On the Outer Hebrides* is the best one —*Mary Schmoller*

7. No doubt that Outer Hebrides is now politically correct – do you wish to be?! I believe WIE are now HIE *Innse Gall* (even more politically correct!) What about *From Barra on her Butt!* —*John Randall*

8. Splash thinks it should be *On the Outer Hebrides* —*Gloria MacKillop*

9. I am not convinced that any of the titles would grasp attention. If the islands are to be named in the title, I think that the Hebrides has more appeal. Personally I would prefer to see something like *Riddoch: Biking from Barra to the Butt – a tour through the Hebrides* —*Alasdair MacEachen*

10. Outer Hebrides is a far better description for the islands, as Western Isles could be anywhere on the planet —*Donald MacAulay*

11. I saw your letter in the *Stornoway Gazette*. Have you considered the 'Long Island/*An t-Eilean Fada*' option? (Not mentioned in your letter among the various possibilities). The name seemed to fall out of favour following association with the Long Island Institute at Lochmaddy, North Uist (Poorhouse to 'Lunatic Asylum' and lastly Lochmaddy Hospital). Maybe now's the time for a relaunch? —*Gordon Wells*

12. You were looking for suggestions for a title for your book about biking through the Western Isles/Outer Hebrides? How about *Lesley on the Long Island*? —*Susan Brekke*

13. Hi Lesley. *Bha mi duilich nach fhaca mi 'n uair a bha thu ann an Leodhas- -co-dhiu,ainmeannan.* I thought of borrowing from both names – 'Western' from 'Western Isles' and 'Hebrides' from 'Outer Hebrides'. Then borrow a word from 'The West Highland Way' – lucky that all this borrowing is free – you then come up with *Riddoch: Cycling the West Hebridean Way* —*Donnie Graham*

14. What's wrong with *Lesley Riddoch 'On The Bike' on the Outer Hebrides*! *but* most definitely 'Outer Hebrides'. Have fun!!!! —*Maureen & Donald John, MacKay*

15. I would most certainly go with 'Outer Hebrides'. I suspect that there are some who wish to get away from the islands' original etymology for reasons of what, in my childhood, were described as 'Papist superstitions', and that this is why the 'Western Isles' became fashionable. I notice that even amongst islanders who I respect there is much division of opinion on this matter today, but personally, I am delighted to see the pendulum shifting again towards Outer Hebrides – and let's be proud of standing on the outer edge of a crazy mainstream – 'When the centre collapses, the periphery becomes central' —*Alastair McIntosh*

16. John MacAulay, a native Gaelic-speaking historian, shipwright and folklorist on Harris has this to say about the etymology in his 1996 book, *Birlinn*:

> The Hebrides, or Ey-Brides (derived from the 'Isles of St Bridgit') are now collectively and politically known as the Western Isles. The Gaelic, *Innis Bhrighde*, has long since disappeared from use, having given way to *Innse Gall* (The Isles of Strangers), a derogatory term from the time of the Norse settlement. According to folklore, at one time all of the Outer Isles were committed to the special care of Bridgit, the Celtic goddess of fire, whose temples were attended by virgins of noble birth, called the 'daughters of fire.' When Christianity first came to the isles it proved easier to institute a Christian Order of the Nuns of St Bridgit than to remove the vestal virgins from their post. The Nuns of St Bridgit were the first Christian community of religious women. Various religious sites, parishes, and individual churches throughout the islands have retained this name, in the form Kilbride, or in Gaelic – *Cill Bhrighde* [*Cill* meaning 'cell' or 'church of'].

17. How about *Castlebay to Cunndal: A cycle pilgrimage* (ride, journey, trip, excursion, outing, spin, tour) *around the Hebrides* (Western Isles). *Cunndal* is the Gaelic name for Port of Ness near the Butt of Lewis. Like most island place names it is from Old Norse: '*unna-dalr*', meaning the hollow of the waves. —*Donald J MacLeod*

Women of the Highlands

Katharine Stewart

ISBN 1 905222 74 2 HBK £14.99

When was the last witch burnt in the Highlands and what was her crime?

Which Jacobite lady led men to war while her Hanoverian husband stayed at home?

Who were the first Highland women to be recorded in history and what did they do?

And how have women's lives changed since medieval times?

Katharine Stewart recounts the lives and legends of famous Highland and Island women, from Elizabeth Grant of Rothiemurchus to Jane Maxwell, Duchess of Gordon. However, the true essence of the book lies in the abiding sense of the thousands of Highlanders throughout the ages who, though they lived under different laws and in far-off times, have together created the history and culture that produced the Highland women of today.

Katharine Stewart's latest book has the authority of being part of the living tradition it describes.
MARGARET ELPHINSTONE

Stories of comfort, healing, gentle revolution and steadfast resolve prove persuasive in Katharine's argument that the Highlands, and Scotland, would not be what they are today without the nurture provided by one gender throughout the ages.
STORNOWAY GAZETTE

The Highland Clearances Trail

Rob Gibson

ISBN 1 905222 10 6 PBK £5.99

The Highland Clearances: one of the most controversial episodes in Scottish history. In the Highlands and Islands the legacy is still immediate and resentful, exacerbated by modern historians' generalisation of experiences and denial of the scale of evictions.

In *The Highland Clearances Trail* Rob Gibson presents the real past of the Highlands, full of its complexities and local variations. From the Strathrusdale Sheep Drive to the Battle of the Braes, he has brought together the story of the Clearances from a Highland perspective, using evidence from Napier Commission reports, bardic poetry and oral accounts.

This book systematically documents the Highland Clearances of the last 200 years, guiding the reader round sights of particular evictions and memorials and providing facts and figures which show the true extent of the destruction of Highland communities. Ordnance Survey grid references and information on access, historical notes and a selected bibliography provide a resource for visitors and students alike. An earlier version of this book has been described as 'a pioneer in eco-tourism' because there is no substitute to visiting the very places where these dark deeds took place.

It is important to get the whole movement into perspective and examine the truth of the matter and I hope that this well-written book will redress the balance.
HIGHLAND NEWS

Crofting Years

Francis Thompson

ISBN 0 946487 06 5 PBK £6.95

Crofting is much more than a way of life in the Highlands and Islands of Scotland. It is a storehouse of cultural, linguistic and moral values, which holds together a scattered and struggling rural population. This book fills a blank in the written history of crofting over the last two centuries. Bloody conflicts and gunboat diplomacy, treachery, compassion, music and story: all figure as Francis Thompson takes us into the homes and the very minds of those who fought so desperately for security on their land.

I would recommend this book to all who are interested in the past, but even more so to those who are interested in the future survival of our way of life and culture.
STORNOWAY GAZETTE

A cleverly planned book... the story told in simple words which compel attention... [by] a Gaelic speaking Lewisman with specialised knowledge of the crofting community.
BOOKS IN SCOTLAND

An excellent social history of crofting in the Highlands and Islands by a writer with a deep knowledge of his subject.
THE SCOTS MAGAZINE

Scotland: Land and Power

The Agenda for Land Reform

Andy Wightman

ISBN 0 946487 70 7 PBK £5.00

Land reform campaigner Andy Wightman delivers a hard-hitting critique of the oppressive absurdities of Scotland's antiquated land laws. His is by no means a purely negative analysis – here are thought-through proposals for reforms which he argues would free both country and urban Scots from the shackles of land laws that are feudal and oppressive.

Andy Wightman's views are controversial, but he doesn't mind a good argument. He is an influential figure in Scottish political life these days. Those who don't agree with his views do pay attention to them, and his contribution to one of the hottest debates of the new millennium is well respected.

Writers like Andy Wightman are determined to make sure the hurt of the last century is not compounded by a rushed solution in the next. This accessible, comprehensive but passionately argued book is quite simply essential reading and perfectly timed – here's hoping Scotland's legislators agree.
LESLEY RIDDOCH

Details of these and other Luath books are to be found at www.luath.co.uk

Luath Press Limited

committed to publishing well written books worth reading

LUATH PRESS takes its name from Robert Burns, whose little collie
Luath (*Gael.*, swift or nimble) tripped up Jean Armour at a wedding
and gave him the chance to speak to the woman who was to be his
wife and the abiding love of his life. Burns called one of the 'Twa
Dogs' Luath after Cuchullin's hunting dog in Ossian's *Fingal*.
Luath Press was established in 1981 in the heart of
Burns country, and is now based a few steps up
the road from Burns' first lodgings on
Edinburgh's Royal Mile. Luath offers you
distinctive writing with a hint of
unexpected pleasures.
Most bookshops in the UK, the US, Canada,
Australia, New Zealand and parts of Europe,
either carry our books in stock or can order them
for you. To order direct from us, please send a £sterling
cheque, postal order, international money order or your
credit card details (number, address of cardholder and
expiry date) to us at the address below. Please add post
and packing as follows: UK – £1.00 per delivery address;
overseas surface mail – £2.50 per delivery address; overseas airmail
– £3.50 for the first book to each delivery address, plus £1.00 for
each additional book by airmail to the same address. If your order
is a gift, we will happily enclose your card or message at no extra
charge.

Luath Press Limited
543/2 Castlehill
The Royal Mile
Edinburgh EH1 2ND
Scotland
Telephone: 0131 225 4326 (24 hours)
Fax: 0131 225 4324
email: sales@luath. co.uk
Website: www. luath.co.uk